More
Than Meets
the Eye

MORE THAN MEETS THE EYE

Carl Mydans

HARPER & BROTHERS

NEW YORK

TO SETH AND MISTY

Contents

CONTENTS

CONTENTS

PART I

1.

I Come to Life

Late one afternoon in 1951, as the sun jumped behind the snow-covered ridges of the Korean mountains, turning the top slush into crystals, a Turkish patrol, shouting incomprehensible words of recognition, struggled back into their lines. Blowing on fingers and staggering awkwardly under heavy weapons and bandoliers of cartridges, they half-carried, half-dragged a poncho in which quivered an incredible bundle.

They moved in miniature through my camera finder, hunched, silhouetted figures against the failing light. I followed them to the medic's tent. Here the Turkish doctor looked at what he had. Wrapped from head to foot in rough bandages and bits of stuffing from a Korean coverlet was a mound that moved. Two holes at the top showed black, glazed eyes.

"Turkish soldier," said the medic as he stood half-crouched beside me with a pair of scissors in his hand. He struggled for his English. "Turkish soldier," he repeated. And then angrily he pantomimed the scratching of a match and the torture of fire.

As the bundle was slipped onto a litter and carried away to an ambulance the doctor rose and faced the mountains. Pointing toward the darkening horizon, he turned to me and shouted: "History!" In exasperation he searched for other English words, but they would not come. "History," he shouted again and then stood jerking his fist into the air, looking wordlessly toward the purple twilight.

What more he would have said about history was now lost. We had no common language and the moment was gone. He may have wanted to express some all-encompassing and penetrating view of our times. More likely it was a deeply personal reflection on that fleeting instant, a moment of reaction and contemplation, an intuitive awareness of the history we are all creating. I waited, but the impulse had swept over him and he turned back to his work. Night fell upon the Turkish brigade and I never saw him again. But his urgent face, his body tense and frustrated against the twilight, and the momentary insight he inspired in me of our place in history, live forever in my memory.

What memory chooses to retain is unpredictable. As a photo-reporter I have witnessed and recorded more than two decades of our unfolding history, much of it violent. But the sweep of our times has been so broad, so complex, that no one mind can encompass it. We have all seen it in bits and pieces. For historians, no doubt, our era will fall into clear patterns of economic and national pressures, the decisions of statesmen and the actions of generals. But for me the memories of the decisive actions I have covered and the world leaders I have photographed have dimmed. Instead I see sharp images and hear clear sounds coming back, over the years, of ordinary souls caught in the convulsions of war and war's aftermath.

Memory is related to background and outlook. Once a fellow reporter said to me: "You think with your eyes." I am sure, because I am a photographer, he meant this as a compliment. Certainly it is true that all my life I have felt the urge to see and report. But now, when I look back at myself as an active and inquisitive boy, I perceive that my questions were more often "what" and "how" than "why." There was much in my young world which I simply took for granted.

A world war raged through part of my childhood; I was eleven years old when the armistice was signed in 1918; and there was much in my family background that was influenced by war. But I was unconcerned with it or missed its implication. My family had come to America to avoid war. My grandfather, a bookbinder from a little village near Odessa, had set out when his sons were still under conscription age to find a place they could live in peace and without having to serve in the Czar's army. After searching through Europe and America he chose Boston, Massachusetts. This was where his sons would live and sow their seed. He moved them and their mother out from under the shadow of the Czarist army and the pogroms, and with this move cut off a family heritage of culture and religion. For my father, once his young feet hit the soil of New England, adopted without reservation the mores and outlook of the New World, resolutely putting behind him the language and religion of his fathers. And I grew up amidst the landmarks of a heritage that I accepted without question as my own: the fields of Lexington and Concord, the heights of Bunker Hill, Boston Common, Plymouth Rock. I never doubted that this was, indeed, the "land where my fathers died." To me the great wars of the world were the American Revolution, the War of 1812, the Civil War, the Spanish-American War, and in all of them American soldiers had fought proudly, for freedom.

Now, in my lifetime, our soldiers marched away to fight in France. And it was all bands playing and flags flying. In my imaginary world of war the colors could not have been brighter or the prospects more enticing. By now my family had moved to the suburban town of Medford, just outside Boston. And from there one memory especially persists: it was in 1918 and the soldiers had just returned from the war in France. I was drawn to a crowd which had gathered on the front lawn of a house on my street. A big soldier was standing there, shaking hands with everybody while his mother stood with her arm reaching up round his shoulders and his father talked about where his son had been and what he had done. I recognized the colored ribbons on his uniform and knew that they meant that he had been a very brave soldier. But this was the first time I truly understood what the word "hero" meant. This was the first real hero I had ever seen. I remember that his hair was fair and his legs, bound neatly in puttees, were enormous. And I remember that someone asked him if he had seen anyone killed in the fighting and how his face changed and how his father spoke for him and

5

said: "Soldiers don't talk about such things."

There was a victory parade in our town a few days later, with bands and many soldiers marching. Most of the others wore colored ribbons also. But my soldier marched at their head. And I ran all the way beside him, trying to walk as he did and saluting when he saluted. For days I used to watch, and sometimes join small groups of visitors who came to his house. I would listen to what was said and then go off and live again in my imaginary world of war.

One day months later when I was coming home from school I saw the neighbors gathered there on the lawn again. But this time when I joined them I saw that the soldier's mother was wiping her eyes with her apron. And I saw his father sitting alone on the porch with his head bowed and his back turned. Each adult avoided me when I asked what had happened. But later my father told me: that morning while I was at school the soldier had taken a pistol he had captured from a German and shot himself through the head.

It was a warm, sunny day when they buried him, and at the cemetery there was a fresh dug grave for him in a lovely green dell. Nearby were the headstones of soldiers who had fought in the American Revolution and the Civil War. He had an American flag over his coffin and an honor guard fired into the air. On my way home I heard adults talking. I followed, wondering, straining to listen and to understand what had happened. "It was the war," they said. "Something happened to him over there." And: "He's never been the same since the war." It was then that I first came to have some vague and flickering comprehension of what war meant.

But new and exciting interests of boyhood soon flooded over that moment of apprehension. We lived on the Mystic River, a winding, snakelike tidal waterway that ran through miles of salt marshes to Boston. Here were spile-studded ruins of shipyards where once were built some of the great ships which fought in 1812, the clippers which carried the American flag to the coasts of China and the harpoon of New Bedford to the South Seas. They still built ships along the Mystic when I was a boy, mostly small craft with gasoline engines and bronze propellers. But one

6

of my earliest memories of school involves a four-master which was being made ready for sea. Each day, out of the school windows, I could see her masts rising high above the roofs and trees. And even today I recall the propelling rebellion which surged within me as I felt the confinement of the school walls holding me from the promise of the masts in the sky.

Years later in a faraway land I used to watch the black-winged bats that came out each evening to flap freely through the blue twilight above the barbed wire of the prison which held me. Then the scene of the schoolroom and the masts and the call of the world beyond returned with amazing clarity. And the same sickening propulsion that I felt as a child watching the masts above the river made prison almost unendurable.

I went to work in the boatyards, after school and weekends, when I was thirteen and it was there I learned to handle a saw and a plane and how to calk a seam, and there I first knew the joy of doing things with my hands and the quiet pride of looking at something well done.

It was natural, in those early years, that I should want to be a shipbuilder. Later a young surgeon, a cousin, took me on visits to the operating theater of the Carney Hospital in Boston. I had already come to revere the craftsmanship of hands—the ship joiner's, the painter's, the fingers of my father as he played his oboe. Now the hands of the surgeon working silently, commanding life and death, seemed to me almost godlike. I wanted to be a surgeon.

Sometime during my last years of high school, journalism caught my imagination. I don't recall now any steadfast interest outside these three fields. And I have since credited myself with selecting the most satisfying and exciting of professions, for in the pursuit of journalism, perhaps more than any other profession, one comes closer to and lives more intimately and imaginatively with the world he loves. This is especially true of photo-journalism; for here one joins mind and hand, and here the reporter must always come in closest contact with his subject. The very limitations of his craft force this intimacy on the photographer. In the course of his own work he rides the fishing trawler through the storm; he descends half a mile into the earth to record the mining of coal; he climbs atop a girder suspended over a river to show the building of a bridge; he follows a soldier into combat. Time and again soldiers staggering under their own gear have come to me to ask if they could help me tote mine. They were not singling me out, as an outsider, for unusual kindness. They were just treating me as they would treat any other soldier.

I know I have spent a great deal of my life feeling wishful about the lives of others. Covering a cattle drive will almost surely bring me, somewhere through the story, to wishing I could be nothing else but a cowhand riding the range. I would gladly have been a sand hog when I photographed them in the muck under a river. I have been a toreador, a jet pilot, an engineer laying a pipe line, a platoon leader. But these are only impulses, triggered by my intimacy with the subject and the thrill of suddenly living another life.

A writer may get his story of bridge building from the ground. But the camera has to be above with the men. No great combat picture was ever made in a headquarters briefing. And no camera that was ever late for an assault was ever "filled in" later by comrades in journalism or survivors of the action. The camera must always be there. And behind it there must always be a man's eye, and a soul.

I was twenty-seven when I first began to use the camera seriously. That was three years after I had graduated from the School of Journalism at Boston University and had worked as a reporter in New York City. Picture journalism in those days was held to be of so little importance and so uninviting that no course in it was offered at the university and I recall only the most passing references to it in my four years there. Those were still the days when Hollywood cast the press photographer as a helpless chowderhead, slightly stooped in posture, following his glamorous, masterminding reporter and waiting in bewilderment for his command: "Shoot that." Now most journalism schools give courses in photo-reporting and in some of Hollywood's more recent productions the mantle of glamour and wisdom has been slipped over the squared shoulders of the photographer.

This miniature social revolution has taken place in the span of a few years. Not long ago a news photographer entered a house through the delivery door. Today he is greeted at the front entrance. But I recall as late as 1940 the class distinction made by the United States Navy. Three of us from *Time* and *Life* came aboard the USS *Enterprise* for a period at sea. The two writers were berthed in "officers' country." I was sent below with the enlisted men. I liked it that way, but it was indicative of the Navy's attitude toward photographers. As a matter of fact, it was not until World War II and under the persistent pressure of Captain Edward Steichen that the Navy took its own cameras from the hands of enlisted men and made the job a respectable one for officers. Today, the U.S. Navy's picture record made by the Steichen group is one of the greatest of the war.

This revolution, to be sure, is an American product not yet widely bought for export. In Britain, the photographer's position is even now by no means exalted. At the annual dinner given by the Royal Academy in London, for instance, the few selected photographers who are permitted to make pictures are hidden behind specially hung curtains which cover them and their equipment from the view of the distinguished guests as one might screen off a plumber who unfortunately had to make repairs during the evening. But even here its recognition is slowly spreading. For picture coverage is the most dramatic development in reporting in our times. By 1936 the products of the new, fast thirty-five millimeter cameras were catching the imagination of editors and readers, and in that year *Life* was born. Its creation was predicated upon a new form of visual journalism. The nation was ready for it and it became an immediate success. Almost single-handedly it brought the photo-reporter to his present respectability.

A year before *Life* came into being I had put the typewriter aside for the camera. I had left New York for Washington to join the Resettlement Administration which merged into the Farm Security Administration. The United States was then fighting its way out of the great depression and I was sent with my cameras through most of the forty-eight states to record the nation's dramatic recovery.

9

I joined the staff of the new magazine when its first issue was going to press. In that year the shadows of another great war began to lengthen.

2.

"Wonderful to Watch"

One scene keeps coming back to me from those early days on *Life:* there was a large room called the bull pen filled with desks and heaped with books and papers, pictures and charts and maps. Young men and women sat among them telephoning, reading, talking, typewriting. An editor came in. "Anyone here an expert on brain surgery?" he asked.

There was a moment's silence and then a young reporter tore the paper out of his typewriter. "Not yet," he replied, turning to the telephone, "but give me ten minutes and I will be."

This was the brash spirit with which we grew in those young years. We expanded with the magic and speed of protoplasmic cells: young men and women appeared, formed departments, and these grew, divided and multiplied until they filled the top floors of the Chrysler Building with throbbing, growing tissue, crammed into offices and overflowing into passageways, all vibrating with brilliance and temper, with ego and expression, with ideas and idiosyncrasies. Like cells we suddenly appeared and pushed about for existence, or perished and were replaced. No idea was too absurd to be tried as a story. Sometimes two people found themselves on the same assignment, each representing a different department. And sometimes when the story came in the department assigning it had moved along to new interests or had died along the way and the pictures, finding no takers, finally came to rest on heaps of others, now repositories for discolored coffee cups and ash trays.

But it was a magazine for expression and creation and for youth, and never mind the fatalities. The death of one creative urge simply cleared the way for another. We had an insatiable drive to search out every facet of American life, photograph it and hold it up proudly, like a mirror, to a pleased and astonished readership. In a sense our product was inbred: America had an impact upon us and each week we made an impact on America.

In the field the small staff of photographers was laced back and forth on the whiplash of ideas brandished by these young editors and assistants. Seldom did we finish one assignment before we were sent hurrying on to the next one. In these first years I had no home at all. All places were alike to me: all stimulating, all exciting and full of people and things to be seen and photographed.

One day stands out in my memory as more or less typical: I began it taking pictures of the processing of skunk fur in the dank basement rooms of New York City's garment district. That same morning I flew to Washington to photograph Congressman Sol Bloom in his Boy Scout uniform and at noon took a chartered plane to Johnstown, Pennsylvania, where a strike had shut the Bethlehem Steel mills and the town was under martial law. Four hours later I flew back to Washington and that night was on my way again, this time to Waycross, Georgia, where I was to do a story on one J. J. Wilder who raised bees. The details of that story have now faded; I recall only that Mr. Wilder was not particularly pleased to see me and that I wired New York "Wrong season for bees" and was sent off again on another wonder of man or nature or science.

Early in 1937 I went to Texas. Holland McCombs, a tall, rangy Texan, *Life's* reporter there, was waiting for me. I remember his greeting: "You ever been in Texas before?" he asked. "No," I replied. "Well," he said. "It's big." That ended our first conversation. It also became the title of our first story.

Holland liked to exhibit Texans to me. I had the feeling also that he liked to exhibit me to Texans. I know one time when we were making pictures of an old and weathered range rider who

struck me as something right out of the Indian wars, I heard
him whispering to Holland, as I circled him with my camera:
"Ain't he a bird!" And Holland whispered back: "Wonderful to
watch."

By the end of 1937 *Life* had fattened into the most spectacu-
lar success in American publishing history. Its staff continued to
grow and its editorial obsession with pretty young women was
reflected in the choice of its employees. Nowhere in my travels
had I seen such beautiful girls. I began to spend more and more
time in the bull pen, for it was here, toward the end of the year,
that I first saw Shelley Smith.

Shelley was slim and lovely and she moved with the rhythm of
a dancer. She once had been one. Her voice had exciting tones
and she laughed a lot. I had never before met a young mind with
such clarity and such searching qualities. She had the wonderful
confidence of youth. One night after I had worked late in the
darkroom I found Shelley working alone in the empty bull pen.
Her desk and the floor around her were covered with books and
pamphlets and sprinkled with sheets of paper all scribbled over
with arithmetic. It was past midnight and Shelley's hair was
mussed where she had run her hands through it and her lipstick
had worn off. She looked as toilworn and distracted as a healthy
twenty-two-year-old can look. I asked her what she was doing.

"I'm balancing the budget," she said with a curious smile.
"You know, for the lead story this week on federal expenditures."

"Balancing the federal budget?" I asked incredulously. "All
by yourself?"

"Oh, no," she said earnestly. "I take my results down to the
accounting department and check them on the adding machine."

I think I was in love with Shelley from the first day I saw
her. But that night I was sure. Our courtship was short and often
carried on at a distance. But six months later, in June, 1938, we
were married in a little church in Brewster, New York.

By the summer of 1939 my assignments had begun to change.
Shelley continued to work after we were married and I continued
to travel. But I was no longer homeless. And my stories were

concerned less with skunk fur and more with the threat of war and America's potential to protect herself. By then the whirlpools of fright which Hitler and Mussolini had sent rippling across Europe had reached the United States; and we were feeling the pressure of Japan in Asia. In mid-July I went to New London, Connecticut, where the Navy had its great submarine base. The editors had recalled that in 1918 Marshal Foch had predicted that "the next war will begin where the last one ended." They had therefore arranged for me to photograph a submarine at sea. That's where I was when the news came that Japan had set up a blockade between Canton and Hong Kong and that the United States had renounced her commercial treaty with Japan.

The last month before the war I worked at the Army Air Corps experimental base at Wright Field. I remember the radios in every hangar and every research laboratory blaring out the hourly flow of news: Hilter and Ciano meet at Salzburg; Hitler demands the Polish Corridor; the German Army marches into Slovakia; Germany and Russia sign a nonaggression pact. The day I finished my story on America's most advanced fighters and bombers Hitler's warplanes bombed Poland and his armies swept across her land. That week Britain and France declared war on Germany and the British liner *Athenia,* with 292 Americans among her passengers, was sunk in the Irish Sea in the first submarine action of the war.

Now *Life* was faced with the problem of photographing a war four thousand miles away. Those of us in New York were reduced to covering small local developments in reaction to the big news. The inadequacy of this was apparent to all of us. Thus on September 13, less than two weeks after war began, Shelley and I flew out of Long Island for Paris. We were going as a photo-reporter team to cover the war at closer hand, and I was to head for the fronts wherever I could. The night before we left, Shelley had completed her research for a story entitled "Neutrality" to appear in the following issue of *Life.* As we flew toward the war fronts of Europe, one passage I was reading caught my attention: "The first great fact about American neutrality," it said, "is that though America may be neutral, Ameri-

13

cans are not. They hate Hitlerism. In that respect, America is far nearer war than it was in 1914."

When we arrived in Lisbon the war seemed even farther away than it had in New York. For one thing, our dramatic flight to the war fronts which had started in a whirl of preparations (we had three days' notice we were going abroad) and a mounting sense of crisis had been interrupted by two cloistered weeks in Bermuda where my appendix, which had burst high over the Caribbean, was removed. But our main trouble was that although we were already styled "foreign correspondents" neither our office nor we had a very clear idea of what that entailed. Today Time, Inc., has one of the largest and most effective foreign staffs in the world. In 1939 Shelley and I were the first of the roving correspondents *Life* was to send afield—prototypes bearing little resemblance to the assured and well-instructed reporters who travel the boulevards and trails today. Then we were green. And so were our editors.

And as we wandered uncertainly along the sunlit and mosa-icked pavements of that steep-hilled balcony of Europe, the war seemed not only far away but inaccessible. We had rushed off eagerly, equipped by our editors with gas masks from the last war, money belts, each stuffed with a thousand dollars in small notes, and Portuguese transit visas. But we had no permit to travel through Spain nor visa to enter France.

I like to think back on those first days in Europe because I was younger then than at any other time in my life—younger than when I was a boy in the boatyards, younger than when I first became a reporter in New York. For although I was troubled by our inability to get at the war, I was enchanted by all that was new to me in the Old World. When we weren't pleading at the consulates, we spent our days exploring the medieval slums that encrusted the hill under the ancient fort and the waterfront along the Tagus River. I was especially excited by the tiny Portuguese fishing craft, with their ancient bright designs and the curious blue eyes which brought life to their prows.

Later, when we had finally crossed from Spain into France, a suave French officer who struck up a conversation with us in a

14

bistro asked about the craft we had seen in Lisbon. I described these little fishing boats in detail, and it was not until months later that I realized, suddenly, that he was an intelligence officer and that we were being grilled about ship movements. I was embarrassed then, but now I'm sure that he never really knew whether we were blushingly naïve or members of that worldly tribe of informed but unrevealing correspondents.

In Paris a cable awaited us. The great British battleship, *Royal Oak*, had just been sunk by a submarine, and since combat along the Western Front had by then lulled into patrol sorties, it was decided that we should leave for Britain where I was accredited to both the Admiralty and the Royal Air Force.

Britain was a sobering experience for us. The nation was quiet and determined; behind a sometimes jocular front there was a spirit of no-fooling. At the airport we were examined politely but thoroughly: our bags were turned out, our shoes examined, all our notes read, the origins of our names questioned, and every page of the paper-backs we carried on the plane was felt over for the pin pricks of a possible code. In London sandbags grew like mushrooms in the damp streets and the wide parks were crisscrossed with trenches. Air Raid Precaution squads staged mock raids in which the victims wore printed signs describing their make-believe wounds. Windows were taped with strips of paper against the shattering blast of bombs rumored to be measured by the ton. And on everybody's shoulder hung a gas mask—that talisman against the most fearful of then known evils.

I spent two months in England that grim winter, among the dockers in the Port of London, the green troops drilling at Aldershot, the county families who had opened their big homes to evacuee children, the young airmen of the RAF. As I remember it, we did not see the sun once and the monotonous gray of rain and fog was interrupted only by an occasional freeze during which roads and railways were blocked by snow and water pipes burst in the houses. The only relief in the blacked-out cities, the cold and fogbound countryside and the foreboding which hung over the land was the warm wry humor of the British who seemed to thrive on discomfort and bad news.

I was in the south of England working with the RAF when the astounding report came over the Moscow radio charging the Finns with having fired on Russian troops and demanding that Finnish forces be withdrawn twenty-five kilometers from their boundary. On the last day of November the Russians bombed Helsinki and began their invasion of Finland. For nearly a week my office wrestled with visas. Then I flew to Stockholm.

One night on a train packed with civilians and Swedish troops and traveling with a British correspondent, I began my trip northward toward the frontier and the little Finnish town of Tornea where Finnish military permissions awaited us. All night and all day we rode through snow and cold. At noon the sun rose, a sickly ball a few feet above the horizon, and then dropped away, lighting for a brief period dark figures of tiny men laboring along the countryside through the deep snow. The Russians could bomb Helsinki, we said. But what kind of war could be fought in the snows of an arctic winter?

3.

"Russians Are Pigs"

Tornea is a sleepy little frontier town at the extremity of the Gulf of Bothnia. Between it and the town of Haparanda on the Swedish side runs the Torne River and in the winter solid ice bridges it, joining the two countries whose lands extend into the arctic night. Across this bridge of ice we walked, that December night, from brightly lighted Sweden into the blackness of Finland.

In black silhouette the town was moving: a mass of passing, flickering cigarette ends, of almost indiscernible figures lumbering under heavy packs; moving to the sound of many boots marching, of muffled voices and the rumble of vehicles. This was our first view of an arctic night war, like a showing of endless footage of underexposed film.

We were expected and the Finnish officer who found us did so by sound and we greeted by feel. He had come through the shapes of darkness calling our names. And when we finally met, it was with a fumbling of gloves and grasping of hands. "Welcome to Finland," his voice said in the precise English which Finns speak. "We have been waiting for you. The world is waiting for you. Yours is a grave responsibility: to see and to tell what you see. Every Finn today looks to your countries for salvation."

We stumbled after him along the ice and snow of the roadway until the black form of a building loomed and suddenly a door opened and we were struck with light and warmth and the sound of singing. When our eyes adjusted we turned to our escort. He was a lieutenant, but he looked more like a poet as he stood before us with a wisp of beard on his chin and a bright ski sweater over his narrow shoulders and he told us at once that indeed that was what he was. This was the beginning of a war that would engulf us all, he said. "The world will sing the song of Finland." And pointing, it seemed accusingly, at us, he exclaimed: "You will see how soon!"

We followed him into the large dining room, crowded with disorder and loud with voices and the scrape of dishes, and as we squeezed past the tables hands reached out and patted us in welcome. They belonged to young men wearing ski clothes and bright sweaters and from them we caught snatches of a polyglot jargon. We were seated at a table already covered with many small dishes of pickled fish and a waitress was pouring beer from a big brown bottle when the lieutenant was called away. Immediately there was a rush for our table and we were surrounded by broad-shouldered young men holding glasses and shouting, "Inglis! Inglis! Welcome. A toast to America and England." We rose to the outstretched glasses.

One young man thrust his hand into mine. "I am Italian fighter pilot," he said. "You fighter pilot too?" We said no. We were correspondents. At this there was a shout of laughter. "I know. I understand," he grinned. "And I am a salesman. I came to sell bicycles. It says so in my passport." He waited for the laughter to die and then he continued seriously: "We are all here together for a purpose. Everybody in this room." And he swung his arm about in a circle. "British, American, French, Italian, Swedish, Danish. We welcome you among us." This was cut short by the return of our lieutenant who made an obvious show of displeasure. Our guests returned to their own tables and the lieutenant moved from group to group of them whispering something that brought quick glances in our direction. The smiles were gone.

When he rejoined us the lieutenant sat silently for a moment, his hands in his lap. Then somberly he spoke several lines of Finnish. "That is from a north country ballad," he said smiling gently. "In English it would read: 'Indiscretion is evil. Among friends there is no evil.'" We waited. "What you have seen and heard tonight must for now be our common secret. This is just a beginning. These are the first of the great armies of the world which will join Finland in her fight against aggression. Already, I am told, the American Navy is on its way and soon it will be followed by troops from America and England and France. You will see," he ended in a whisper. "Finland will be the battlefield of the world. Together we will crush the Russians. Until then the Finns will show the world how to fight and how to die."

Sometime in the middle of the night he put us aboard a troop train for Rovaniemi on the Arctic Circle, headquarters for the Finnish forces of the north.

When we arrived, I learned that the first major battle of the war was then being fought some sixty miles north, on the Kemi River. I left at once in a whitewashed staff car, traveling through snow embankments which at times towered over the car and squashed against us as we skidded from side to side. Above us was the clear blue-black of an arctic heaven, blazing with a dome of stars I had never seen before. Momentary sweeps of color made constantly changing patterns as the northern lights danced through the skies. The countryside was quiet, a world of forests and ice and unending snows.

The fighting was almost over as we walked up the snow-banked path that led from the road to the river. In the sickly half-light we followed its stained track onto the ice. Here the Russian dead spotted the river crust. They lay twisted and lonely in their heavy trench coats and formless felt boots, their faces yellowed, eyelashes white with a fringe of frost. Across the ice the forest road was soiled with battle, strewn with weapons and ammunition, with bits of uniform and woolen clothing, littered with papers and letters and pictures, with sausages and bread, gloves and shoes. Here the bodies of Finns lay with bodies of Russians. Everywhere were dead trucks and sleighs, dead tanks with blown tracks, dead carts, dead horses and dead men, blocking the road and defiling the snow under the tall black pines. Here, in a winter of nights with no days, on an obscure river north of the Arctic Circle, in snow that engulfed a man on foot to his bayonet belt, exhausting him and making him stagger like a dying insect, in temperatures that solidified the lost or wounded into frigid death, here the Finns met the Russians at the Kemi River and stopped them in the first great battle of the war.

A Finnish officer reconstructed for me the battle that was ending. A Russian division that had been at war games in Karelia had suddenly turned and crossed the frontier into Finland. Into the dark night it moved, a single column in the deep snow along a single road through the forest. A lumbering seventy-ton tank led the column, filling the forest silence with the explosions of its motors. Behind came the infantry, on foot, in carts, in sleighs, on Mongolian ponies.

Almost from the moment of invasion Finnish ski patrols paced the column and watched it silently from the familiarity of their own forests. Then, when the snow and cold had slowed it and spread it into a long, thin line, the Finns came out of the trees and hit it at the center, cutting the infantry from its supplies. The column stopped. Finnish ski units sealed the road at both ends. For days there was no escape from Finnish fire, no shelter from Finnish cold. The Russians were trapped. And here, in one of the loneliest and darkest battles of history, numb and dumb with cold, they were overrun and died in frozen heaps.

Now, as we walked among them, tiny crystals of frost settled

19

over the dead and the debris, giving the field a soft and lacy quality. The rap of guns and the boom of artillery finishing off the battle across the forest seemed strangely detached and far away. Their sounds were muffled and echoed our footsteps as we moved along the battle road, erect and quick as one would walk through a graveyard at night.

The sun had gone again and now the moon was rising, making tiny sparkles on the snow. We recrossed the Kemi River, falling in with a ragged column of troops who were coming out of the battle for relief. No one talked and the dark world was filled with heavy breathing and the scrunch of many feet on the snow. Then we heard shouting and yelling ahead of us, a frightening sound in the prolonged silence, halting the troops and sending us to the protection of the snowbanks.

When we heard the laughing we went on. The road had widened into a little village and a crowd of soldiers had filled it. I walked forward into the group and pressed in among the figures and saw the black heap around which they circled. It fluttered! It was a man standing with two blankets hung over his head, one dragging crazily down his back into the snow. Then I saw the eyes, wild lights furtively flicking left and right, and the tongue moving over an indefinite mouth.

A Finnish officer came up to me and pointing with a helmet which he swished like a sickle, screamed, *"Ruske!"* I lost the rest in the unfamiliar language.

The prisoner ducked his head and jerked back and forth. The body shook. A Finnish soldier suddenly thrust a lighted match before the face and the arms flew up in involuntary reflex. The soldiers roared with delight. Another soldier pushed in before the Russian. We could hear him yell something and then the metallic click as he snapped a cartridge into the chamber of his carbine. Then he shoved the barrel between the Russian's eyes and the soldiers again cried out with delight, their derisive yelps echoing and calling back from the forests on both sides of the road.

A Finnish officer peered at me in the moonlight. He put his

flashlight on my yellow arm band and read aloud: *"Sanomaleh-timies."* He looked at me. "Journalist," he repeated in English. Then he said to me: "He is Russian, this dog. He is like all Russians—dogs."

Two men with rifles were now prodding the prisoner forward. The little group waded over the snowbank and into a low-roofed wooden schoolhouse. For a moment after we brushed through the blackout blankets into the brightly lighted room we all stood like bats turning our heads toward sounds. Then we could see. School benches were piled one upon another in a heap on one side, blackboards with faint white images lined the other. A table with a bare electric bulb dangling above it stood in the center. Fifteen or eighteen officers and men, all heavily clothed, sat or stood about. On the table was a map, several automatic weapons, a nest of German grenades and a steaming teapot. Behind it sat a broad-shouldered Finnish major, his pale eyes impassive and his firm mouth controlled, neither stern nor smiling. Across the expressionless face a scar ran from ear to chin.

The Russian, still trailing his hood of blankets, was shoved before him and the major went into his interrogation without introduction. The replies came in dry whispers and the men in the room laughed loudly with every answer. He was forty-two, a dairy worker from Leningrad where he had a wife and three sons and a daughter. He thought—he struggled with himself to bring out the right reply—he thought that his unit was on the Helsinki front. The room roared with laughter and the soldiers pounded their rifle butts on the floor. Kemi River was hundreds of miles north of where he thought he was.

The jeering audience was crowding forward and suddenly a soldier slipped up behind the prisoner and yanked the blankets from him. The Russian whirled with a tiny cry of fright. With a quick frown the major barked a command and his men moved back. Then, his face once more impassive, he paused before starting his questions again. When he did his voice was more gentle, almost soothing, and the interrogation was soon ended.

Reaching forward, he offered the prisoner a cigarette. The Russian stared at him and at the outstretched hand. His tongue, large and white, licked his cracked lips and he slowly raised two blackened and bloodstained hands toward the cigarette. He hes-

21

itated, then looked full into the eyes of the Finn. Suddenly tears welled down his dirt-cracked face and rolled off his encrusted, padded uniform. The room went silent. Gently the major placed the cigarette on the corner of the table and turned away as if to study the papers before him. For a long moment he sat withdrawn in silence while the Russian continued to tremble, his face now smeared where he had rubbed at the tears with the padded cuff.

I reached in my musette bag for my camera and flash gun. The major looked up. "You want to take his picture?" He beckoned to me. I stepped forward to move the Russian about facing the camera. He was rigid and shied from my touch like a mare. I turned him about and he moved slowly, reluctantly. I waved several soldiers out of the background and the prisoner watched me frantically. As he looked about and saw himself standing alone his knees sagged further and knocked audibly in the silent room.

"It's all right," I said assuringly. "I'm only taking your picture." But the major did not offer to translate. I held my camera aloft to show him but he only cringed away from me. Through the finder I saw his hands move up slightly in front of him and then drop. I flashed.

The Russian wheeled around, screaming. He sagged to his knees and grasped the table leg. There he remained, head pounding the table, weeping, stuttering Russian.

For a moment no one moved. Then, in shame, some of the officers and men slipped out of the room. The major jumped up and gently raised the sobbing prisoner. "You're not hurt," he repeated soothingly. "You're not hurt. We are not shooting you. We are taking your picture." He reached for my camera and held it to the Russian's wet face. "Look through the window." He spoke as one would speak to a child. "See through the window."

The furtive eyes flickered about the room. Then one eye caught the finder and two black hands reached up slowly and took hold of my camera. For a moment he peered through it at me and into the little group of Finns who waited quiet and embarrassed. Suddenly there was the flick of a smile, then a

22

laugh. And then as the major held him he shook with screams of laughter.

Now the whole room was laughing and half a dozen hands were poking cigarettes at him. Someone put the blankets back over his head and we followed him out through the blackout curtains. Outside, the major turned him over to some guards and again he was surrounded by a gathering of soldiers in the moonlight.

The major was walking away when he heard the fierce, threatening cries of his men again and he whirled about, barking an order. Again there was silence. Then, as the major passed me on his way back to the schoolhouse he stopped, hesitated before me, and started on again. Over his shoulder he said harshly in English: "Russians are pigs."

4.

Night Train to
Haparanda

The arctic war in Finland was the first of its kind in our times. Since then floating ice fields have been converted into air bases and radar stations, and arctic military exercises have become important phases of training schedules. In recent years great progress has been made in human survival in the frozen regions of the world, but in 1939 clothing and equipment for subzero weather were not much advanced over those of the Middle Ages, and the cold was a terrible adversary.

It was more than the cold, though, that hampered the correspondents covering that war; it was the Finns themselves. They were intent on keeping their losses secret even from their friends.

The best that correspondents could do was to organize trips for themselves and these, invariably led by a Finnish conducting officer, were inexplicably delayed along the way and either never arrived at the scene of battle or arrived only at its very end. As far as I know, no foreign correspondent ever witnessed a Finnish defeat. And even on a field of victory where the corpses of Russian and Finn lay commingled I was forbidden to photograph the Finnish dead. If we managed to elude our conducting officers long enough to get stories of Finnish reverses they were snapped up by the censors. At least one correspondent was thrown out of Finland for trying to evade censorship.

Thus until the very end of the war the news which got out was of an unbroken series of Finnish successes. Months later when I read the *New York Times* for this period I found the following sequence of front-page headlines: "Russians Retreating in Arctic from Finns," "Finns Victor on Central Front," "Finns Drive Ahead on Three Fronts," "Finns Push Battle over Foe's Border," "Gains on Soviet Soil Reported by Finns," "3000 Russians Die . . ." The world was prepared for a Finnish victory.

This, of course, was absurd. Finland was magnificently brave and her military campaign was one of the proudest in history. But she was a tiny country, with almost no air force and no reserve, pitted against a giant. Her only hope of survival, as the poet of Tornea had predicted, was with outside help. But the Finnish success story had minimized the urgency and very little help came. By the end of February it was clear there was no longer any hope for Finland.

The night train from Helsinki was packed. Soldiers with their kits and civilians with their huge bundles blocked the passageways but the usual humor of a troop train was absent. The Russians had broken through at Summa and Finnish resistance was collapsing. The war was lost. And I was on my way back to Haparanda on the Swedish frontier.

The train lurched and I turned from the window where ice crystals were re-forming over the little clearing I had scratched.

Outside in the moonlight the snow fields and the black forests I had seen so many times in Finland were moving by. Inside, the three Finnish officers who shared my sleeping compartment were already stretched out on their bunks. They had nodded when I came in but none looked at me again. And none spoke until the next morning, when the train was approaching the frontier.

We were dressing in the narrow compartment. Suddenly the tall colonel turned to me. "You are an American," he said. He was shaving and he stood swaying with the train, a straight razor held delicately away from him. The others did not look at me. The colonel began to shave again. Then he stood over me, wiping the cream from his face with a towel.

"You are leaving Finland," he said.

I looked at him, suddenly feeling cheap. "Yes," I said in a half-whisper.

He threw his towel on his bunk and pulled on his tunic. He had cut his cheek and a tiny line of red was swelling into a bubble. "At least you will tell them that we fought bravely." I nodded.

When he buttoned the collar of his tunic his hands were shaking. "Your country was going to help," he began again. Then louder: "You promised and we believed you." Then he screamed: "A God-damned dozen Brewster fighters and no spare parts was all we ever got from you. And the British sent us guns from the last war that wouldn't work."

The other men were dressing. Their backs were turned. The train had come into the station. I was picking up my gear when the colonel seized me by the shoulders and spun me about. His fingers dug into me. Then he let me go and dropped onto a bunk and wept convulsively.

The others slipped out of the compartment. The colonel rose as I was leaving. He wanted to say something but he fought it back. As I left he put his head out of the compartment door and watched me go. When I looked back I noticed that the tears had run into the blood on his cheek and together they stained his face.

25

5.

"Parachutistes!"

The lights of Swedish Haparanda were garishly bright, the food shops seemed opulently filled and the people had too much color in their cheeks. As I wandered among them I had an urge to shout at them or to pull on their coat lapels and point across the river into the darkness and say: "Don't you know what is happening over there? Have you seen the dead and dying? Do you know what war is like?"

I learned later that everyone coming out of a war into a neighboring atmosphere of peace has similar impulses, sometimes almost of hatred, for the people who live in tranquillity next to lands at war. Now as I stood in the snow still wrapped in my Finnish Army sheepskins and looked back at Finland I seemed to have been there for years. It was, in fact, a small war, curiously compact: invasion, resistance, defeat, all within a hundred days. But something about it clung to me like an unwholesome smell, evoking images I wanted to forget.

Shelley awaited me in Stockholm and we began at once a story about Sweden under the threat of war. The impact of the fall of Finland was beginning to reverberate and military and political prognosticators were talking portentously about the rest of Scandinavia. Sweden was in full mobilization. Flags flew at half-staff "for the death of Finland" and everywhere the Swedes talked nervously about the danger of attack on the homeland. Every able-bodied man was a soldier and if he was not wearing his uniform it was hung neatly in his bedroom with

26

his rifle beside it. And every soldier thought of himself as an intelligence officer and every member of his family his assistant. I was arrested everywhere: in Stockholm in front of the Royal Palace, at the University of Upsala, at a railroad junction in the lumber country of the north, in the port of Göteberg. Always it was a well-meaning citizen who challenged me. As he accused me of spying, a crowd gathered. Then the police came and took me away. At the local station house the men in authority were always courteous and after examining my identification papers sent me along with kind wishes.

And so we progressed through Sweden, from city and factory through the great forest areas to military centers, always delayed, always a little behind schedule, until on our return to Stockholm we found a cable from our office asking me to leave immediately for Rome. Shelley stayed in Sweden to wind up our story while I flew to Italy where, after nearly two years of being turned down, *Life* had finally and inexplicably received official permission to photograph the Fascist state.

It was a frustrating experience trying to photograph Italy in the spring of 1940. In Sweden the obstructions of overzealous civilians were smoothed away by placid officials; in Italy it was officialdom itself that hampered me—though fortunately they were almost always either lacking in zeal or quite delightfully inefficient. When there were no loopholes in their regulations there were weaknesses in their guards. My days became a game of double talk and surreptitious pictures. May 9, 1940, was designated the Fourth Anniversary of the Founding of the Italian Empire. On the steps of the enormous, white marble Victor Emmanuel Memorial Monument in Rome, Mussolini was awarding medals to the mothers and widows of soldiers who had died in the Ethiopian campaign. I had come with the usual Propaganda Department permits and passes, with the usual result: two blackshirts followed me and managed to move in front of my camera whenever I raised it. However, as Mussolini and his entourage came down the steps of the monument I was able to make one quick exposure, shooting between the shoulders of my escorts. I was seized for my effort. I protested. "There must be some mistake," I said. "You have been following

27

me all morning. I am here by invitation of the Propaganda Department." I produced my passes.

They brushed them aside and hurried me on. "We know," said one in a low voice as they pushed me through the dense crowd. "But we too are being watched and followed." Somewhere along the way they melted into the throng and disappeared.

What happened to them after that I do not know, for that night the Germans began their invasion of the Lowlands and the next day I left Italy for France. Later, however, when *Life* printed the picture I had grabbed between the shoulders of the blackshirts and captioned it, "The elderly butcher-boy of Fascism struts out," our entire staff in Rome was escorted to the airport and expelled from Italy. It was not until the fourth of June, four years later, that we were able to return. At that time I came back in with the head of a column of Mark Clark's Fifth American Army.

In May, 1940, when I arrived in France, German Panzers rolled steadily through crumbling French defenses and Paris kept her head averted and tended to her business. Restaurants overflowed, tailors took fittings for delivery in sixty days, the walks were crowded with strollers and baby carriages and people dozed on the brightly painted park benches. But the city, outwardly calm, even gay, was on the verge of panic.

Soon restraint was to give way to nation-wide hysteria. There were previews to this. The most frightening came a month before the great city was to be abandoned. It was a fine afternoon and the wide avenues were swathed in sun under a cloudless blue sky. I was in our offices on the Champs Élysées reading the discouraging news which was coming off the ticker. A girl burst shouting into the room. Her hands were shaking and her face was blanched. "They have come!" she screamed. "The German parachutists. They are here. They are landing all over Paris!"

We rushed to the window. The sky was bright and empty. The Champs Élysées was quiet. The scene of the strollers below was unchanged. Someone tried to calm the girl. "But I saw them myself," she protested. "They floated down right in front of my window." She pointed again to the Champs Élysées. Then: "See!" she exclaimed. "Look below. Everybody down there has seen them too!"

It was true. Something had happened below. The whole pattern of the holiday groups had suddenly changed. People gathered in clusters all along the wide street. They stood with necks craned, their faces to the sky. Traffic stopped and there was a din of voices and a movement of excited gestures. We rushed down to join the crowd.

"Have you seen them?" someone asked us.

"Seen what?"

"The parachutists! The Boches are jumping on Paris. See, the sky is full of them!"

We looked up. There was neither parachute nor plane. We moved from group to group. Everybody had seen them: "The Boches!" "The parachutists!" "Seven planes!" "A hundred planes!" "Twenty parachutists!" "A thousand parachutists!" "Green parachutes!" "White!" "Orange!"

We asked the police. They had seen them too. We stopped some flying officers. They had seen them and were leaving for their station. They grew more excited as they talked to us. They began to run down the street. We got a taxicab. They were easy to get for the drivers were all standing beside their vehicles with their necks craned. All over Paris it was the same thing. Everybody looking up. Everybody pointing somewhere.

Late in the afternoon we ran it down. There it was, on the edge of the city—remnants of a barrage balloon. It had broken its mooring that morning and had been floating free over the city, its dangling steel cable damaging roofs and chimneys. A French fighter had climbed aloft and shot it down. When it burst, its fabric floated down in bits and pieces, each personifying a repressed fear, each taking on the shape and color of the grotesque nightmare of France before its fall.

I had arrived in Paris on May 12 with a permit to stay ten days. It was my problem to get it extended and to obtain authority to go to the front. This, in their panic and indecision, the French denied me until early June when everything was already lost. Then, suddenly, my permission was granted and at a moment's notice I was put on a military train bound for Verdun.

But in the morning when I arrived, I was met by a French officer who told me brusquely: "It is my duty to see that you return at once to Paris." When I protested that I had been promised conduct to the front he said bluntly: "There is no longer any front. There has been a major breakthrough at Sedan." I was to wait for him, he said, and he would see that I was taken safely back to Paris.

It was a beautiful morning and it had all those qualities which poets discovered long before armies attacked in Panzer envelopments. As I waited outside the station the morning warmth and the smell of earth and horses stirred vague, remote memories. The grass and the new-leafed trees were soft as fur. Green moss painted little designs over the sandstone front of the hotel across the street, crawling in the sun along the masonry and into old bruises left by artillery and shrapnel from the last war. Over the doorway was chiseled the word "Verdun." What a magic word it was and what images it inspired of a French Army that rose to greatness on these rolling hills and stood in its own blood to turn back the German invaders.

Then in the distance I heard shouts of command, the rattle of equipment and the step of men and horses. Out on the road I could see them coming toward me in a column. When they approached they stuttered and slipped over the rounded cobblestones. They were tired men, bearded and soiled. They had no vehicles save ammunition carts and a few supply wagons pulled by horses. And there was no exchange of welcome between them and the few townspeople who passed them on the street or watched them from their front gates. This was another French Army in Verdun, a dispirited one moving back through a dispirited city.

It was one week later. The car in which we were traveling

was an American convertible Auburn supercharger, bright red and with an abundance of chrome. Our office had bought it when the first talk had swept the city that Paris might be abandoned and a premium was put upon anything with wheels. We had paid a ransom for it. It was neither the color, the shape nor the symbol for flight but those were days when hasty decisions were made and we were glad to have it.

Sometime after midnight on the tenth of June word had spread through the city that the government had packed in the night and fled in secrecy. By sunup the great exodus from Paris had begun and the odd assortment of vehicles from our office there had joined the stream of traffic southward.

We assembled at Tours where the government rested briefly in semishock, meeting in old buildings and cafés and restaurants. And when the news came that Paris was to be declared an open city, Andrew Heiskell of *Life* and Max Corre, a French Army lieutenant attached to the Ministry of Information, and I decided we would go back to photograph it.

By now traffic had swelled to a struggling, halting, pushing, suffering stream of people in convulsive hysteria moving southward like a huge school of fish fighting blindly against each other in fearful, instinctive flight. With Lieutenant Corre riding the running board and screaming abuse at the traffic which continually forced us off the road, we pushed the red supercharger relentlessly against the current. The jam tightened with every mile as tributaries fed into main arteries. Fine limousines crawled alongside broken-down carts, creaking trucks filled with whole factory staffs and families, and vans of exclusive Parisian shops moved abreast of bicycles and baby carriages and handcarts. And trudging and bumping along on foot, men, women and children moved on slowly, piteously laden with possessions.

Everybody was there: the expensively dressed and the shabby, governmental bureaucrats lugging attaché cases and sausages, military officers riding in staff cars accompanied by their wives or mistresses, children lost and crying, soldiers wandering aimlessly, some having deserted from their units and some having been dismissed with dispirited blessings. Slowly down the roadway they crawled, offering little aid to each other, passing without a glance those who were broken down or who begged gasoline, pausing only to relieve themselves by the side of the road or to pass along wild rumors.

And watching them by the hour in fascination, farmers and their families stood silently in their barnyards until, with the sudden and inexplicable action of a crystal forming in a solution, they too grabbed a wagon and a few possessions and rolled out of the comfort of their homes and off the lands of their fathers and into the fighting stream.

As twilight came, the struggle against the traffic had exhausted us and as we neared the village of Roncevaux, some fifty kilometers from Paris, we pulled off the highway and followed a narrow country road into a wheatfield. We would sleep here, we agreed, and go on into Paris in the morning. It was quiet except for the evening birds, and we ate from cans without speaking. Then we slipped into sleeping bags and lay down on the grass and watched the stars slowly brighten in the heavens. A few bits of clouds drifted by and it began to rain a little. We got back into the car, sleeping bags and all, and fell asleep.

We were awakened by shouts, almost in our ears, and by flashlights piercing our eyes. Turning round in my sleeping bag like a bug in a cocoon, I felt the cold end of a gun against my forehead. Then a huge cocked trigger and an enormous hand, blurred and out of focus, filled my world. Behind it a voice shrilled: "Come out without making a false move or you are a dead one." There were many men, I could see now, with guns and pistols and dogs. Within the car we were all struggling with the same dilemma: how to get out of a sleeping bag, within a car, without making a false move.

Corre protested and received a clout over the ear. A clubbed head has a sound of its own and we did not protest again. "*Parachutistes!*" voices exclaimed. "Boches!"

Out of the car we rolled and were stripped of our sleeping bags. They prodded us along a sandy road, with our hands extended over our heads, barefoot and stumbling in the blackness. With guns at our backs and the hot voices still in our ears we came into a blacked-out village. A shadow crowd surrounded us, pushing and threatening. "We have bagged a good catch tonight," we heard them say. Then we were shoved roughly through the crowd and into a small building lighted with a single swaying lantern. With this we could see our captors. They were old men in peasant coats and berets and corduroy trousers, standing in long, grotesquely moving shadows. They carried pistols and bird guns. One had a face like a football. He thrust it close to mine. "In the last war," he yelled, "we were the soldiers of France. Today France has no soldiers. The blood has gone out of their veins. They have no honor!" He looked round as the others nodded. These were the Garde Civile.

We were taken upstairs and pushed into a room. We were in total darkness and we bumped into chairs and tables and felt for the walls. In the next room we could hear them telephoning. They were angry and they shouted, calling for the Garde Mobile. When these came we were taken again into the room with the lantern. We found that they had searched our car and found our papers and were examining them now. These men of the Garde Mobile were erect, young and efficient. They read our papers and questioned us briefly and then they shook their heads.

"These are American journalists," they said to the old men.

"German parachutists!" shouted the Garde Civile.

The young men and the old men quarreled before us. "Friends of France," argued the Garde Mobile. "Look, their papers are perfectly in order." They held out our identification cards and passes in the light of the lantern.

"Good papers, certainly!" yelled the Garde Civile. "All parachutists have good papers. If these have good papers it is only proof of their guilt." They swung their weapons and the Garde Mobile moved in between us and led us back into the dark room. A shadowy figure brought us cigarettes and we lit them from the end of a piece of glowing cord. They tasted like string and our throats were parched. We could hear them in the next room. "Cowards!" a voice was shouting. "Is there no blood in your veins?"

Someone had tiptoed into the room. "Come with me quietly," he said in a low voice. "You must go now. We have brought

33

your car up from the field and it is ready for you. The motor is running. You must get in it and drive away at once. The Garde Civile have lost their senses. We cannot hold them back much longer."

He led us out of the building and waited while we got into the car. As we drove away we could hear footsteps running behind us in the night.

Ten miles south of Paris the stream of traffic had thinned to a trickle. We stopped at an army gasoline dump. One soldier was left. He was slovenly and unshaven and he remained seated on a broken chair when we came up to him. The Germans were now in Paris, he told us, and there was only a small French tank unit between us and their advance forces. He was waiting for a lorry to pick him up and soon he would be gone too. If this was true we had no hope of getting our story. We could not take Max Corre into a city already occupied by the enemy.

A little farther down the road we ran into the tanks. They were rumbling southward. "It is true," they said. "We are the last defense. The Boches are behind us." We turned in their dust, southward.

Back at Tours the next day we discovered that the government was already fleeing south again and the great flood of refugees followed along after it like the crest of a wave. We drove with them, tired and dulled, the hours lengthening into days.

Then one morning in the middle of June we were rolling through a tiny valley of green pasture bespeckled with white daisies. The sun was high and hot. Cars still crowded each other bumper to bumper and the people who rode in them were stained and crumpled. For days upon days they had lived in their cars and in the fields and a kind of herd numbness had grown upon them.

When a bearded soldier carrying his hat in one hand and a rifle in the other walked slowly into the traffic it stopped. Standing in the middle of the highway he raised his rifle overhead, turning it slowly like the needle on a compass pin. He shouted and the drivers turned off their engines so that they could hear him.

"Go no further," he yelled hoarsely. "It is the end. They have sold us out like rabbits. The government has capitulated to the Boches."

A great silence settled upon us. Slowly he lowered his rifle and tears ran down his beard and dropped on his chest.

Then, as the news spread, the sound of weeping filled the valley.

PART II

6.

Half a World Away

Shelley was waiting for me in Lisbon, that detached little portal through which we had entered Europe and the world of war. There was nothing more that we could do there now and our editors cabled us to come home.

This was the summer of 1940 and America was building up her national defenses. We were not yet committed to the war, but our neutrality was precarious. In Europe France had fallen, England carried on alone. In Asia the Japanese were biting deep into China and were threatening Indo-China. They had bullied the British into closing the Burma Road and were trying to bully us out of using the British naval base at Singapore. Our answer was to send more of our warships into the Pacific for extensive naval maneuvers. In September I was sent to photograph these war games at Pearl Harbor.

Here was a new kind of military operation for me: slick, shiny, rolling under Polynesian skies on the soft seas of tourist posters. Aboard the USS *Enterprise* the crews of machinists and fuelers and plane handlers wore shirts and wind helmets of bright red, yellow and blue. Each morning on the flight deck they gathered around a briefing officer as eagerly as a football squad listening to their coach. It was a mechanized, synchronized, dangerous game for them. Then we were only playing at war. Europe was half a world away and Japan lay far across the blue Pacific. And when we came ashore we were immersed in the gay colors of seemingly everlasting peace: sparkling beaches and bright bathing suits and flashing flowers and lush green trees, all daubed against the blue sky and the blue sea bearing its gray-blue fighting ships.

I shall always remember in these bright colors my last look at Pearl Harbor that year before the war. From the crest of the green hills that rise behind the base, I looked down upon a massive blue fleet of battleships and cruisers, all tied bow to stern and side by side, reflecting themselves motionlessly upon a blue-tinted mirror. The next time I saw that scene it was in smudgy black and white and I was sitting in a prison camp reading the Japanese-edited Manila *Times,* its entire front page plastered with aerial photographs of the American fleet smashed and burning and sunk.

Toward that fate Shelley and I sailed in December, 1940.

7.

Chungking

At first we could only hear China and smell it. The twentieth-century air transport which found a hole in the weather and skillfully landed us on a spit of sand in the middle of the Yangtze River was again enveloped in yellow mist. As we walked cautiously across the primitive field we could hear voices near and distant running the scale in a pleasant singsong. And there were smells, evil and new—and yet intimately familiar and human. The rolling mist boiled clear in places and we could now see the steep cliffs of the city with its tiers of bamboo shacks which clung to them. This was the ancient city of Chungking.

Shelley and I had come here on our first assignment in Asia, to photograph this capital and military headquarters of China's resistance against the invading Japanese. For three and a half years the war had been going on, and China's back was against the wall of the Himalayas. Now, this summer of 1940, the Japanese were trying to knock her out from the air, bombing Chungking as Hitler had bombed the cities of the Lowlands. We had flown in from Hong Kong over the Japanese lines that stretched inland along the coastal plains. Now we stood with the land of China under our feet, and as the fog parted saw the black mass of sandstone that was the city of Chungking, the hills towering in irregular forms over the confluence of the Yangtze and Kialing rivers. Here was the last embattled stronghold of the Chinese government, a city swollen with refugees and battered by daily bombings. Many hands had chipped into the heart of its rock and the crowded life of the city flowed in and out of the tunnels which honeycombed the hills.

Lean little men with shaven, scaly heads and wiry brown bodies picked up our bags and, breaking into a quickstep and chant, took off for the city. But we were told that we must ride: the steps up the rocky sides of the city were too steep and we could never keep pace with our coolies. But ride what? These, said the man from the Chinese Ministry of Information. And he pointed to some frail bamboo seats slung to bamboo poles. Grinning, rag-clad coolies stood beside them. We glanced back at the American-made airplane, glistening silver where the mist parted, and hesitated before this new conveyance. For there is a reluctance on the part of those who have come from the frontiers of our age to move backward too rapidly. And if the frail chairs caused concern, the thought of being carried by human beasts of burden brought repugnance.

But since our Chinese host faced no such conflict and was already sitting in his chair, shoulder-borne, we stepped testingly and awkwardly into ours and were swung aloft and carried away feeling like fattened hogs on the way to market. The progress was slow up the steep stone steps. The hammock-like chairs forced us to lie back and our stomachs rolled and gurgled. But the impact of China on the newcomer is overwhelming and we forgot our uneasiness as we were absorbed in the ever-moving, fleeting scene of human action around us.

Chungking in the winter is a dank brown. The brown mud of its roads sticks to its people as it does to the walls of their shack houses and shops. It clings in great blobs to their straw sandals and converts the wheels of the rattling and repatched rickshas from circular to irregular elliptical shapes. When the sun shines, says an old legend, the scrawny, scurvy dogs of Chungking bare their fangs and howl. It is a city of endless hovels, yet a city where life is lived in the open. The shops and shacks have a roof and three sides and the business within them spills out into the street. There rice is polished with pole and wooden mortar by the gutter. There the chairmakers split their green bamboo poles and stack them to dry and itinerant barbers snip at the close-cropped heads of their customers. There whole families live and work and eat. Tiny daughters hold tinier brothers so that they can urinate through open, padded pants into the gutter. And there, in the ever-running stream at the roadside, the women pound their frayed cotton clothing and wash their vegetables.

We were transferred at the top of the city steps from sedan chairs to rickshas. But the men who pulled us had the same lean brown legs and arms and patched blue jackets and trousers as the men who had carried us. We rolled on bumpy wheels through the throngs and slime, the smells and chanting song. The life of a ricksha coolie is short, but with a knowledge of his art he may gain himself a month or two. On the pull uphill the artful coolie lowers his shafts and bends his knotted body almost to the ground. On the downhill stretches he tips his passenger helplessly backward as he pulls the shafts up under his armpits and rides them, his feet touching the ground only to keep balance. "Hiya! Wei! Wei!" he yells as he skims through the crowds.

As we were alternately dragged and whirled up and down the hills of the city we heard, at one point, the engines of our plane gaining altitude as it headed back for Hong Kong. We saw it come up over the city and as it roared directly above us felt the throbbing vibrations of its tremendous power. Then it was lost in the mist. That world was gone; our new one was the straining, sweating body before us.

Late in the day we pulled into the compound of the Press Hostel. It was quiet and the setting sun made a pink glow in the steamy sky. In the compound were patches of green grass. A Chinese policeman wearing a black pith helmet, black sneakers and a padded black coat eyed us while he fingered a German Mauser which hung from his belt on a piece of braided straw. We were home, Shelley and I—two more correspondents with a shocking ignorance of the East, come to see and say things about it. Home was one tiny brown room. It had a brown mud floor, brown mud walls, a brown discolored straw roof and one brown-framed window without glass. In it were one small table, one bed and one chair, brown. But we were made welcome.

Long after dark we started out of the compound for dinner with a mixed party of Chinese and Western newspapermen. We gathered in the street outside the gate.

A woman came from behind us out of the darkness. "Li! Li!" she screamed. She fell to her knees, supplicating, bowing, crying for money. The Chinese with us tried to brush her off but she held on to us, screaming and pointing at a pile of stones in the darkness near the gate. On it, arms and legs spread wide, lay a dead, naked child. The woman wept and shouted frantically. Then she picked up the inert baby by one foot and held it aloft before us like a butcher with a plucked chicken. We dropped money at her feet and moved away quickly along the muddy road. But her cries seemed to shut out all other voices and followed me through the crowded streets.

In front of a shop, lighted by flaring tung-oil lamps, a man swung past us with an empty bottle hung on a piece of straw. The bottle suddenly broke free and smashed on the flagstones. There was a rush and a scampering movement from all directions and we were jostled by urchins grabbing, fighting each other, for broken bits of glass. In the stalls we were passing we could see in the wavering light the secondhand wares for sale: twisted, rusty nails; a single shoe; broken china bowls; frayed and patched clothing. And everywhere were the filthy beggars, dressed in rags, thrusting forth their tin cans or chipped rice bowls as they cried, "Give. Give."

The impact was exhausting, the cries of the beggars penetrating deeper and deeper as we reached the restaurant. We climbed to the second floor of the dimly lighted building, a ruin of bamboo and mud rebuilt upon a ruin of a ruin. We sat at a big, round table in the steamy heat of many bodies, eating hot food. The smell was new and wonderful, the room was crowded with people who ate with gusto, talking in high voices, poking chopsticks at each other as they shouted, making one feel, as they pushed the food down with pleasant little noises, that this was man's most uninhibited and glorious moment.

But the beggar woman with her knotty black hair holding the naked child by one leg kept flashing back upon me. She blotted out the room and the food and her cries of supplication drowned out the sound of Chinese laughter. The wine helped, warm rice wine to be tossed down in a gulp, and finally it and the delicious food and stimulating talk threw the beggar woman and her child out of focus. Indeed, by the time we left the restaurant late at night and stepped out into the quiet streets, a rolling arm-in-arm group making our way homeward amid imperfectly sung American songs, the image of the woman and dead child remained only in the complexities of my subconscious.

But back again at the compound gate I looked, almost expecting to see her standing there in the moonlight holding the child toward me. I knew that such apprehensions were only my own shame and sense of guilt turning me toward that heap of stones. But then I saw something moving in the shadows. Irresistibly I stepped nearer. It was she. There she sat, with her back to the wall, a patch of moonlight across her dirty face, her twisted hair askew. Her eyes gleamed as she watched me without moving. By her side I could see a dish of white rice. But there was something in the shadow of her arm. It was the child! It was stirring! It was nursing at a long, dark breast, its tiny hands playing and punching at it like a calf stimulating the flow at the udder. The mother covered it defensively with a bit of quilt and she glared at me defiantly. Then I understood: in starving China any ruse is a fair one that adds a few more days to life.

44

8.

Uncommon Drama

A little group had gathered at one of the main intersections of the city and was staring curiously at a large billboard on which was hand-painted the map of western China. At the center was Chungking, a black circle to which were attached long arms like those of a clock. At the end of the longest, now pointing nearly due east, were fixed three miniature wooden airplanes.

It was morning and the sun was beginning to drink up the night mists. The dust in the street was drying again, the life of the tradespeople moving in and over the vague remains of the bombed buildings assuming a lazy drone. The crowd in front of the billboard was transient and absently conversational, like those that pause to oversee a building excavation or glance at an unusual window display. Shelley and I, on our way to take some early morning pictures, stopped for a look at the map. Coolies with water buckets slung over their shoulders joined us for a minute as an excuse to rest. Government clerks on their way to the office paused beside us. A woman carrying a rooster in a cagelike bamboo basket set it down while she adjusted her thick pink cotton stockings, rolling them below the slit of her skirt. Near her stood a slim woman of better class, the tiny spray of jasmine in her oiled black hair sending out a piercing sweet smell over all of us.

Around from behind the billboard a soldier appeared. He climbed on a box and reaching on tiptoe slid the toy planes down the arm toward Chungking. As he pushed them over the border from Japanese territory a murmur sounded from the crowd. We all looked up toward the nearest tall building where an empty flagstaff stood against the sky. And as we watched a great, round red lantern was hoisted up the staff to hang at the top. A strange and fleeting pause interrupted the buzz of the city as the people saw the signal and knew that an air raid was coming. Soon a second lantern was raised, the urgent alarm, and the entire population of the city emptied into the deep, dark tunnels, waiting there hunched in the darkness for the bombs. When the all-clear sounded they would flood out again to pick up their lives aboveground. And thus, day after day, did China live in that year we came there—that year before Japan's attack upon the West—a continuing, outlandish mode of life.

Indeed, my whole memory of China is one of uncommon drama. No doubt it has been heightened by the circumstances of the war which denied us the conditioning of the coastal cities with their twentieth-century façade, and dropped us deep into the Middle Ages where we alighted like creatures from a space ship. No human beings I had ever seen looked so unusual or lived so remarkably. Not for months did it occur to me how unusual we looked to them. As a consequence we and they had the busiest time regarding each other. Much of my peering was through a camera view finder and on crowded streets my horizon was often limited to an eyeball which zoomed in to look through the other end. Once a bold stranger gripped the camera to steady it as he peered so that the two of us held it between us, eye to eye on the view finder.

No country has more humor than China—or more misery. Once we were climbing a steep, dusty road in the hills of western Chungking. It was busy and the human beasts of burden sang a cadence as they panted along under creaking loads. We were tired and plodding, with our eyes on our feet. Abruptly on rounding a sharp curve we came upon an old man kneeling in a hole by the side of the road. He was in tatters and his face was yellowed and his eyes rheumic and glazed. He held forth an old and withered arm and a rusted beggar's can to the traffic that moved impassively by him. Later, when we returned along the same road and rounded the bend, the old man was no longer in the hole. He was lying by the side of the road, dead. And already in the hole, kneeling and holding forth a rusty can, was a boy in rags who, like an actor on cue, had come quietly from the wings for a brief appearance on the China stage.

China's drama is not lost upon the Chinese. Especially when it concerns a foreign visitor, they are not always willing to let a fact stand in its way. We were planning a story on an old Chinese family, one of ancient lineage who lived, unchanged by time and war, behind the tall walls of their ancestral home. Peking, of course, was the place to find such a family but that part of China was already in Japanese hands. So we went instead to Chengtu, the cultural center of western China, an ancient capital.

With the help of Chinese and American Christians, who in turn enlisted the aid of the Governor of Szechwan, we found General Chen I-tin, a scion of an ancient family with a fine old home on one of the quiet, tree-lined streets of the city. He was a glistening fat man, round-faced, round-bodied, smiling and gross. He was delighted when he learned of our interest and he met us ceremoniously at the first gate and walked us through the front courtyard where the footmen were washing down the rickshas and the women hung up cabbages to dry, into the rock garden of the second court where his grandchildren were playing with the goldfish, through the household pharmacy where a male nurse was compounding deer antler powder and into the kitchen sheds where the cooks were steaming rice and slicing strange vegetables, slabs of dried duck, black fungus and soft cheesy bean curd. In the daughter-in-law's courtyard a childish amah was playing with a baby and in the courtyard of the first wife we passed Mrs. Chen praying in her little private Buddhist temple. In the ancestral hall, the center of the big house of the first court, a maid was lighting incense before the ancestral tablets as she did twice every day. General Chen stopped here to show us the scrolls that recorded his family tree.

This was a mistake, for Shelley is a relentless seeker after small truths. I was busy with my pictures when she came to me with the facts. After painful questioning and some fumbling

47

and stumbling, she had brought General Chen's true family history to light. He was, in fact, a soldier of fortune, an orphan, from Honan, who had proved himself so agile in the civil wars among the robber barons of the west that he had himself become a warlord. With his political power secure he had bought this fine old house together with its family records and the ancestral bodies themselves in a family tomb outside the city.

But even Shelley, struggling through an unwilling interpreter, could not find out what had happened to the original family. And later, when General Chen accompanied us to the second gate to say good-by, I could not help but feel that he carried himself with the air of a man whose grandfathers had always lived there.

Once there was a man in China with two heads. He lived upon the south bank of the river at Chungking and we used to see him as he climbed the steep embankments hauling water in double buckets on his bamboo pole. He would bend under his load until one head looked down upon his feet. The other, which hung from the back of his neck on a thin cord of tissue, dangled and rolled upon his shoulders. Of course it was not truly a second head. But it was exactly the shape and size of his real one and the top was covered with hair and it gave the illusion that it was looking at you.

One day he came aboard the American gunboat, the USS *Tutuila,* which lay off the river bank. Twice a week the gunboat's sick bay was open to the villagers nearby and he had come for some help with a leg infection that was not responding to the village doctor's concoctions. The American surgeon was fascinated by the coolie's second head and after an examination told his interpreter that if the coolie wished he would remove the growth which had been such a bother to him all his life. There was no danger, he assured, no pain, and it could be done with one snip of the surgeon's knife.

The coolie was aghast. Reaching one protective hand round his second head, he rushed past me and over the side of the gunboat and into his sampan without waiting for the leg dressing.

48

He never again came to sick bay. And each day the surgeon, from the decks of the *Tutuila,* watched him labor up the hill ashore, carrying his load of yellow river water, while the second head, rolling about, looked down upon the barbaric foreigner who lived upon the river.

Early in 1941, I photographed two faces. The first belonged to Lao Kung, our coolie, and I remember him best when his name was shouted through the Press Hostel compound and he came running heavily toward the voice, his huge, bare feet slapping the ground, and his head pushed forward like that of a faithful dog answering a call. Lao Kung was perhaps twenty. He had no hair at all on his face which was large and flat and Mongolian. He wore a perpetual smile which made you think that he understood what was said and liked what he heard. He swept the earthen floor of our room every morning, swishing the dust about with a shock of straw and whenever there was an air raid he piled all my cameras and photographic supplies and all our bags and books into two huge baskets that swung from a bamboo pole and trotted with them into the shelter two hundred yards away. A stronger back I have never seen. But his mind was not quick and sometimes he was the butt of jokes to which he turned an appealing and pained expression of confusion.

He disappeared during one of our trips away from Chungking and I scarcely thought of him again until long after I had left China. But now, in some obscure way, his face has become fixed in my memory alongside another I photographed that same day. It belonged to a man named Chou. He was a small-boned man in a dark frayed suit and dirty shirt and his unshaven face was black with whiskers. But his eyes were clear under heavy arched brows and his movements quick and his hand delicate around the Chinese brush with which he was writing. He sat in a tiny unheated room in Chungking preparing reports for Yünnan. Now, years later, when I see Chou En-lai's picture in the newspapers his face is clean and smoothly shaved and his clothes of good quality. And then I see Lao Kung and I wonder if he too has shoes on his feet and warm clothes on his back and if he still comes running heavily when he hears someone call.

9.

"Big Buddha in Cave"

Chungking, as China's wartime capital and military headquarters, bore the brunt of the air war. But the Japanese armies stretched from Manchuria to Indo-China. They garrisoned the large cities in strength. In the vast land mass of China, however, they could do little more than hold lines of communication. Here they were spread thin and harassed by guerrilla bands. But there were even more extensive areas of China where there were no guerrillas and no Japanese. Here indeed the war for the Chinese was remote. It conscripted their sons and was blamed for increased taxes. Otherwise it was just another evil force, more distant and less disastrous than floods and famine.

In June, 1941, we traveled through some of this country on our way to the front lines that lay along the Yellow River on the Shansi-Honan border. Long before, in their first great push of the war, the Japanese had advanced as far as the mountain ridges that skirt the north bank of the river and this spring, in a sudden thrust, they had gained the river bank itself. Since this was the most active and accessible front during our time in China, Shelley and I, with Mel Jacoby of *Time*, were on our way there. We had flown to Lanchow, the capital of Kansu, and from here our goal was Tungkwan, five hundred miles away. There were no airplanes, no trains, no automobiles. Our fastest means of travel was public bus. We secured our tickets and spent the night at a travelers' inn. We were to leave at dawn.

When the loess dust from the Gobi does not obscure the summer sun in Lanchow, the morning countryside is lighted with a golden brilliance at five o'clock. But in the small courtyard of our inn darkness still lingered and the greenish clay paving was wet and slimy with the emptyings of chamber pots and wash-basins from the small bedrooms that surrounded it.

Outside, however, morning had arrived with its hard, dry light and a foretaste of its heat. In the fields surrounding the town farmers were already at work. And in the caravan yards the camels were loaded for the day's start along the bright high-way of the old silk route, northwest around Tibet. In the street before us the traffic of the day had begun. Loaded rickshas, sway-ing sedan chairs, hand-drawn wagons with ungreased wooden wheels shrieking wildly, took turns at jostling the slow-moving coolies who waddled painfully under huge loads hung from bamboo poles across their shoulders. A line of boatmen trotted single file toward the muddy flats of the river carrying their rafts of inflated pigskins on their heads.

Now and then a laboring truck passed, a reminder that the twentieth century had progressed to newer forms of transport. But these were so broken, so patched and mended, that they merged indistinguishably with the ancient scene and gave no il-lusion of the new among the old.

At the doorway of the inn the Chinese passengers had already gathered to await the bus that was to carry us over the Six Dishes Mountains to Sian. Their bulky bedrolls, washbasins, baskets of squawking ducks and chickens, and their assortment of imitation leather valises formed little heaps about which they stood pro-tectively, listening for the bus. When it arrived, its radiator al-ready steaming from its short trip across the city, it pulled up well short of its passengers. The driver, a fuel conservationist, had turned off the engine some distance away and had misjudged his momentum. There was a rush for the bus and a hauling of bundles. The rear door was stuck fast but undaunted the pas-sengers boarded anyway. Like pirates climbing the rigging of a prize, they scaled the sides of the high, square wooden body, pushing and pulling their bundles with them, and entered through the open windows.

In a moment the three long wooden benches that served as

seats were filled with passengers, their baggage heaped around them like clumps of earth around the roots of newly planted shrubs. Containers of nervous chickens, bundles of vegetables and sacks of rice appeared miraculously atop the bus and hung from its sides, defying the law of gravity by virtue of a ridiculous piece of twisted straw.

In this confusion, so dear and familiar to the Chinese traveler, we three foreigners were left standing by the door of the inn looking helplessly at the driver. But he, a machine-age man, a person above the common run in unmechanized China, stood apart. In great detachment he surveyed the bus and its load. People were no concern of his; engines were his field.

We were rescued by a plump young man in the uniform of a minor government official. He hurried up to us, puffing with concern, the tight neckband of his tunic seeming to force his breath out in involuntary gasps. He told us his name was Lee and that he was sent by the Ministry of Information to see us safely to Sian. He also addressed our traveling companions. This he did with the most possible talk, gesture and heavy breathing. We understood almost none of it. But the passengers listened attentively, for in China all such discussions are made available to the nearest citizens and frequently their advice is asked and even accepted. From time to time one of the nearer passengers picked up the conversation and relayed it trumpet fashion for the benefit of those farther inside. After each such assist we received appreciative looks and pretty soon, after a great shuffling and moving of bundles and people, a space was made for the four of us at the far end of the bus and we climbed in and sat.

I looked around uncertainly to judge popular reaction to such unwarranted privilege and found that all the eyes riveted on us were friendly and the smiles genuine and even hinting of admiration. This struck me as unusual. For the gaze of the country Chinese upon the foreigner is commonly filled with curiosity, often with incredulous laughter, almost never with any hint of admiration. I leaned over to Mr. Lee. "What were you telling everybody?" I said in an unnecessary whisper.

"Oh," replied our guide and interpreter, "they asked where you were going and I told them to Sian-fu." This appeared to us to be scanty information for such a lengthy and animated conversation but it is not uncommon in China to ask an elaborate question through an interpreter, receive paragraphs of Chinese in return, and finally have translated the neat reply: "He says yes."

The driver, satisfied that the time had come to start, climbed into the truck cab that comprised the front part of the bus. His assistant labored at the crank. The bus heaved and shook, settled into a steady rattle that eased us down into our seats and settled the paraphernalia of the trip about us. The sweet smell of the alcohol fuel filled the bus for a moment and we were off.

The road and countryside out of Lanchow were flat and undistinguished. We were more concerned with our fellow passengers and with the sputtering engine which promised to demand a good deal of attention. After considerable effort the driver managed to jerk his gear shift into high and we were bouncing along the level country road to full throttle, a speed we judged to be about fifteen miles an hour despite the fact that the speedometer needle quivered at zero. Streams of fine dust began to pump up through the broken floorboards, filling the bus and settling over the heads and clothing of the passengers, reducing inequalities of dress and baggage to the uniform neutral hue of corn-meal yellow.

The gentleman on the center bench opposite me was a generous fellow who carried sunflower seeds in the two breast pockets of his dust-covered coat. We faced each other so closely that we had to fit knee past knee like meshed gears, but he more than made up for the mess of shells which fell upon my lap by providing me with small handfuls of seeds to chew. But the most impressive thing about him was his eyeglasses. Made of heavy brass, they pressed heavily upon his nose and clipped tightly behind his head. It was moments before I noticed that they had no lenses. "They give him face," explained Mr. Lee. "He is a merchant on a business trip and they give him face."

This last was shouted at us above a series of bangs and crashes directly behind us. The driver wrestled with his machinery in an effort to bring the bus to a halt and then leaped off. We caught a fleeting view of him as he galloped back down the road behind us in a cloud of golden dust. By the time we had climbed out and joined the others alongside the highway, the driver and his assistant were limping back. Between them they carried the gasoline tank which had dropped off. Sloshing with the odd-smelling fuel, it was deposited at our feet and, as everybody else sat comfortably on the small hilly shoulder of the road, it became quite evident that Mel and I had been chosen, not only by the driver but by our traveling companions as well, to take charge of reassembly of tank to bus. Since the tool kit consisted of a tire iron and a length of pipe we gained little face by our efforts among Chinese who, accustomed to the lack of modern tools, can perform miracles with a twist of rice straw and an iron bar.

But we got it on and soon were snugly fitted into the bus again and pounding down the road toward the first foothills. The radiator steamed like an enormous kettle, occasionally erupting into a fountain of boiling water, and the engine missed noisily. Finally it stopped and the driver turned and signaled us to dismount with him. His friendly gesture was repeated by the passengers who nodded knowingly and waved us from the bus.

The trouble was with the spark plugs. They needed cleaning. There was no wrench, but between the driver's discouraging kit and several small camera tools I carried, Mel and I managed to pound the plugs out, clean them, and pound them in again. When the engine started smartly at the first yank of the crank we were the only ones who showed surprise.

As we chugged along toward the rising hills most of the passengers dozed easily, leaning one against the other, holding bits of cloth for dust masks over their noses. But at each sudden stop—and we counted fifteen that first day—they woke to look inquiringly at us and we were urged out of the bus to assist in the repair work. In return we received increasing deference from our fellow travelers and on the second day, when we acquired a new passenger on the middle bench, it was obvious by the intense discussion and unabashed pointing that he was being briefed about us. When it was all over he rose, swaying a few inches above his bench and, clasping both hands before him, moved head and hands up and down several times in unison. We bowed back. He was a tall Chinese in a blue gown. He had a wispy gray goatee, and from a wart on his right cheek hung several other long hairs which he tweaked occasionally with a yellow finger nail two inches longer than the rest. "He is a rich man," said Mr. Lee, ignoring our interest in what had been said about us. "The long nail shows that he does no manual work. This gives him face."

The bus developed new troubles. It could not make a full left turn. The road up the mountainside had been a relatively gentle pull but the descent was steep and twisting. We strained forward to calculate each oncoming bend. We relaxed when we saw a right curve coming. On turns to the left we sat alert, suffering through the driver's agony as he hunched his shoulders, pumped his brakes nervously to make them hold, fought to get his gear shift into reverse, backed up, and finally worked his bus around the corner panting like a rider on an unwilling horse. The other passengers, happily unaware of anything unusual, slept down the mountainside and only awoke as we pulled out into the level of the Kansu-Shensi border. Here we drove into a wide courtyard, a sort of graveyard of broken vehicles, which was the government checking station where police stopped all traffic for inspection.

We were all ordered out of the bus and a control officer asked for our credentials and tickets. Mr. Lee watched as we handed over our Ministry of Information identity cards. Then he produced his own papers and turned and wandered away. The other passengers, in more characteristic fashion, continued to press around the control officer as he slowly read our papers. Suddenly one of them, breathing excitedly in the officer's ear, began to exclaim. The whole group became animated. The man with the goatee led the discussion, pointing at us with his long finger nail.

We looked for Mr. Lee and saw him walking listlessly down the road. When we caught up with him he exclaimed: "I knew they would find out sometime, but I thought we could reach Sian first."

"Find out what?" we demanded.

"Find out that you are only correspondents."

"Only correspondents!" we pressed him roughly.

"Yes," said Mr. Lee looking uncomfortable. "The first morning I told them you were American fliers come to fight for China, and Mrs. Mydans was a Western-style nurse."

"But why?" we persisted.

"It gave you more face," said Mr. Lee.

There was an embarrassing silence and then as we started back for the bus I asked timidly: "But now, Mr. Lee. What will happen now?"

He shrugged. "They will no longer ask you to repair the engine," he muttered. Then he increased his stride and outpaced us to the bus.

The vehicle was loaded when we got there and as soon as we were seated the police waved us on and we continued into the valley. Mr. Lee went to sleep at once and we concentrated on the scenery, avoiding the eyes within the bus. The heat increased and the road straightened and the passengers dozed. I must have also, for suddenly I was jerked into awareness by a grinding of brakes and a shouting within the bus. Half the passengers were jumping out of the door, some were going out the windows. Suddenly I realized that all seemed to be waving, shouting and beckoning to us. Our immediate reaction was defensive. We held our seats and looked for Mr. Lee. He had disappeared.

Then we spotted him in the crowd outside the window. Puffing and actually smiling, he also was waving and calling us to come out. Everybody was laughing. Everybody seemed friendly. And at last we caught it from the man with the lensless glasses: "Come. Quick come," he was saying in a surprising revelation of English. "Big Buddha in cave!"

We followed him out of the bus and stood with him and Mr. Lee as the rest of the passengers, the driver and his assistant, all hurried off across the hard fields toward a cliff that we could just see behind a line of ancient cypress. As they continually turned and beckoned to us, we started after them at a jog.

"This is the famous Ta Fu Tze Buddha," panted Mr. Lee beside us. "They want you to see it and take pictures for America."

In the cool caves Shelley and Mel ostentatiously took notes on the height of the Buddha, his age, and the quantity of gold leaf that covered his enormous head. The passengers waited in watchful silence. Then I crouched below the towering figures and, slowly and impressively as I could, raised my camera and made the picture.

On the way back to the bus the gentleman with the whiskers

was beside us talking volubly. Mr. Lee was voluble too, and excited. He translated: "He says it is a great honor to have American correspondents here. Your presence, he says, gives much face to China."

When we were all loaded into the bus again and rattling down the valley road the man with the lensless glasses leaned forward and with a wonderful smile handed each of us a little pile of sunflower seeds.

10.

A Little Cloud

The fighting had ceased all along the river by the time we reached Tungkwan. The Chinese soldiers lay within the massive brick and adobe walls of its ancient fort which for centuries has commanded the Yellow River; and from its towering, crenelated battlements they watched the Japanese, dug into caves on the other embankment, watching them. Now and again there was an exchange of a round or two of shells. That was all.

We made what we could of the story and left the quiet river front, traveling westward by army truck across the dry, yellow countryside. Near Paoki an army colonel awaited us. He had orders to conduct us through his area. It was a very hot day and we walked for several miles over a rolling, roadless plain. The sky was clear and blue and along its edge, far to the west, was a tiny line of gray no bigger than a man's hand. As we came closer it formed into an elliptical fence. It grew higher and higher and suddenly it towered over us. We entered through an old wooden gate which hung on broken hinges. It had been propped ajar for us, all askew, and gave the feeling that it had not often been opened. There were Chinese soldiers at the gate wearing weathered uniforms. They carried German Lüger pistols on long wooden stocks and they watched each of us as we entered.

We were in a compound of yellow dust encircled by sharp gray stakes. All around us against the bright skies of north China was a fringe of barbed wire: the horizon. We were in a prisoner-of-war camp. It was the first I had ever seen. Everything in the prison was worn and aged and tired. The buildings were old and stained and the piercing sun laid bare the blemishes. Inside we found men lying or sitting in the shadows, or bent over little tasks. They did not look at us and they seemed vague and formless. A few worked at rickety looms of old bamboo and knotted string. Slowly they wove spiritless cloth with spiritless hands.

They were Japanese. Once they were soldiers in a faraway land. Now they were prisoners with yellowed faces and stained teeth. Their bodies were wrinkled and wasted and their ribs showed and their legs were large with beriberi. They moved listlessly and their eyes looked nowhere..

Long after we left China, I saw them. And even later, after I too had been a prisoner, I saw them. So that today the faces in my own prison camp and those in the yellow compound in north China are sometimes indistinguishable. And the barbed-wire horizons have merged into one.

11.

Makeshift and Make-Believe

We frequently relive our lives in the light of later events, history giving point and emphasis to otherwise disorganized impressions. Such are the moments I recall of the last months in Southeast Asia before the Japanese overran us there.

It was late in 1941. Shelley and I had come out of China and were in Malaya, doing a story on the great Singapore fortress which was a linchpin in Western defense hopes. With other foreign correspondents who had converged there as the tension in the Far East mounted, we were invited to witness a test of jungle fighting put on by elements of some of the newly arrived Indian Army.

We met in the bar of the Raffles Hotel where the latticed doors swung gently under the slow-revolving fans. Our conducting officer explained the operation very carefully to us, spreading a map out upon the bar. "The country to the north of us is thick jungle, as you know, and quite impenetrable to an army of any size. However, this morning we have dispatched a Sikh battalion straight off through this area. Their objective is this secondary road," he tapped the map, "twenty miles from their starting point. They will attempt to reach it by this evening. We shall drive around. If any get through we shall meet them as they emerge."

That afternoon, when we came up the black-top road, we found the entire battalion sitting in the shade of the jungle belt by the highway. They had been there some hours.

A few days later the same correspondents gathered again to witness a test firing of some of the big guns that protected the Singapore base. They were emplaced on the island of Blakang Mati, a small green hummock off the southern coast of Singapore proper, and they had not been fired for a long time. Green shrubbery and even some young saplings had grown up in front of them. The guns were fifteen-inchers, commanding the ocean approaches to the harbor, and when they were fired their enormous blasts tore up the shrubbery and withered the saplings' leaves.

Behind us the trees grew bigger and stouter. "What happens when you shoot that way?" Shelley asked the artillery commander.

"Oh, we don't shoot *that* way," the officer explained. "That's Singapore. We've got jungle to protect us there—miles and miles of it, quite impenetrable."

In mid-October we went to Manila to report on the defenses of the Philippines. General MacArthur, who was there as military adviser to President Quezon, had recently been recalled to duty in the American Army as Commander of the U.S. Armed Forces in the Far East. We were to show his over-all plans and the matériel he had at his command. This, we found, was one mixed American-Filipino division, an assortment of service troops, a few airplanes, a few tanks, a small unit of Marines recently evacuated from Shanghi.

For six weeks we traveled around the country photographing these and the tender young Filipinos—often barefoot, often drilling with sticks—and the green boys of our National Guard units who were arriving to fill out his strength.

In a boatyard in Manila we saw four torpedo boats under construction. Four were already in the water. This was the Philippine navy. At Clark Field, our only heavy-bomber base on Luzon, the shortage of aircraft was so acute that the commanding officer contrived a substitute to mislead Japanese reconnaisance. He had local Chinese craftsmen build replicas of the P–40 fighters and B–18s out of bamboo and canvas. They were so skillfully constructed that at first I didn't recognize them as fakes. And as it turned out the trick was tragically effective. For on their first attack, at noon on December 8, the Japanese concentrated on these bamboo illusions parked along the edge of the field next to the barracks and mess hall where the officers and men were at lunch. And thus by a bizarre twist of fate these make-believe planes helped to destroy their makers.

MacArthur had as well, of course, Cavite, the modern well-stocked navy yard with shops and drydock for our fighting ships, and Corregidor, the rock that guarded the entrance to Manila Bay, with its deeply tunneled fortifications and heavy-gun emplacements. No enemy could, or ever did, get by The Rock. As in the case of Blakang Mati, they didn't have to.

We finished our story on December 1, and that night we were invited to the annual party to celebrate the Army-Navy football game. It was the biggest American social event of the year, but this year it never really got going. The tables that were set out on the lawn of the club were never occupied by more than a few couples and the giant scoreboard that stood on the edge of the sea remained blank. The Navy ships in the bay had been blacked out, and a sudden radio silence cut off the play-by-play account of the game.

There was little dancing and no gaiety, and it was not until early morning that we learned that the Navy had beaten the Army, and no one really cared. For by then it was generally known that there had been a major alert that night, that officers had been recalled to their posts and that ships had quietly sailed away. And now, as night turned into the dawn of December 1, the guests who remained sat uneasily at their tables staring out past the empty scoreboard toward the dark sea beyond. For the feeling was strong upon us that somewhere out there in the distance the Japanese fleet was moving and that war was just over the horizon.

In fact, although we did not know it, at that very hour President Roosevelt was receiving the most ominous reports from Secretary of State Hull on his talks with Japanese envoys. And the Japanese fleet had indeed been seen operating in the China Sea. And that morning General Homma arrived on Formosa to join his Southern Army where it had been staging for the invasion of the Philippines. It was on that day also that he received his orders to attack on December 8.

12.

The First Roundup

It wasn't until years later, when I heard how General Mac-Arthur, Commander of the U.S. Armed Forces Far East, was informed that Pearl Harbor had been bombed and that war in the Pacific had started, that I felt less embarrassed about how I, foreign correspondent Far East, learned that we were at war. By chance a warrant officer in Manila, who happened to be lying awake in the early morning hours enjoying dance music short-waved by commercial radio from the United States, heard the report of the Japanese attack when an announcer cut in on the program with a flash. He telephoned MacArthur's chief of staff who in turn passed the news over a private wire to the general who was asleep in his penthouse atop the Manila Hotel. The time was 3:30, December 8, on the west side of the international date line. This was an hour after the Japanese had launched their attack.

Nobody telephoned me and I awoke four hours later. The sun was yellowing the city and a refreshing breeze was blowing in from the bay and the world seemed good. I could hear José pushing the morning paper under the door and I lazed in bed for a moment looking across the room at the big black type of the headline. Suddenly my mind came into focus and I knew what it was. I shouted to Shelley and jumped out of bed and picked it up. I read aloud: "Pearl Harbor Bombed. We Are At War With Japan."

Like us, Mel Jacoby had been switched from Chungking to Manila. He had just been married and he and his bride Annalee had a room near ours. I reached for the phone. Mel answered. "Mel," I said, "the Japs have bombed Pearl Harbor and we're at war." There was an annoyed voice and the telephone clicked. Mel had hung up. It was the kind of humor, he told me later, that he supposed newlyweds had to expect. I telephoned him again and by then he was reading his own newspaper.

There was, as always, the reluctance to forego old habits even in the face of world-changing events, and that morning in Manila, when the great war in the Pacific had at last begun, the city reacted slowly, shrinking from the truth. Mr. Chen, my Chinese tailor, arrived at the appointed hour carrying over his arm a white linen suit cut and roughly basted. He had to be sent away. Felixberto, the chauffeur of our hired car, had asked if he might come late that day so that he might wash the car. He washed it and came late and as a consequence we did not find each other until nightfall.

When I went past the yacht basin that morning I saw some men painting a small sailboat a lively red. Later I photographed it being thrown upon a fire built of other boats to keep them from falling into the hands of the Japanese. And during a quick visit to the High Commissioner's office I noticed two gardeners resodding several spots in the lawn. Just before I was imprisoned I saw a contingent of barebacked Japanese soldiers digging it up again and emplacing a cannon.

As the morning progressed the calm of habit and the comfort of doing familiar things began to give way to nervousness and insecurity. There were reports that Baguio and Davao had already been bombed and soon the air raid sirens in Manila were wailing. I was on my way to headquarters when I passed a unit of Philippine Scouts proceeding down the road, helmeted and hung with gas masks. I turned to follow them. "We're going to round up the Japs," the American officer told me tersely when I caught up with him.

Manila's Japanese community lived in the Quiapo area. They were mostly shopkeepers and artisans whose homes were in the small frame buildings, fitted tightly along the narrow streets of the area, that served both as living quarters and commercial establishments. Usually this was a busy section, with the open-fronted shops full of bright goods and the Japanese characters on the signboards giving an Oriental touch to the tropical city. But this morning the streets were deserted and the shop fronts were boarded over. A few dogs scampered away as the Scout contingent turned into the first street. The American officer, a captain, halted his men and re-examined a typed list of names and addresses he carried.

"This one," he said to the Filipino sergeant beside him. The sergeant called to his men and they ran about making a semi-circle in the street, their bayonets fixed, as though they expected an attack. A crowd was gathering behind us and the soldiers waved them back, warning them away from danger.

At that moment the door of the shop began to open and the Scouts froze, rifles thrust forward. The crowd behind us scattered like a flight of frightened birds. Slowly, from the side of the doorway, a little head emerged into the sharp morning sun as though thrust there on the end of a stick. For a moment it hesitated and then rode out timidly on the shoulders of a tiny man bent forward slightly under the weight of a bulging camper's haversack. He paused indecisively and bowed. A nervous half-smile wrinkled his face as he bowed again and again. Then he turned toward the open door and motioned. A stout little woman bent under another backsack came out. She bowed. And then she too turned and motioned inside. Nothing happened. She beckoned again. Then two little boys wearing Tom Thumb backsacks came running and after them a tiny girl, all clutching blindly for their mother and burying their faces and as much of themselves as they could in her skirts.

A feeling of misery overwhelmed me as I watched them huddle helplessly, clutching each other, frightened and at bay. And I think the captain felt it too for he stood a long time watching as though he were but a spectator. Then he suddenly jerked into action and shouted an order and the Scouts relaxed and lowered the rifles. He waved reassuringly at the little family. Then a truck rolled up and they were helped aboard with their baggage, the children still clinging to their mother and she talking to them quietly, her face bent down, trying not to see the Filipinos who had gathered nearby.

And so down the streets we went, musket butts pounding at doors, until we had them all gathered in the streets ready to be taken away for internment, frightened people blinking in the sun, holding on to their bundles and their children, turning away their heads when they saw me raise my camera.

For two years now I had witnessed the afflictions and calamities of war. But I had never been a participant. I had viewed them with something of the attitude of the doctor who knows the danger of the disease but who has never really suffered the pain. The time was soon to come, though, when I would feel the pain, for there was to be a turnabout and I would be the one standing with my bundles waiting for a truck which would take me away. And there would be a little man with a camera who would circle me, too, with maddening persistence, photographing me in my hour of degradation.

13.

Phantoms up the Road

In the first two days of the war the Japanese knocked out our air force at Manila and Clark Field and our naval base at Cavite. Then they landed in the north and in the south.

To the local population—American and Filipino—softened by long, warm years of peace, the situation was so bad that any elaborations on reality might seem to have been unnecessary, and yet they thought up many a nightmare to compound the terror that now gripped them. In Manila air-raid warnings were sounded constantly and at night nervous guards shot wildly at moving cars or at windows that leaked light. Often the sound of one nervous volley would be followed by the spatter of firing all over the city.

According to many there were parachutists dropping behind us, assault forces coming up the rivers and uprisings of enemies hidden among us. I remember hitching a ride on a provost marshal's car rushing to investigate a report that Japanese had landed at the mouth of the Pasig River. When we got there we were told that they had seen no enemy *there* but they had heard that Germans in American uniforms had come ashore at Legaspi.

After each bombing a rash of eyewitness stories described flashing lights and colored flares signaling to bring the attackers in over their targets. At Clark Field an American officer told me how a mirror tied to a tree had brought the Japanese bombers in on its beam. And at the Bay View Hotel we too observed and reported a flashing light which appeared each night across the city from us. Twice, teams of American officers worked from our window trying to triangulate its position. But it continued to flash right up to the surrender of the city—and after it, its operators presumably having changed sides.

The first Japanese landings were small and at far-distant points. We expected their major assault would come at Lingayen Gulf, a hundred miles north of Manila. I had been photographing the shambles of Clark Field and decided to go on up there. Near Rosales I found Lieutenant Colonel Arthur Nobel, who was organizing demolition teams and instructing Filipino farm boys in the preliminary technique of guerrilla tactics. He came out of a cane field with news: there had just been a full-scale landing assault at Lingayen and the shore defenses had shot the hell out of it. The bay was filled with floating bodies and the beaches were strewn with Japanese dead and MacArthur had credited the 21st Field Artillery with having repulsed the first big landing of the war.

I drove on fast to Lingayen but there was nothing there—no bodies and no signs of battle. Filipino soldiers were stringing up old barbed wire which had been reclaimed from nearby farms, and gun crews were lying resting beside their weapons. Otherwise the long stretches of yellow sand were empty. An American major joined me on the beach. "Looking for bodies?" he asked, his lips twitching in a curious smile. I felt suddenly embarrassed. "Well, that's what headquarters reported," I replied defensively. "I heard there was a big battle here."

"That's what I mean," the major replied. "Everybody wants to see the bodies and the wrecked boats. There are no bodies and no boats, though God only knows why we aren't all dead. There was no battle. This is just a green division and they've been shooting the hell out of shadows all night long. First one let go and then another. Finally the whole division opened up and the whole gulf was blazing—but there never was any enemy."

As far as I can learn now, the false battle of Lingayen Gulf on December 10, 1941, still stands in the records as the first major reverse of the Japanese in the war.

Twelve days later, however, the Japanese did come over the beaches at Lingayen. But by then I was back in Manila involved in plans to get out of the Philippines. For by that hour it was perfectly plain that we were now within an isolated garrison five thousand miles from base with our air force destroyed and our navy gone and our troops moving to Bataan for a last stand. The surprisingly rapid Japanese military successes in Malaya and Hong Kong, in Thailand and on Wake and Guam had sealed our fate and we knew that we must either get out or be taken.

Mel and Annalee Jacoby left the city on an ammunition barge headed for Bataan but each of the plans Shelley and I made for escape aborted. Ships were sunk or boats sent away in the night. Most of those plans are now mercifully fuzzy in my memory. But one I recall clearly; perhaps because it was the last hopeful one. A ship had come through the mine fields late in December to fuel and then make a run for it. The captain invited us to go along. But on the afternoon of the day we were to leave, a lone Japanese bomber found her sitting near the break-water and sank her as we stood there and watched. She went down by the tail with her bow and foremasts and bridge sticking up ugly and symbolic of our last hopes.

Years later she was still there just as I remembered her. And during the final mop-up of Manila, which took place in the port area and among the sunken ships in the bay to which Japanese soldiers and marines had fled for their last desperate stands, I was aboard the LCM which put an assault landing party onto the old wreck. Three Japanese on her fought to the end and died horribly, cornered and defiant. But a fourth surrendered. And it is an odd turn of fate that here aboard this sunken ship which to me had grown so large a symbol of my own captivity, I should make my only picture of a Japanese surrendering in combat.

As the year began to run out the ring closed around us. But our editors, reading news reports of the Philippines through censorship, were not yet aware of how fast and how far our military position had shrunk. A cable from them requested: ". . . another firstperson eyewitness story but this week we prefer Americans on the offensive." Shelley's reply, worded for censorship, as were so many in those days, was the last message we got through. "Bitterly regret," she cabled, "your request unavailable here."

Early in the morning of January 2, the Japanese entered Manila. They came up the boulevards in the predawn glow from the bay, riding on bicycles and on tiny motorcycles, their little flags with the one red ball looking like children's pennants. They came without talk and in good order, the ridiculous pop-popping of their one-cylinder cycles sounding loud in the silent city.

We had waited too long. It was too late, now, to get out. But the blow of this realization was softened when we saw that the soldiers were obviously under restraining orders. There was to be no massacre; we could forget the horror stories of the Nanking occupation. We could expect to live—but in what manner we would have to wait to find out.

I recalled the judgment of a captive in the last war. "Being a prisoner," he had told me, "is not a happy thing. First you are worried that you will be killed. Then when you are not killed you think, 'Well at least I can sit.' And then you find out that it is not the way you like to sit."

That's the way it was with us in 1941. For one thing, the little dream of "at least sitting" presupposes an organized prison camp with the captors providing some sort of program for the basic needs of our prison life. But the Japanese had no program whatsoever. Their only instructions to us as the roundup swept the city were to "bring food and clothing for three days," an order, we were soon to learn, that was based on their own confusion and indecision and lack of any plan except to seize us and dump us within prison walls.

PART III

14.

Santo Tomas

It was late in the day when they took us. A truck came by loaded with other Americans and we were put aboard and driven to Santo Tomas University on the outskirts of Manila. We turned into the main gate of a great dusty compound, the sunset red behind us, and when we were ordered to dismount we jumped down with our suitcases and looked around us at the darkening grounds. Heaped about us were the bags and bundles of those who had come before us, their owners all moving aimlessly, seemingly at cross purposes, flowing in and out of the gaunt building.

The truck swung round and headed out of the compound and for a moment we stood where we were, looking after it, realizing we could not go that way ourselves. We were prisoners.

Inside the building we found the hallways overflowing with bewildered men and women and crying children. People were carrying things and bumping into each other, sometimes asking questions and going off without waiting for answers. We wandered along the concrete halls with the others, peering into the classrooms that lined them. They were already crammed with either men or women. The Japanese had decreed that husbands and wives must not remain together.

At last we found a place for Shelley in a small barren room

with thirty other women, and in a nearby room a spot on the floor for me among a crowd of men. A single light bulb glared overhead in a swarm of insects and the men around me shifted and sighed and coughed as they lay on the concrete floor. No one spoke. For a long time I lay awake assessing how I felt: defeated, trapped, cut off. All these I might have expected. But more than these I felt the burden that is so heavy on all prisoners: lack of self-respect.

In the morning there was work to do—food to be found for breakfast for Shelley and me, our surroundings to be learned and a place to be made for us. And with these small worries a sense of life returned. Some of the prisoners had contributed the coffee they had brought with them to a communal brew and we found a line forming for it and joined it. The sun was rising and people began to feel more hopeful.

"We'll be out of here in a month," the man behind me said.

"A month!" someone challenged. "A week. We'll have American troops in here in a week."

Then the man who stood ahead of Shelley, a stout prosperous-looking citizen wearing an expensive Panama hat, spoke up. "You know," he said in a faintly Teutonic accent, "this is my second prison camp." All at once everyone was listening.

"You've been interned before?" someone exclaimed.

"Yes," he said. "In the last war I was traveling in Canada. I was a German then, on business, and when it began I was rounded up with the rest of the German community." A faint smile came over his fat face. "I remember those first days in the camp. We were all saying how soon we would be out. We even told our Canadian guards. 'Just a few more days,' we would say to them."

"And how long were you there?" several asked him eagerly.

"Till the end of the war," the ex-German said. "Four years."

There was a silence along the line as we began to shuffle toward the coffee, step by step, in a movement that was soon to become routine.

The Japanese had provided nothing for us beyond the empty buildings of the university set in their weedy compound. Before we came, soldiers had gone through and marked in chalk on the door of each classroom the number of prisoners who were to sleep there and whether male or female. Then they had set a guard at the gate and a patrol around the walls. Their orders, so explicit about rounding us up and interning us, had evidently made no mention of feeding us or providing any other necessities. We were simply left to fend for ourselves.

From this situation grew an extraordinary arrangement which came to be known as "the fence." Though we sometimes used the term in referring to the concrete wall, the stretches of barbed wire, and the iron-picket fence which surrounded us, more often the term meant just a small section at the front of the compound near the main gate. This was the place where the Japanese allowed the Filipinos to come with food and bedding and all the other things we needed to keep alive. At first they simply threw things to us as we crowded on the grass inside and they on the street outside. Later the Japanese, having provided us with a minimum allotment of rice and cereals from the Philippine Red Cross, regulated the traffic at the fence, systematizing it and cutting down on our contact in an effort to keep the more than material things from entering the camp. But in this last they failed. For all the months that we were there the Filipinos continued to bring us not only their food but this constant evidence—so desperately needed—of their friendship and loyalty.

Inside this new world of ours it was remarkable how quickly order was formulated out of chaos. Almost overnight the prison camp swelled to a crowded active community, a little city, in effect, isolated by battle, filled with refugees, and lacking in almost everything that we had considered necessities. Two things we did have in abundance: time and know-how. There was never anything that had to be done for which there could not be found an expert.

We started from scratch and despite the shortage of materials, repaired the lighting, flushed the choked plumbing, built showers and toilets, organized church services, established schools, set up improvised hospital facilities, evolved a democratic government with an elected executive committee to treat with the Japanese commandant, and made our own laws within those imposed upon us by our captors.

There were doctors from all over the Far East. There were dentists who came in with full kits of tools. One could have his teeth pulled, his hair cut, his shirt mended, his fever soothed. He could have his child taught by the same teachers he had had outside and he himself could study French, Spanish, music appreciation, etymology, or half a dozen other subjects. He might contribute his time to teaching such things, or to digging pits for the refuse, or picking the worms and warehouse sweepings out of the communal rice before it was cooked, as Shelley did, or to mopping the floors of the camp hospital shack and carrying bedpans for the dysentery patients, as I did.

We even had a police force. This, like our other community functions, grew out of necessity. In the first days it was agreed among us that for the good of the greatest number a small representative body would be chosen to treat with the Japanese and front for the rest of us. And since the Japanese commonly dealt group punishment for individual transgressions it was in our own interest to police ourselves. Our powers of law enforcement were limited, however, to public censure, for the most unpardonable breach in any prisoner-of-war code is to report the offenses of a fellow prisoner to the enemy.

Social disapproval in our confined world was dramatically effective in most cases although of course there were some whose social I.Q. was so low that public censure had to be fortified. A lady who was infested with head lice and refused the medical attention prescribed by the doctors was put in an isolation cubicle in the hallway. And once or twice a man who could not otherwise be persuaded to behave found himself in the back of the compound within a circle of men who walloped him into a community consciousness.

The problem of teen-agers—and even husbands and wives—seeking to be alone in the dark corners of the buildings and courtyards was dealt with by a self-elected body, the "Morality Patrol," and thievery was handled on at least one occasion by sending the culprit out into the busy compound hung front and back with two large placards reading: "I Am a Thief."

The Japanese commandant and his staff observed all this without comment. They wanted just one thing: to keep us there and to keep us quiet. In the first weeks they had done their part to show us what they meant. Three men, all young and single, had escaped one night by going over the wall. It was not hard to do. Next day they had been recaptured and brought back into camp. Here they had been systematically beaten so that their screams could be heard by all their fellow prisoners. Then they had been tried *in absentia* by a military court and sentenced to death. Four other prisoners, the chairman of our internee committee and the monitors of the rooms where the three men had slept, were taken from the camp next day to the North Chinese Cemetery and forced to witness the execution. It was explained to them, quite carefully, that in the future should anyone escape his roommates would be held responsible.

After that there were no more escapes. But from time to time, as the quiet, hopeless days went by, a prisoner might receive a summons from the Japanese military headquarters at Fort Santiago, and in the midst of our apathy a little pool of fright would form. It might come at any hour and its total effects accumulated within every one of us like the agents of the gamma ray, silent, penetrating and degenerative. Someone usually whispered to you that you were wanted at the commandant's office. And there a Japanese officer was waiting to take you away. Or you were simply rushed out to a car and you disappeared through the prison gates. Many never came back and there were various stories of what happened to them, all unpleasant. Some, we heard, suffered awful punishment and were then thrown into the old Spanish dungeons below Fort Santiago. And indeed, a few of these were still there, wasted and bleached and sunken-eyed, when we liberated Manila three years later.

But the most terrifying were the ones who did return. It wasn't what they told us that was so disquieting. It was what they wouldn't tell. When they were dumped back in the camp they simply turned away from others, or limped off, or lay silently day after day in the prison hospital, looking at the ceiling while the doctors dressed their bruises. I remember a friend of mine who was returned. He was a representative of Press Wireless, a press cable service which had handled much of the news filed from Manila before its fall. He had been gone for more than a month and when he came back he was emaciated and his body bruised, his wrists and legs ulcerated under the marks of ropes. I met him next day standing alone in the compound looking strange and vacant.

I said, "What happened?"

And he replied, "Nothing."

After a while he said: "Don't talk. Don't ever talk in here," and walked away. He never told me anything more.

At last I got a summons, too. But I was not taken to Fort Santiago. I was simply ordered to report to the commandant. "They have found out who you are," I was told. It was almost five months after we had been interned and our first commandant, a colonel in the Imperial Army, had been replaced by a civilian ex-diplomat by the name of R. Tsurumi who feared the military Japanese as much as we did.

Mr. Tsurumi was sitting in his office waiting for me and looking uncomfortable when I arrived. He rose and bowed and I bowed and he introduced me to two Japanese officers who remained seated. One was in uniform without insignia and the other was a colonel with a handle-bar mustache and a long sword in a gold-encrusted, black-lacquered scabbard which stood between his knees.

"The colonel has just had a report about you," began Tsurumi, laughing nervously. "He says you are a famous photographer. He has seen your pictures of China in *Life*. He has come here to give you a camera and take you out of camp so that you may continue your professional work."

"The colonel is very kind," I said. "There is nothing I'd like more than to take pictures again. But of course I cannot; I am a prisoner." Tsurumi translated and the colonel sat watching me impassively.

"The colonel says you will no longer be a prisoner," the commandant explained. "He will take you out of here. Your wife too. You will both be free. And this week we are having our great victory parade in Manila. General Homma will review the victorious troops who have conquered Bataan and Corregidor. And you will photograph this historic event."

I told him as politely as I knew how that I was very grateful but that I couldn't do that because our countries were at war and if I took such pictures my country would consider it a grave offense.

I waited for their exchange in Japanese. Then Tsurumi said eagerly: "We will ask your executive committee for permission."

I tried to smile. "I'm afraid they have no authority with my government."

"We will not tell anyone it is you," the commandant persisted. "We will keep it secret whose pictures they are."

"That wouldn't be fair to me," I said. I had been watching the colonel and his face had not changed. But I made my point direct to him. "Please explain to the colonel," I said to Tsurumi, "that if I take pictures for you here I shall always be a man without a country. Please tell him that if the Japanese newspapermen who are prisoners of the Americans should work for the American Army—taking pictures and writing stories—they would be disowned in Japan. In the same way I would be disowned by my country."

At this the colonel suddenly rose and without waiting for Tsurumi's translation said in English, "I see. I see." Then he bowed slightly and looked at me. "I understand," he said. "You may go." And I was dismissed.

I was never again asked to do propaganda work for the Japanese.

Somehow the months passed by, the months of settling down, the months of boredom, the months of heat and the rainy season. We worked to keep ourselves from starving; we worked to keep ourselves from thinking; we entertained ourselves and we told each other stories.

In the absence of food the women took to writing recipes, wonderful concoctions of all the things we hadn't eaten for so long; in the absence of news we took to reporting rumor.

77

Prisoners of war live on these hopeful rumors. And in the telling of them they often achieve moments of great satisfaction, for the spreading of news gives a measure of importance to a man who has lost his identity. And thus the stories grow and change, each teller adding that new bit that will make him the center of attention. Sometimes, if the community is small enough, a man's own story will return to him so changed and embroidered that he doesn't recognize it as his own at all, but takes it as a confirmation from another source and adding just one final touch, sends it on its way again.

But there are usually a few shining lights of good judgment and sane humor who manage to walk above disaster. Spike Heyward, who had spent twenty comfortable years in the Philippines, was one of them. He shared my room with thirty-one others and in all those months we lived together I never heard him pass on a rumor or even bother to comment upon one—except once. We had as a roommate also another old Philippine hand, but a man of a different temperament. He lived his prison years from optimistic rumor to optimistic rumor, most of them so patently absurd that it is embarrassing now to remember that an adult conveyed them in sincere belief.

One evening he rushed breathlessly into the room with another piece of news. We all knew that he could not possibly have had contact with the outside world, yet he called out in excitement: "Listen to this! I've just gotten it from an unquestionable source." He stopped and waited, swelling with importance, while many of his roommates circled him. Then he lowered his voice. "They're landing in the morning," he said. "The biggest armada in history! They'll be here tomorrow. By morning we'll be free!"

"Landing where?" someone asked.

"Landing right on Dewey Boulevard, with MacArthur leading them. General MacArthur will be in this camp for breakfast tomorrow morning!" He stood proudly among his listeners while a buzz of talk grew around him. Then I heard Spike Heyward speak up in his deep, resonant voice from across the room.

"MacArthur!" he said. "Well if he's coming in here, better tell him to bring his food and clothing for three days." The room

78

laughed and the rumor-monger subsided.

But often a man would tolerate no contradiction if he thought he was in possession of an exclusive piece of news. Nagged as we were, each man by his own secret sense of failure, we needed that instant of superiority when we knew something that another didn't know. To question a man in this state was not always wise. I had a sad and rather frightening experience with this.

It was toward the end of June, 1942. We had been prisoners six months. Corregidor had fallen, MacArthur had gone to Australia, and Southeast Asia had been overrun. And in camp our hopes had reached a bitter low. Stories of MacArthur's coming up over Dewey Boulevard with the morning sun had fewer takers. Tempers were short and patience running out.

That morning those of us who walked down to the fence in the hope that some Filipino friend might have sent us in some food did so listlessly. I was on my way down when someone passing stopped me. He was tall and wearing wooden clogs and ragged shorts that had been cut from trousers of better days. The skin of his waist was brown and wrinkled and folded in flaps. Once it had covered a larger stomach. Above it a voice said: "You heard the news?"

I moved on without raising my head, but the voice followed me. "You heard the news?" it repeated. "That *Time* and *Life* photographer, Carl Mydans, was killed in Australia."

I stopped and looked up at him. There was a bearded face under a floppy straw hat. "Killed in a plane crash with General George," the man said. "Spanish friend of mine down at the fence just told me. Got away from the Japs and made it to Australia and then went and got himself killed there. That's the way it goes, isn't it?"

I stood for a moment looking at his stained teeth and sagging jowls. No men can hate each other more than prisoners. "That's one you're wrong on." I heard my own voice full of vicious triumph.

"Wrong," he yelled, stepping toward me. "Wrong! Why, you son-of-a-bitch. What the hell do you know about it, sitting here rotting in this lousy prison?"

"Because . . ." I said. And then I stopped. I realized what

had happened. Mel was dead. It was an easy mistake to make; we had been confused before. So Mel had gotten out, and now he was dead. I nodded and walked on.

15.

Lucy

We knew her husband long before we met Lucy. He was in Chungking when we were there, involved in some venture with the Chinese government which he referred to only vaguely and which we took to mean supplying ammunition or weapons or some such business to the armed forces of Free China. He was young and handsome and he talked continually of his two loves: Lucy and the U.S. Army Air Corps in which he was on inactive reserve. And it was not surprising in those last months of 1941, as war became imminent, that he should chuck China and head for Manila, where he had arranged for the arrival of both Lucy and a new commission in the Army.

By chance we sailed together on a Dutch ship which carried us from Hong Kong to Manila and we were there when Lucy ran up the gangway and into his arms when we docked at Pier Seven. He smothered her in kisses and she bent in his embrace, looking fresh and young in her colorful Hawaiian print dress and smelling seductively of *pikake* blossoms. And that night when we all had dinner together under a starry sky and at a table dressed with orchids they were so effusively happy in each other's presence that Shelley and I left them early.

We never saw him again. For, as it turned out, not only was his commission waiting for him but his travel orders as well.

And sometime that week they took him out of the Philippines and back into China.

Lucy continued to live at the Bay View Hotel for a while, waiting for a ship to carry her back to the States, but she had lost some of her nerve and she was at loose ends and the smell of *pikake* was less engulfing. Once, when we met her at the Army-Navy Club, she asked us pertly as she turned a shapely foot on a high heel: "Who's he married to, anyway? Those airplanes or me?"

We lost track of her after the war began and I recall first seeing her again standing in the food line at Santo Tomas, holding an empty powdered-milk can for a cup and a tin pie plate for a dish. She was still rocking on a high heel and wearing a dress that looked as if it had just come from the laundry. But her blond hair was not as lustrous as I remembered it and was darker at the roots.

"Well," she said as I greeted her. "That husband of mine has sure got us fixed up good. There he is, somewhere in China. And here I am in this dump. Nice going."

The months of prison camp dragged on and the men grew beards and women wore less make-up. We all became thinner and shabbier. In the early months Lucy came in and out of our lives with irregularity. Now and then she would join us in the food line and sit with us for a meal. Or sometimes she would just come and talk. Then there were long periods when we would pass each other in our daily tasks with little more than a "hello" or a "hi." It was mostly when she thought of her husband that she came to us, for so few prisoners had known him that we became a kind of comforting link. In time, however, she came less and less and finally she stopped visiting us altogether. After that when we did meet the subject of her husband was avoided.

By now, like so many of us in this new world with its steadily lowering horizons and its warping pressures, she had changed. She wore her hair a dirty blond, a color she managed with some prison-concocted bleach, and her dresses were faded and unpressed. Her high heels were gone and she clicked about on wooden clogs. She had, however, lost only a little of her femininity and beauty. And when she walked through the compound, her hips swinging gently and her breasts outlined seductively in an old shirt, men stopped and watched her as tired and almost forgotten urges in their wasting bodies came alive again.

The crowd she ran with had changed too. Now it was mostly the young merchant sailors whose ships had been sunk, or those holding camp jobs where, it was said, there were pay-offs: the kitchen staff or the food supply detail, whose company she shared in their shacks during the day and in shadowy corners of the buildings at night. They had in some way opened a channel into the prison supply of sugar and made fermented juices that gave her both lift and remorse. And as time went on Lucy alternated between these.

Then one day late in August she came to see us once again. We had been in camp nearly eight months and suddenly the commandant had announced that he would send 130 prisoners to Shanghai. Who, he wanted to know, would like to go?

Lucy was asking our advice. Should she go? Did we think, she was saying in effect, that if she were on the same continent as her husband things would be better? We could not answer her. We were not sure ourselves just what the commandant meant, whether this was a bona fide proposal or some kind of trap. Later we learned the history behind his offer: when we had first been interned about a hundred refugees from China, most of them women and children, who had been caught in Manila on their way to America, had petitioned the Japanese for permission to return to their husbands and homes in Shanghai. No one, of course, knew what had happened to the petition after it reached the commandant's office for no answer had been given. Now, more than half a year later, after it had virtually been forgotten, after the commandant had been replaced, an order came from Tokyo to return 130 prisoners to Shanghai.

Our new commandant knew none of this background. He only knew he had his orders. And many of those who had originally petitioned to go had changed their minds. As in most prison camps, a psychosis had crept through Santo Tomas like a fog, darkening everything outside the fence into a frightening unknown and drawing the prisoners closer and closer together for comfort and security. Now it was unthinkable to venture out across the sea.

The commandant had trouble filling his quota. The more he urged his prisoners to leave, the more they suspected a trick: they were to be used as guinea pigs in odd experiments in Tokyo; they were to be slave laborers in the Manchurian mines; they would be sunk by U.S. submarines before they got there anyhow.

But some of us, after learning what facts we could, decided to try our luck. Here was a chance at least to get out of Santo Tomas, perhaps of reaching China, even of getting through the lines to freedom. Shelley and I were among those who registered to go. We looked up Lucy once again and tried to persuade her to join us, but by that time she had changed her mind. "Oh, what's the use," she said with her old evasiveness.

I don't recall seeing her again in those busy last days until just before we were leaving. Several big one-time U.S. Army buses driven by Filipinos and still painted with the hasty brush strokes of another era reading "Keep 'em Flying" had come into the compound and drawn up in front of the main entrance. And there we all assembled with our baggage tied into bundles and old valises. Much of the camp gathered round to watch our departure, their faces showing a last-minute mixture of envy and compassion, some wishing us well, some wishing they had earlier thought the better of it and decided to go themselves, and some still muttering words of doom.

But we—all of us—in our best clothes which hung loosely around our skinny bodies, had only shining faces. For at last we were off. To what fate we could not know; but after all this time behind the walls we were going out. And when we were all in the buses with our bundles and the drivers began to roll the vehicles slowly down the prison driveway toward the gate, the crowd broke into cheers and waves, and a few followed calling out and blessing us.

They dropped back farther and farther as we picked up speed —all except one who kept coming for us, running hard and waving her arms and shouting violently. It was Lucy. She caught up as we neared the gate.

"If you see that God-damned husband of mine anywhere out there in China," she screamed, "tell him if he wants any wife left he'd better hurry up and get me out of this place."

She dropped behind and we lost what she was saying. But as we turned out into the road we could still see her running and shouting madly and waving her arms at us.

I saw her years later, the night we liberated Santo Tomas. By then her hair was mousy brown and she looked different: thinner and older. And when she talked to me it was in a strained half-whisper. "Have you see him?" she asked. "Have you heard anything about him?" And I said no. For I had not yet learned that he was dead; that he had in fact died long ago, even before that day we left the Philippines, shot down somewhere over China where we first heard him talk about flying and the girl he loved.

16.

The *Maya Maru*

The *Maya Maru* lay alongside Pier Seven, one side of her swathed in the late afternoon sun looking bright and promising and the other dark and cluttered and ominous as it grated against the cap of the wharf. On the dock, intermingled in her shadow, were the cargo and passengers she would soon take aboard: nervous, stamping horses captured on Bataan and still wearing the brand of the U.S. Army on their thin flanks; Japanese troops lugging and pushing their worn fighting equipment and making gruff monosyllabic replies to their shrill and voluble prostitutes who trotted after them like faithful pets; Axis Spaniards and Italians and stateless Nansens and third-party Hindus and Lithuanians and White Russians; men, women, children and horses all milling among the piles of luggage and freight heaped upon the dock and waiting anxiously for the word that would start them up the gangway. Into this came the buses from Santo Tomas, and we all climbed out and added ourselves and our bundles to the disorder.

It was dusk when the word was finally given and then everybody just formed into a great circular mass and pushed blindly toward the ship's steep gangway while Japanese voices yelled incomprehensible orders and the horses, hanging helplessly in belly straps, screamed in terror as they swung out over our heads into the ship's hold.

We carried disorder with us as we pushed and tugged our gear up the ladder to the well deck. There Japanese soldiers and civilian officials, their arms and legs spread like those of sheepherders at the gates of a corral, worked us toward tiny hatchways. A Spaniard revolted, holding up the movement and making himself heard above the noise. "This is no way to treat your friends," he shouted at a Japanese official.

"Who are you?" yelled the Japanese.

"I am a Spaniard," he answered haughtily. "An ally."

"If you are," replied the Japanese spitefully, "all the more reason for you to suffer with us." And with both hands he pushed the Spaniard through the hatchway. There was no distinction: soldiers, allies, enemy, we all went through the hatches together and down the steep ladder. It was dark in there and smelled of urine and horses and the heat struck us in waves as we panted under our bundles and felt the sweat slip over us.

We came out onto a level within the hold and found ourselves looking down a series of gaping hatches. A neighing horse was lowered past us hanging grotesquely in a sling and we bent gingerly over the unguarded edge to watch until it reached the outstretched arms of barebacked soldiers standing below us in a small open square surrounded by horses packed like fish in a can.

There were no bunks. But two tiers of wide shelves lined the hold and on them a scattering of old straw and oddments of clothing indicated where the previous occupants had slept. And without direction we all took possession of a few feet of untidy deck or shelving, sitting or lying with our gear, panting with exhaustion and the heat and slowly crowding closer and closer as more and more people squeezed in among us. The Spaniards and Italians and third-party nationals disappeared into shelves behind the ladder well. We prisoners took the section one side of the open hatch above the horses, and the Japanese troops and their Formosan women moved into the section opposite. And when the planking of the hatch cover was put in place the Hindus pre-empted that area, setting up a kind of buffer state with their jars and heaps of rags and clay cooking stoves where they lived their tribal lives as though there were skies above and land beneath.

That night we ate from the small stores we carried with us, rolled sleeplessly in the stifling hold and brushed at cockroaches and waterbugs which scrambled over us, but at dawn when we felt the engines throb we climbed a ladder onto the open decks and watched as we maneuvered through the harbor and turned seaward into a pale morning light. Along the horizon we could see the shore which fringed the Bataan Peninsula and to the left, in open water, a hummock: Corregidor. Between these the ship's head found its course and we stood out to sea.

Few among us had sailed these waters since the war began. As we passed between the battlefields of Bataan and Corregidor the chatter died away and we crowded the rails, each gripped in his own thoughts. On a point on Bataan a flag fluttered. It was Japanese.

Now we were entering the mine fields and were ordered to go below. It seemed more familiar now, more like a home for us— such is the adaptability of man. We took our places along that section farthest aft which was already recognized as the Santo Tomas area while the other passengers—the soldiers and the neutrals—crept into theirs.

Thus for two weeks we lived, we prisoners lying squeezed together, dreaming, talking, or quietly watching the little worlds which lived within the angle of our vision. There was our own, supine and strangely detached, reduced, under pressure of prison life, to a herd community with common features: unhealthy bodies, ill-fitting clothes, and a lassitude of will.

There was the cockroach world on the underside of the shelf overhead, vigorously moving in swiftly changing patterns which constantly caught our eye and snatched us from apathy for long moments, drawing us into their exciting domain busy with thousands of little feet running thousands of little errands.

There was the rat world, the only one below decks that appeared conscious it was sharing its domain. Often we looked each other in the eye but without any fellow feeling for they fouled our possessions and scrambled over us at night, going at our clothing and foodstuff with shocking voracity. I recall the expression of fright and revulsion of the prisoner who slept alongside me when he awoke one morning to find that his prized watermelon had gone. He had gotten it from a Filipino on the dock before we left and had slept with it guarded between his feet. In the morning only that part of the rind remained which had been in contact with his soles. It had been eaten away into a corrugated fringe which was a repulsive replica of his toes.

There was the horse world below us, shifting, sighing, smelling, and the Hindu world on the hatch top which we gazed upon from our shelf as though we were looking at another planet. All day one old woman pounded red powder on a granite slab while the men slept with cloths wound around their loins and women and children squatted and combed and picked at each other's hair or fanned smoke rings out of their charcoal-burning stoves. Often their children urinated on the deck and once I protested to the women about it; but they just looked past me neither seeing nor hearing and giving me the uncomfortable feeling that I had lost my earthly presence.

And finally there was the world of the Japanese soldiers on their shelves across the hold who lived their life as though floating in celestial space over the heads of the Hindus. They had their own mores and conventions, soldiers and their women lying together, sleeping, dressing and undressing, laughing, playing odd games, and making love as often as the girls could manage.

We saw very little of the girls on deck. Their duties kept them mostly below. And that was well for us, for they showed none of the friendliness of the soldiers, snarling and spitting at us, often pushing us roughly aside when we were on deck while their men watched from a distance chuckling and nudging each other and sometimes giving us that look proud parents give when their children are naughty and cannot be expected to know better.

All of us prisoners made a conscientious effort to preserve a hostile attitude toward our enemy. We were more successful in this when we came in contact with the civilian Axis nationals, but with the Japanese troops we soon felt the tug of friendship. We tried to compensate for this by putting on our most meticulous manners and were deliberately correct as we waited in line for food or privy, offering our places to the Japanese soldiers who invariably refused with the same fixed smiles so that we enacted on the cluttered deck little scenes reminiscent of a children's dancing class.

There was one lieutenant who was so concerned about the conduct of his men that he followed them around like a mother bird, watching and picking at them. And one day, as we turned into the trough of the sea on our zigzag antisubmarine course, rolling and wallowing in a sharp blow, he ran shouting at a soldier who had tossed a banana peel overboard. This unfortunate lad had thrown it into the wind and it had been returned inboard, dropping into our group with a wet slap.

The officer brought the soldier before us, both of them having difficulty, in the ship's roll, to muster themselves with proper military bearing. There they stood facing each other at stiff attention, looking like wooden soldiers carved off balance, one moment erect and the next tossed and scrambling at our feet. And all the while the officer was yelling the riot act he was interrupted by these undignified gambados until he was finally able to steady himself and administer punishment to the unseamanlike soldier: a punch in the face. Then as the lad went down, properly struck and instructed, the officer, breathing hard and brushing off his uniform with the backs of his fingers, said to us: "Just a young soldier. You must forgive him. He is not yet trained."

We were screened by four destroyers which skirted the convoy like porpoises, sometimes running wide of us, silhouetted along the edge of the horizon, and sometimes coming in close, dipping seas which ran white off their backs while sailors hung to the stanchions and gun turrets.

The *Maya Maru* was some three thousand tons, a small freighter converted to a troop ship by the simple expedient of fashioning some wooden shelves in the holds, bolting some steam cooking vats to the well deck, and projecting over one side three board privies lashed to the railing on a few planks. She could carry thirteen hundred troops and her austerity was a constant reminder to us of how easily and speedily the enemy could convert to war and how astoundingly little they needed.

She mounted three guns: one on her forward deck, one on her fantail, and one in a gun tub on the after end of her bridge house. They were faithfully attended night and day by crews who were incessantly diligent, wiping and polishing, springing to action on alerts and snapping through drills with high spirited shouts. We were closest to the gun aft of the bridge house and were soon familiar with the daily routine and activities of its gunnery team.

At first our voyage had been marked by intermittent rain which kept the topside wet and often cool. But on the third day out the weather cleared and the sun shone bright. And one afternoon as we lounged about the well deck and the gun crew above us sat listlessly at its battle station we noted a strange white line showing near the breech of the weapon. A couple of gunners noticed it too and rubbed their hands over it. But it remained and by the end of the day had gotten longer and wider. At last it became quite obvious: the gun was wooden, and the veneer which had been formed round the breech had shrunk and was curling up, leaving an area of unpainted wood as naked and stark and eye-catching as a bit of white thigh showing through a split skirt. And for the rest of the voyage, especially during alerts when the gunners sprang to their weapons, our eyes would return irresistibly to the patch.

On the fourth day out from Manila the Formosan camp followers all came up on deck in new satin uniforms and sat together combing their hair and making up their faces and looking out to sea. Someone saw land and the girls shrieked with excitement. Again we were all sent below and the hatchway above us covered with a tarpaulin. We could hear it being roped in place and it was clear that whatever our destination we were not to see the coastal installations or follow our course of navigation.

It was dark and hot below and we waited in our separate worlds listening to the noises ships make as they get ready for port. Then one of the Formosan girls began to shout shrilly and we watched her in the dim light climb to the top of the hatchway ladder. Soon we saw why. There was someone up there looking out through a rent in the canvas. It was Jimmy Stewart, a young American architect who had come to the Philippines with a good reputation and had tarnished it at Santo Tomas. He had chosen to run with the troublemakers in camp and had been involved in several escapades for which he was ostracized by the more respectable prisoners. He was unperturbed, however, and treated his critics with a laugh. And this is what he gave the Formosan girl, pushing her away and putting his face back to the hole in the canvas. She, of course, was infuriated but the soldiers just chuckled indulgently as they often did on deck and remained in their bunks until word came that we could all go topside again.

It was sundown by then and pleasantly cool and we were making our way through the narrow neck of a harbor. It was jammed with shipping: naval craft, transports, freighters all swinging at anchor and loading supplies and troops from barges nesting at their sides. Warehouses and industrial plants stood on the waterfront, a steel mill blew white plumes into the air, and planes rose from fields either side of the harbor entrance. I realized this must be Takao, Formosa's greatest port. We had heard, when we were in Santo Tomas, that it had been destroyed, but it was not damaged at all.

Jimmy Stewart was sitting by himself on a pile of rafts when I climbed up to him. "What did you see?" I asked him.

"I'll show you someday," he said.

And he did, more than a year later. We had been exchanged and were en route home aboard the *Gripsholm*. "You remember Takao?" he asked. I nodded. "I don't have much of a reputation in this crowd," he said. "But you persuade the State Department representative on board to get me a T-square and a drawing

90

board and a place to work and I'll show you something."

I did and Jimmy went to work. First he cut his shoes open and assembled figures he had written inside their linings. Then he began to draw. Slowly the Formosan coast appeared, the course into the harbor through the mine fields, the industrial plants in the port area, the air bases. At our first neutral port of call on the exchange trip, U.S. Naval authorities boarded us and they hustled Jimmy off the ship with the drawing rolled under his arm. It was, they told him, the first good look they had had of Takao since the war began. However, his contribution was classified as secret and he returned to the ship that night with no better reputation among his prison friends than when he left.

Years later I came into Takao again on another troop ship. This time it was full of Chinese soldiers fleeing the mainland at the end of the Communist war. We docked virtually in the same place we had in 1942. But the scene had changed. The entire port had been smashed into a shambles. Its huge concrete wharves had been blown into mountains of rubble. The steel mill was gone; the warehouses were tumbled down with wild grasses growing out of the ruins. And as I sat there I thought of Jimmy Stewart again, wondering what part he had played in the destruction, and of the Formosan girl who in all those war years was the only one who publicly gave him his due.

17.

Shanghai

The *Maya Maru* lay at Takao for two days and then headed north, hugging the China Coast, and at noon on September 21, after more than eight months in Santo Tomas and ten days on the transport, we docked at Woosung, on the Whangpoo River. Late in the afternoon a tug took us the few miles upriver to Shanghai and we tied up alongside the jetty on the Bund as night was falling. There was no blackout and the city lights were startlingly bright. Groups of men stood in the background under the pontoon lights, watching us land. They were dressed in white jackets and shorts, starched and immaculate, redolent of a life we had almost forgotten.

A Japanese civilian official had taken charge of us and when we were all off the tug, standing over our piles of luggage and waiting the meek and awkward wait of prisoners, he called out: "Line up for roll call," and we fell into our accustomed positions and answered to our names.

"Any questions?" he asked when we had finished.

We all stood there dumbly. He waited, but no one spoke. "All right then," he said. "You may go."

No one moved.

"All right," he repeated impatiently, raising his voice. "You may go."

There was a hush. We remained at dead stop.

He stepped forward, annoyed. He shouted: "I said you may GO."

Still we stood there. Then someone said in a tiny voice: "Go where?"

"Go where!" he yelled. "Go to your homes. Go to hotels."

For just another moment we remained. Then we broke. We pushed. We tripped over baggage. There were little groups of people coming in, meeting, shaking hands, kissing, hugging. But the rest of us ran. Out into the almost empty streets of Shanghai we ran, our baggage seemingly hanging on to us without weight or burden. We started off first one way, then another. Someone shouted, "The Palace Hotel," and we all turned again, running up the Bund.

The lobby of the Palace glittered with lights and was crowded with a mixture of people: Chinese, Japanese, Europeans. A Eurasian stood behind the reception desk. For seconds we faced each other, he waiting and we waiting. Nearby stood several Japanese officers talking. Instinctively we edged away from them. Almost in a whisper I asked, "Do you have any rooms?" And he replied in what seemed a shout, "Would you like them over the Bund or in a more quiet part of the hotel?"

At this the Japanese officer glanced up and walked over toward us. I stiffened. But he only bowed slightly and reached past me across the desk for his key. I think it was at that moment that I felt the strange war world of Shanghai fall into perspective, and by the time our Chinese room boys came for our bags and we followed them across the busy lobby to the elevator we were already ourselves becoming part of it.

When we arrived, Shanghai was one of the most remarkable cities of the war. The Japanese had seized it the day they bombed Pearl Harbor, emerging with a small force from their quarter of the internationally partitioned city like men from a Trojan horse, putting landing parties on board the several small British and American gunboats which lay off the Bund, and carting away to prisons those whose names had long been on their blacklists.

But otherwise their enemy continued to live and operate within the city, still occupying the most imposing houses, sharing with high-ranking Japanese the best apartment buildings and hotels, and often eating in the same restaurants. This illusion of a free oasis in a world at war grew from the fact that though the Japanese were able to take the city they were not yet able to make it run. For Shanghai was the economic and industrial heart of China and for years its complex pulsations had been directed largely by the British, French and Americans. Until the Japanese were prepared to take over themselves it was important that the enemy be persuaded to keep the city living. This the Japanese accomplished with stick and carrot. And by the time we came to Shanghai they had done so well that they had displaced most of their enemy from the desks of the great commercial enterprises and were dismissing the last of them from the apparatus which governed the city. And the hour had come to display before the Chinese the inglorious end of the Westerner who in a hundred years had built upon the mudbanks of an obscure tributary the largest city in all of China and one of the greatest seaports in the world.

Outwardly, that September of 1942, the city looked much as it had during the golden era of the white man, that period between the wars when a moderately paid junior executive could live the life of extreme luxury, employing a staff of servants, belonging to several expensive clubs, filling his cellar with French wines and his living room with the best Western furniture and the rarest Chinese curios. The streets of the International Settlement and the French Concession were still orderly and clean and busy, the Chinese crowds still sprinkled with figures of well-dressed, well-fed Westerners. The hotels and the restaurants and night clubs were full and the race course in the heart of the city crowded on the weekends.

It was only on second look that we noted that the traffic was almost exclusively ricksha and pedicab and that the automobile had all but vanished from the great tree-lined avenues and the narrow Oriental streets. And the Bund, now a quiet stretch of quayside, presented little evidence that once it had been choked with the traffic of great ships which piled the river front with freight and merchandise from every port in the world.

Our commanding hope in coming to Shanghai was to escape through the lines into guerrilla country which we had heard led to Free China. But our plans for a getaway were frustrated almost immediately when the leaders of the escape ring with whom we were negotiating were suddenly arrested and the Japanese tightened their control on all movements. After that we could find no one willing to become involved. There never was another escape during our months in Shanghai. And our hopes, therefore, were centered again on repatriation.

Within a week after our arrival the last phase of the Japanese' slow seizure of the city went into high gear. More and more of the city was placed out of bounds to enemy nationals. Teams of Japanese began to call unannounced at the big houses and fine apartments to survey the furniture and possessions and to attach stickers to those that appealed, forbidding their removal and earmarking them for seizure.

Now, with increasing frequency, we were questioned by men from the Kempei-tai who wanted to know what company we kept, what we did with our time, and where we got our money. The truth was that we supplemented the sixty U.S. dollars a month we were allowed to draw from the Swiss Consulate by borrowing illegally from Chinese acquaintances who were glad to take the risk in order to get rid of the puppet currency in the hope of repayment in American dollars after the war. But of course we could not say that. Each of us supplied his own lies and most of us got away with it. Those who didn't went into special prisons.

As enemy nationals we were not only watched and questioned, we were marked. We had been issued broad red arm bands which we were ordered under military law to wear in public. Each arm band was numbered and each stamped with a large letter: "A" for Americans, "B" for British, "N" for Netherlands and "X" for others such as South Americans. But if the intention was to degrade us it failed, for most of us wore our arm bands as the insignia of our nationality in which the circumstances of the war had given us an even greater than normal pride. Nor did we find any increased unpleasant reaction from the Chinese as a result of publicly showing ourselves to be the enemy.

But the arm bands did make plain the shifting status among the varied nationalities in the international city. For the enemy nationals, once top dogs, now found it expedient to walk with circumspection down the streets they once treated as their own. While the Japanese, who had formerly stayed pretty close to their own section in Hongkew, were now the ones to stride with swinging gait and authoritative laughter along the crowded sidewalks of the city.

Only the Chinese appeared unaltered by this great change. The few remaining members of the upper class usually friendly to the West found it wiser not to associate openly with enemy nationals, but men like Old Wang, our room boy in the Palace Hotel, were under no such compulsion. Wang was tall and meticulous, with transparent yellow skin stretched taut over his thin face. His step and manner were refined and his memory seemingly so crowded with images and sounds of the past that he appeared not clearly aware of what was then happening in China. Each morning at dawn, while we lay in bed, he came in to light the fire in our room. He turned down our sheets in the evening and drew our baths and would have laid out our evening clothes had we had any. And always he showed us the deference that the Chinese gave the Westerner before the war.

One day he proudly brought his nineteen-year-old son, Young Wang, to see us at the hotel. And while the old man stood silently in a corner of our room, his son sat with us at tea and talked about China with the certainty of the new generation. That night Old Wang told us that his son would come to our room every day to teach us Chinese. Shelley protested that this might not be wise, for we were constantly watched by the Japanese and such frequent visits might endanger his son. But Old Wang politely waved away the warning saying that only honor could come to the Wang family from such visits.

Young Wang came every morning and one day Shelley told him her fears.

"Oh," he smiled. "Never mind. I also come every day to the rooms of the Japanese officers in the hotel to teach them Chinese too." And he gestured with his slender hands, the gesture of a juggler who is sure of his technique.

It was during these days of Shanghai's great metamorphosis that Shelley and I went to visit the Bells, a large and prosperous American-Chinese family who lived in Hongkew and owned a lumber factory. All the Bell children had been born in China and they lived in an enormous house, busy as an ant run with the comings and goings of servants, relatives and visitors, everybody switching in and out of English and Chinese as though the two were one language. The huge house, shadowy and darkened by the restrictions on electric power, seemed endless and was piled in confusion with bags and burlap sacks and straw valises of possessions, some ready for the Japanese who had stamped them with confiscatory stickers and some packed and waiting for the hour when the Bells would be rounded up and interned.

Outside through a window we could see a small group of Japanese, notebooks in hand, surveying the stacked lumber in the adjacent yards, preparing to take over the enemy property. And inside, in a great room which in the emergency had become living room and kitchen, the Bell family with their friends and relations sat at a long table with Mrs. Bell at the head, enjoying her children's jokes and the clatter and confusion around her. From the far end of the room came a sizzling sound and the delicious smell of Chinese food cooking and we could see a little man with a ragged mustache bent over steaming pans and *kongs*.

"We think he's the best cook in Shanghai," Mrs. Bell told us, chuckling and pointing in his direction. And then as the cook himself began to serve, sliding the heaped dishes along the table, she added: "He likes to cook so much he's taken over our kitchen."

"He's an old friend?" I asked .

"Old friend!" laughed Mrs. Bell, enormously enjoying the question and watching the laughter travel down the table. "He's a Jap. He's one of those fellows you were looking at out of the window. They're cleaning us out of everything we own. But we like his cooking and while we can we're enjoying it."

Even the most respectable, the most impregnable of American and British families lived from day to day in the same way, keeping up a front and taking what came. I remember especially a visit Shelley and I made to the home of the American doctor, Tom Dunn. It was Christmas day and there were a lot of people there, drinking eggnogs and talking cheerfully and helping themselves to cold turkey from a great teak table. We all sang carols and played with the children and Dorothy Dunn joined us in telling funny stories about Japanese ineptitudes.

But Tom was not there. And though we talked lightly about him, as though he were away on a brief trip, we all knew that he had been taken only a few hours earlier, in the middle of the night, and was already in prison. And we knew, too, that for any of us tonight might be our turn.

18.

Mary

Our roundup for internment was orderly. As a matter of fact, like the city in which it took place, there was probably nothing quite like it anywhere else in the entire world. In Shanghai the Japanese had not yet felt the deterioration and hopelessness of the war, which in the end brought retaliation upon her prisoners, and we were far from the heat of battle and its often brutal influences. Our places of internment had long been selected: old college buildings, tobacco warehouses, mission compounds. Our names had been posted with the dates of our call-up and we had been given plenty of time to collect what bedding and clothing we would need. We had chosen our own British and American representatives to act as liaison between their countrymen and the Japanese, and the collecting points from which we would be picked up were published in the Japanese-edited English-language press.

In a sense, we interned ourselves. On a clear crisp morning in March, 1943, we came quietly out of our homes and hotels with bags and bundles and cots and pots and bargained with the waiting ricksha boys for a price. Crowds of curious Chinese gathered. The reaction was mixed. For the Europeans before them still presented many of the outward marks of the white men they had once known. Immaculate creatures, with an extra layer of flesh under their well-fitted tweeds, with red faces and long noses and their fine shoes rubbed to a shine, they called for rickshas in voices conscious of a superiority too long assumed to be modified now by the fate at hand.

Each departure of a group of rickshas, carrying very erect

passengers or stuffed high with baggage, left behind little eddies of silent, watching figures. The ricksha boys wormed their vehicles into the crowded streets, were lost with their loads in the confusion of massed bodies and high voices, padded through the lighter traffic of Frenchtown, and finally hauled their fares into a growing jungle of baggage and uprooted people on the lawns of the once staunchly American, and exclusively Western, Columbia Country Club. This was the collecting point, well chosen by the Japanese as a fitting place for the Chinese to view the final degradation of the white man.

The British and American community in Shanghai was composed of two groups: those one knew and those one didn't. The old-China-hand families and the representatives of respectable foreign firms provided one. The other came from a jumble of China Coast lives: seamen; Blood Alley bar hands; bamboo Europeans who had found their way or been deposited by circumstances in Shanghai and had stayed on by one means or another; those who had married Orientals, and their Eurasian offspring. These latter lived on a kind of threshold and a limited number moved through both groups.

Within the memory of many were the days when members of the first group would provide funds and arrange forcible passage out of the country for certain members of the second when it was decided that their conduct hurt the standing of the Europeans in China. But in a changing world this had been discontinued and now for the past year the social barriers had been crumbling under the common fear of the Japanese. But as they gathered awkwardly on the wide lawn in a kind of end-of-the-road resignation their baggage and utensils, planned for prison life, still carried the distinctions of the levels on which they once had lived. Fine leather valises with engraved initials and cheap straw bags tied with rope, bedding neatly wrapped in new canvas covers and piles of frayed and discolored Chinese coverlets made neighboring heaps over which their owners exchanged friendly remarks with forced good cheer.

There were of course some among us whose provision for the future was negligible and in some cases pitiable. And each of us noted with absorbed interest what the others had brought. A man in a frayed suit, with lined face and bloodshot eyes, wandered about unsteadily with nothing but a soiled pillow and a pair of worn shoes in his arms and stopped to watch enviously as a family of four, seated on their considerable collection of belongings, shared a Thermos bottle of coffee. Another, a tall thin American in an aging pea jacket, who, in search of some object, had undone the yellow tung-oil sheet in which were wrapped his effects, looked up to find a score of eyes measuring his future. He shrugged quickly with a flush of annoyance, and then relaxed and laughed.

And there were always Japanese intensely wandering among us, looking, looking, and never seeming to find what they were looking for. One stopped before a girl who was seated alone on a little pile of possessions. She glanced at him quickly and then arose slowly, showing that frightened uncertainty of a pretty woman before the conqueror, undecided whether to be attentive and obedient or haughty and disinterested. The Japanese left and she sat down again.

This was the first time I had seen Mary. She was petite, beautifully formed, and perhaps eighteen. Her eyes were large and brown and at the corners there was just the suspicion of something Oriental. Her clothing was undistinguished and inexpensive and the heels on her black shoes were a little too high. On some the choice might have looked cheap. She caught me looking and smiled. It was a wonderful smile. As a matter of fact, looking back on those early months of prison life, Mary's smile is one of the pleasantest memories.

Mary came into prison camp with few friends. But she was not long without them. In a new life where one's past meant little, Mary found herself for the first time in a world that wanted and needed her. She was a constant volunteer for camp duties and was frequently to be found among those performing the most unpleasant. She worked in the scullery. She was on the floor-scrubbing detail. She did laundry for mothers with too many children and she sewed for the men. She had little to say, for she was painfully shy. But it made people feel good just to have her near. Partly it was her smile. But mostly it was that intangible business of happiness, for in the universal misery of prison life, Mary was happy.

In time we began to know something of her past and to understand why. Mary's father was an American who had drifted to the China Coast many years ago. He had married a Japanese girl in Shanghai, fathered Mary, and drifted away. Mary was orphaned when still a child. And after a period of being passed from family to family was finally taken into a French convent in Shanghai. Here she grew up.

Mary's father, who was so briefly part of her life, left her with but one possession. This she came to cherish. At her birth he had registered her as an American with the U.S. Consulate. And in that cold and heartless city of the homeless it grew on Mary that she had a home and she felt the first surge of pride in belonging to someone. In class-conscious Shanghai this crashed no social barriers. But as she grew into early womanhood, the pains of orphanage were softened by the knowledge that she was part of a bigger family. She was no White Russian with worthless Chinese papers, no wandering European with Nansen passport, no "stateless national" with the memory of Hitler's purges. She had a place in the world. She was American.

But it was not until she was within the confined and barbed-wired world of prison camp that Mary finally found herself at home. She never saw the irony. She was too busy being wanted and being loved and being happy. Then, one day, it all changed. The word flashed through the camp before Mary really understood. That morning a Japanese had come into the compound and had disappeared into the commandant's office. When he left the commandant had issued an order: Mary must leave camp. Records had just been produced to show that Mary's mother was Japanese. This, he announced, made Mary a Japanese. She would be released that night and sent to Japan.

"But I am an American," said Mary later, when she was brought before the commandant by a small committee of Americans. Never before had she been so defiant and articulate. "Japan is not my country," she protested. "I have never been there. I don't even know the language."

The commandant looked away from the other Americans who were standing there. He was uncomfortable and embarrassed. "It is all a mistake," he explained to Mary. "You are Japanese and we feel ashamed that you have been kept here with these people. We are sending you home tonight."

Mary began to weep. "I am not Japanese," she cried. "I am American. I will not go to Japan."

The commandant's muscles tensed. "You are Japanese," he repeated harshly. "You will obey."

That night at sundown, carrying a little straw valise and wearing her black, high-heeled shoes, Mary was led out of the compound by the commandant. Most of the camp had quietly assembled to see her go. She turned at the main gate and paused for a moment looking back. She waved slowly before she disappeared.

After that none of us ever forgot Mary. In fact, one of the first things I did when Japan surrendered and I entered Tokyo with the vanguard of the occupation troops two and a half years later was to try to find her. But there were no records and no basis for search in that burned-out and beaten country: only desolation, with survivors hunting for survivors and hurrying past American uniforms with heads averted.

One such head passed me, one morning in Tokyo. It was pretty and it was suddenly familiar. Its owner, dressed in a faded frock, was disappearing in a crowd of hurrying Japanese as I stood watching for a moment. And then I knew: it was Mary.

When I caught up with her she was at first nervous and embarrassed. She looked at her dress and at her shoes and said she was sorry they were so frayed. We walked to the Tokyo Correspondents' Club and sat there for a long time before she would talk. And when other correspondents in their army uniforms came into the club's lounge she appeared distressed and on the defensive. Once she made an almost involuntary motion to leave when two American officers passed by, looking for someone. It was as though a servant had been caught sitting in the master's chair.

"You're among friends," I assured her. "These are all Americans and British."

"Americans," she whispered. "I know. But I am Japanese. This place is out of bounds for me." She had a frightened look and she gathered her skirts about her tightly as though to make herself smaller. A Japanese bar boy brought us drinks and I nodded reassurance. She sipped her drink. Then she began to talk. Mostly it was about old friends in prison camp. She avoided as long as possible the years between her departure from Shanghai and our present meeting. Then slowly she talked about them.

When she first arrived in Japan she had insisted that she was American. This shocked those who tried to help her, and in time she was passed down to those who could handle her better. She was beaten. But she never broke. Ultimately she was sent to a rope factory and there, as a laborer, she spent the rest of the war.

"I was never trusted there," she said proudly. "I was called 'the American' and treated as an enemy, locked up at night and always under guard when I worked.

"I'll always remember the day of the surrender," she said. "Everybody in the factory was huddled around the radio. But I couldn't understand what was being said. Later people began to smile at me. Some offered me food and candy. Then the manager came in and told me the news. 'We have been good to you here,' he said. 'Please tell the Americans when they arrive how good we have been.' I had a wonderful feeling.

"That night I was freed by the factory and the manager took me into his home in Yokohama. 'You will wait here for the Americans,' he told me, bowing low. 'My wife and I will be your servants.'

"It was more than a week before the Americans arrived. And for more than a week I hardly slept." She stopped for a moment and I asked her how it was when the Americans finally came.

"I was in front of the Grand Hotel when the first of them came into Yokohama. The soldiers were nice to me. They gave me food and they all said the same thing: 'Hey! Here's a gal who speaks English!' And when I told them I was an American they sent me to an officer. But all the officers were busy. They said that maybe they would have to fight for Tokyo.

"Later, in Tokyo, they told me I would have to be screened

and they asked me for my passport. But I never had a passport, and my records are all in Shanghai. When I told them my mother was Japanese they just shook their heads.

"So then I applied for work with the occupation. They took down my history. And they filled out a card and wrote across the top: 'Japanese National,' and sent me to one of the U.S. Army billets in Yokohama. Ever since I have worked there as a waitress, living in a little shack with the Japanese girls. And I'm not permitted in any of the places Americans go."

She looked around. Her eyes were dry and her face drawn and her red callused hands nervously twisted a little kerchief she had rolled into a soiled wad. The next day we visited the American Red Cross in Tokyo. Together we told her story.

It was several weeks before I saw her again. She was in a new dress and she wore white gloves over her red hands. Her shoes were black and her heels were high and when she walked up to me they clicked musically. But it was her face I saw first, and her smile. It was beautiful. She took my hands and said breathlessly: "Today I am an American again. I have my passport and I'm working for the American Army."

And then, as she squeezed my hands in ecstasy, she said: "Oh, how wonderful it all is! Wonderful! It's just like the old days when we were all in prison camp together."

19.

A Lost American

Our prison camp was in Chapei, on the outskirts of Shanghai, and had once been part of Great China University. The war between the Chinese and Japanese for control of the city in

1932 had been resolved in this area of flat and fertile farm-land, and in the fighting much of the university had been laid waste. Over the years, some of the ruins had been restored. The rest moldered until hasty and makeshift repairs prepared the buildings and a section of the old battlefield for us.

The rations the Japanese allotted us in Chapei were meager and soon there was a widespread variety of deficiency diseases among us. But as always, someone with knowledge and experience stepped forward in the emergency. This time it was a missionary from North China who told us how to supplement our diet with the Chinese soybean. Himself an expert in primitive improvisation, he planned and directed a project within the prison to manufacture soybean milk by grinding the beans. He found two old millstones partly buried in the mud bank of the creek that ran along the edge of our compound and had us set them up with two long staves laced to the upper stone. Teams of eight prisoners spelled each other, walking the grind-stone round and round by the staves like plodding Missouri mules.

Each day I worked a shift and one morning while I was plodding round I became slowly conscious that someone in a Japanese uniform was present and watching me. When at last I brought my thoughts back from some distant land and looked again I saw that the Japanese was Kazunaro Uno. He motioned to me and I left the stave and we walked away together.

"I suppose," he said, looking back toward the grindstone detail as we walked along a pathway, "that under the circumstances this is the only way it can be done but, Christ, it's degrading. Like a lot of animals. Seems like they could find some other work for you here."

"Oh, I don't really mind it," I replied. "I don't have to do it, you know. We're all volunteers. It may seem odd to you, but in here we're all Americans together and the work we do for each other doesn't strike us as degrading."

He turned and looked at me and I saw that his face was flushed and I regretted deeply what I had said. For Buddy Uno, as he was more widely known in the West, was one of the most tortured souls I had ever known: he was an American in a

Japanese uniform. And though I was defiant and bitter toward him when we first met, as I came to know more about him it had become painful to me to add to his anguish. Despite his guarded and sometimes crude cover-up, I came to realize that Uno deeply loved the country of his birth. And when as a correspondent for the Japanese Army propaganda corps he came to visit me in prison camps in the Philippines and in China, we presented a contrast not lost upon either of us: I in frayed and ill-fitting clothing hanging on a thin frame and he well fed and handsome in a tailored uniform, a star on his cap and cigars in his pocket.

He used to bring me small gifts: cigarettes and canned food, and we would talk nostalgically about America and about when we were both newspapermen there in better days. And all the while we knew that we were both prisoners, I hoping to go home again and he knowing that he never could. And as time went on I felt his shame for what the Japanese had done to me and he must also have felt mine, as an American, for what had happened to him in America long ago.

For it was there that Buddy Uno, dressed in another uniform, stitched with merit badges, was turned about and sent off on one of the loneliest and most heart-breaking roads a youth can travel. It finally led him across the ocean and back to the land of his forefathers, there never to forget his hurt and never to forgive those who turned him from the land he loved.

It happened in Salt Lake City in 1926. Buddy was then thirteen. The First Presbyterian Scout Troop was marching into a Salt Lake hot springs club, to an outing it had for weeks been promised. As it was entering the gate in march formation, the manager who had come there to welcome them called to the scout master. "Just a minute," he shouted. The scout master stopped the column part way through the gate.

"Say," the manager said, pointing at Buddy. "Isn't that a Jap boy there?"

"Jap boy!" echoed the scout master in surprise. "You mean this lad here? Buddy Uno? Why he's a First Class Scout. He's got more merit badges than any boy in the troop. He's of Japanese origin all right, if that's what you mean. But he's an American, and we're proud to have him in the troop."

"Yes, I know all that," said the manager. "But he's still a Jap and no Japs can come in here."

There was a dreadfully long moment while the manager and the scout master stood aside together and talked, and Buddy remembers that all the while he was so tense that he shivered. Finally, the scout master came over to him and bending low whispered: "I'm sorry." And Buddy was turned around in front of the entire troop and sent home. He walked slowly all the way, crying openly and wishing that he could crawl away and never be seen again. "When I got home," he said to me, "I put my scout uniform away and never wore it again. I never told my family what had happened."

Perhaps he never told anyone else. But that day, sitting in the prison camp with the gulf wide between us, it just came out. It was the only time while I was a prisoner that he let his guard drop. And at that moment, when tears filled his eyes, I saw how he must have looked as a little boy those many years ago when he walked away from the country club wearing his scout uniform for the last time.

20.

Fujita

The years have softened many offending sounds and soothed a host of haunting memories. They have not, however, done much for Fujita. He was a little man with a barrel chest, powerful legs and short arms. He was unusually hairy and his small, black, shifting eyes matched in color the hair which stood heavily on his head and ran down his arms to the backs of his wrists. His head was so enormous that it gave the illusion that there was no neck and that his Maker had in some manner created an imperfection, a second so to speak, in the production of humans. By the fate of war, Fujita was second-in-command of our prison camp.

He laughed frequently and loudly. But it was never contagious and he appeared to be undisturbed by the fact that he enjoyed a world of humor alone. When the first tentative arrangements for an exchange of prisoners were revealed to us, it was the camp commandant who solemnly made the announcement. But it was Fujita who found most pleasure in it.

"You're all happy!" he bellowed as he stomped into one of the crowded sleeping areas that night. The prisoners rose slowly to their feet and waited. "Happy!" he shouted again, despite the fact that no face would reveal any such emotion in front of him.

"But soon I hope we shall meet again." He grinned. Then suddenly, with a jerk, both stubby arms rigidly forward in simulation of a bayonet thrust, he lunged at the nearest prisoner shouting, "Meet again. Like this! Like this!" And roaring with laughter he walked out of the room and we could hear him far down the hall still noisily registering satisfaction with himself.

In our tiny universe Fujita was a power, a ruler of men. And unlike the commandant, who was a gentle and timid creature, Fujita enjoyed the war, his place in it and the rein it gave him.

One hot August morning the camp awoke to the plaintive cries of a Chinese beggar. In answer to the basic urge of hunger and ignorant of what the compound before him enclosed, he had wandered into a forbidden area outside the barbed-wire fence and was reaching through it, tin can in hand, repetitiously wailing the beggar's chant.

It was not long before the captain of the guards and two soldiers were upon him and from the distance we could see him being dragged away. Later that morning Fujita was observed making an unusual survey of the trees within the compound. He was accompanied by the captain of the guards. Finally, pointing to a low-branched mimosa near the outer barracks, he dismissed the captain who saluted and walked away, his sword clanking behind him. Fujita sauntered off into the main building.

At noon hour the captain of the guards clanked back into the compound. Behind him were two soldiers marching stiffly, rifles on the shoulder, trailing a rope between them. The end of the rope hung from the neck of the Chinese beggar who followed at a stoop, crying and clasping his hands together, wandering off to left and right like a bewildered animal at the end of a leash.

As Fujita barked orders and the soldiers tied the beggar to the tree, the prisoners who had been watching turned their backs and walked away. All day in the hot sun the beggar hung against the tree on the cords which bound him and called for water and for pity. At dinner hour few prisoners ate much of their ration and that night the beggar's cries filled every room with depression and sleepless men. Next morning he was gone. But the rope still dangled from the tree as though waiting for his return—"Or," as each prisoner felt within himself, "for me."

Several of us had been working on a camp census for the Japanese and that afternoon we brought our report to the commandant's office. A counter-like bench separated the area where the prisoners could go from the sanctity of the commandant's headquarters, and over this bench Fujita greeted us with a laugh.

"The news is good today, gentlemen," he said. "All your planes which attacked the Shortland Islands yesterday have been shot into the ocean. Soon you will have no more planes." He laughed again.

The roaring of his mirth was interrupted by pitiable cries and moans within the office and across the bench, over his shoulder, we saw a human heap lying on the floor near a rusting iron stove. It was the Chinese beggar. His hands were tied behind his back and he was lying in a circle of water. On top of the dead stove was a large white porcelain teapot, decorated, Japanese fashion, with brilliant orange blossoms. Sitting nearby, in a collarless shirt with yellow sweat marks about the arms, was the captain of the guards. He was relaxed, legs crossed, elbow in hand, smoking a pipe.

Fujita took our written report and with his stubby arms resting on the bench, began to read. Behind him the body on the floor stirred and struggled slowly to sit up. The captain of the guards smoked and watched as one might watch a grounded, fluttering butterfly in its last hour.

"Your totals don't match ours," muttered Fujita as he continued to read. We said nothing. The beggar began to wail again. He tried to bow in his awkward position. His voice rose.

Fujita pondered the papers for a moment and then, as though footing a column in his head, he walked slowly, holding the papers before him, to the figure on the floor. His arm pointed at the dead stove and the captain reached for the teapot. He put his pipe carefully on the stove lid and then with one hand seized the shaven head of the now screaming Chinese and jerked it backward. With the other he poured water from the spout of the pretty teapot into the nose of the helpless man. The beggar's cries were reduced to gurgles as he struggled in convulsions and water splashed from his mouth. Then he collapsed again and sprawled inert in the puddle on the floor. The captain of the guards sat down and again busied himself with his pipe. Fujita came back to the bench.

"Your figures do not match ours," he repeated. "Perhaps you do not know how to count." This was said with heavy sarcasm. Then he laughed again. "Only five ships sunk at Pearl Harbor! Five! You Americans can't count or you are liars!" He looked at us with a grin. We said nothing. "You report a victory at Guadalcanal. Can't you even count your own dead?" The laugh again.

With a black ink stick and a Chinese brush he mixed a pool of writing fluid. Then in flashing strokes he wrote a message in Japanese down the margin of the first page of our report.

He looked up and saw us standing there. "Go on!" he said as his arm shot out, signaling us to leave. "Go on. You Americans don't even know what the truth is. You can't even count!"

As we backed off and walked hurriedly away we could still hear his laughter—and, as a faint counterpoint, the whimper of the Chinese.

21.

Turn of the Tide

We knew when the war had turned. We felt it first as a moment of intuition. Then it grew into a thrill as the surging flood which long ago had left us behind like flotsam was flowing back to float us free again. By August, 1943, it had reached a crest. Mussolini had resigned, the Anglo-American landings in Sicily were firm, the Japanese had abandoned their toehold in the Aleutians and the American offensive was sweeping through the Solomons.

This we read between the lines of the Japanese press reports. But it was the Japanese themselves with whom we had contact who kept us best informed of the turn of fortune by displaying through word and manner their growing uneasiness.

Nothing disclosed this more than the breakdown in their own relations: their bickering and brawls, their disputes and fall-outs, which spread among them like an infectious epidemic as the outlook grew more and more ominous for them. In our last months in China they were quarreling openly before us, often using us as sounding boards for ridicule and disparagement of fellow Japanese. I remember especially a scene in Commandant Tsurumi's office which took place toward the end of my prison days. I had come there on some camp business and the commandant, an academic man who had spent some years in the consular service in Vancouver, began chatting with me and had gotten into a discourse on Japanese traditional conduct. A staff assistant wandered into the office. It was a hot afternoon and he was clad only in a pair of floppy underpants and he stood beside us listening and rubbing the sweat off his stout red body with a towel. Tsurumi winced and his discussion lagged. At last he stopped and, pointing to his assistant, said to me: "Look! A coolie has come into the room."

In mid-September it was at last announced that plans for repatriation were complete and lists of those to be included in the exchange were posted on the camp bulletin board. The commandant called me in for one last talk. The time had come, he felt, for our two countries to discuss peace. Perhaps I might suggest this to my government when I got home.

"Everyone wants peace," he said. "Is it not so?"

I agreed; everyone wanted peace.

"This war is no good for your country and no good for mine," he continued sagely.

Again I nodded.

"We cannot understand," he said at last, "why the United States would not permit Japan to have Asia—and Germany to have Europe. We Japanese would all be happy to have your country take over South America and Canada."

They divided us that last morning in prison: those of us who were going home forming into long lines across the compound, waiting beside our bags and bundles for the captain of the guard and his soldiers to come and examine and seal them; and the rest standing at a little distance, watching. We didn't say much back and forth. We had said it all before, awkwardly and painfully, we who were leaving never quite finding the right way to talk about it, and those who were not being overly helpful as we packed and overly generous in telling us how happy they were that we were among the chosen.

When the buses came through the gate and drew up near us, there was a sudden restlessness among the prisoners who were watching us. They moved about and pointed and we could hear a drone of excited conversation. For days, everything that we said and did within the prison was concerned with our departure. But not until this moment, it seemed, when the buses arrived to take us away, did the real impact of our leaving strike those who were to be left behind. A few began to wave at us and some turned their backs and walked away.

While we were loading into the buses the little prison band began to play and everybody followed us toward the gate singing "God Bless America." And when we were at last out of prison we could still see them through the open gate, waving and waving. And long after that we heard their voices.

22.

One for One

The exchange ship *Teia Maru*, like so many other things the Japanese called theirs in those days, belonged to somebody else. Before she was seized by the Japanese Navy, she was the French motor ship *Aremis*. She was seventeen thousand tons, with accommodations, including steerage bunks, for seven hundred passengers. After our last pickup of prisoners along our route, we were fifteen hundred. But we, who crowded her rooms and beds and bunks, who slept on chairs and floors, in the holds and on hatch tops and decks, who assembled with equanimity at the always-waiting shower and toilet lines, who often ate standing because there was no room at the tables, had long ago learned that lack of privacy and of personal facilities was a way of life. And still prisoners in mentality, we still felt the comfort of the herd.

It was not until we had had some days of ocean and skies and wide horizons that our perspective broadened and the attitude and manner of the prisoner began to wane. Then a revestment of individuality made its way slowly through the group. And with it came an awareness of discomfort, a return of intolerance, and an indulgence in complaint about conditions and companions.

There were no strangers among us as they came aboard from various ports along the Asian coast. Some had known each other in the Far East for years. Some had shared prison camps. Some had never met before. But all were bound into a kind of companionship in misfortune.

They came by small boat from the beaches of Stanley Prison Camp at Hong Kong, waving and looking up at us with strained, bright faces. They climbed the ship's ladders from launches in San Fernando Bay in the Philippines, calling names in tight voices. And we picked them up along the winding Mekong River near Saigon, ill with the fever of the jungle and the war.

They carried all they had in a few bundles and they looked pitifully shrunken and aged, wearing clothing too large for them and making their first steps aboard with caution and their first words in prison tones until they gained the assurance that it was all over and that they were in fact going home.

It was a strange voyage indeed: inboard an overpopulated, self-absorbed civilization, carried through space like life on a planet; and outboard a silent, empty eternity which enveloped us in a great arch from horizon to horizon. Once a Japanese submarine surfaced and ran along beside us in a little white streak of foam, but no life showed aboard it and it was as impersonal as a following star. And once or twice we saw smoke far off, lying on the ocean, but it caused no more interest than a rain patch in the sky. In a curious kind of way, we became dissociated from the universe. Never before in the war, or again after, was I so detached.

But this feeling altered as we neared the port of exchange in Portuguese India. By then Shelley and I had become painfully subjective, wavering between crests of elation and depths of despair. We shared long periods of depression and talked of hiding away at home from people we knew and of avoiding familiar places. We were frightened. It was a kind of anxiety illness, a combination of fear that life has gone on and left you behind and of self-pity that you are no longer wanted, that there is no job for you, that you are finished. Later I came to understand that many people who have been shut away suffer this way when they come out into the world.

On the twenty-sixth day, however, a surge of excitement went through the ship and carried us along too: at dawn we had passed some small fishing craft and by the time the sun came up out of the Arabian Sea we had picked up a pilot and were standing in toward the Indian coast. Ahead of us was the neutral port of Goa, where we would be free.

The long, modern dock area was empty of ships, and a row of black cranes stood immobile with their necks askew like great sea birds dozing along the cap of the wharf. The inner harbor was dotted with the bows and superstructures of sunken vessels, sabotaged early in the war, we learned later, when their German and Italian crews prepared to take them to sea loaded with the manganese which was mined nearby. After that, little more than tides moved in and out of the harbor and a few indolent Portuguese police and reclining Indian caretakers watched over the fine godowns, vacant of everything except the lingering smells of spices and copra and dried fish.

A few clusters of people were waiting on the nearly deserted quay, and as the tugs pushed us broadside to the dock, there was shouting and waving back and forth. But Shelley and I who stood together, pressed by the crowds against the rail, saw it all in a fuzzy kind of way. In one of the ironies of our lives, the great moment we so long had talked and dreamed about was dimmed to gloom by a wave of depression. We saw the small group below us waving and heard the shouting. But we dared not believe it included us until a voice beside us repeated urgently: "It's you they're calling, Shelley. Right below. They're calling you and Carl."

We looked down into the little knot of men in khaki bush jackets and shorts, their faces turned up and all of them yelling at us. Suddenly we recognized them: they were old friends, newspapermen, all laughing and waving sun helmets

—all but one whose face was strained and who kept shouting through his cupped hands: "Virginia? Where's Virginia?"

All at once we were ourselves again. The tragedy of another can, in a flash, reduce your own imaginary troubles to nonsense. It was Frank Hewlett. We had known him in Manila as a fellow newspaperman. When the Japanese came in, Frank and Virginia had parted, Frank to go to Bataan and Virginia to remain in the city as a nurse at Santa Catalina Hospital. The course of events carried Frank to Corregidor and ultimately to Australia. It led Virginia to imprisonment in Santo Tomas. And there, under the stress of war and separation from Frank, whose fate she never learned, she lost her mind. The State Department had listed her among the repatriates, and here, now, her war-correspondent husband was waiting for her. But at the last minute the Japanese had ruled she was too sick to travel. She had been left behind in prison.

This was not the sort of thing you could shout from the side of a ship. We appeared not to hear him. Anxiously he tried others along the rail. But nobody else wanted to hear either. He was back at us again, urgent. "Please," he called. "Where is Virginia?"

"We'll come down as soon as we can," Shelley shouted back.

"Better wait for me," a voice behind us said. It was Dr. Hugh Robinson, a missionary doctor from North China and one of the truly great men of our Santo Tomas days. "I was her doctor," he said in his direct New England way. "It will be better if I tell him first." And he went down the gangway with a special State Department escort.

Later, from the ship's rail, we spotted him walking down the quay with Frank. They were a long way off and they looked small. They stopped and we watched them standing together and we could see the little motions of Dr. Robinson's hands as he talked. And it was as painful as though we were there.

It wasn't until the next day that the exchange ship *Gripsholm* came. Sharp eyes found her coming hull-up over the horizon, and though she looked no bigger than a fly climbing over a window sill, we set up a great shout and there was dancing on the decks and a clapping of backs.

Perhaps none of us left the decks that afternoon. We stood there watching every move the Swedish ship made as she entered the harbor and was warped alongside the dock. She was made fast a diplomatic distance from us, but not too far away to keep us from regarding with an eye sharpened by experience and an interest whetted by vindictiveness what the Japanese were doing on their decks, or they, with equally un-Christian motives, what was happening on ours. And I must say they appeared more consistent than we. For while we presented a patchy, uncoordinated front, seemingly without will or purpose, they held military drills on the decks of their ship, engaged in mass calisthenics and sang fierce and dedicated songs.

On the third day after the *Gripsholm* arrived, we were exchanged. We simply came off our ships, single file, and forming two great semicircles, one well inside the other, walked slowly along in opposite directions, toward our own vessels. In some ways an observer might have mistaken one group for the other. We Americans and Canadians were brown-faced, slimmed to an Oriental sparseness, dressed in faded and ill-fitting clothing and carrying straw bags and baskets. The Japanese were stout and overfed, wearing the latest American fashions and carrying the best American luggage. They shouted in good spirits and once, as the lines halted, some of them fell into a football formation, running through a series of plays with an imaginary ball and calling signals in loud American accents. They were still coming off one end of the *Gripsholm* when Shelley and I, moving along our line, climbed the gangway at the other.

On the ship's deck there was a little knot of waiting people. But I did not see them very clearly. For, as hands reached out to help us aboard, someone said, "Come on home," and our composure crumpled and everything went out of focus.

We walked a few steps and a big man appeared before us. "I'm Bill Langdon. State Department," he said. "I've been waiting for you. I've got this old thing that I've never been able to work myself and I thought you might like to borrow it for the trip home." And from behind him came a hand holding forth a camera and a packet of film. "Take it," he urged. "It's

117

yours for duration."

And there on deck, not more than five yards from where we stepped to freedom, I turned the camera on the still-arriving repatriates and made my first picture in twenty-two months. And even now, these many years later, I remember the moment in detail: the feel of the camera, the forms moving through the finder, the sound of the shutter making the first exposure. And it was this last that I remember best. For exactly at that instant I heard the voice at the head of the gangway again: "Come on home," it said. "Come on home."

And then I heard Shelley: "Let's go down and get the two lines exchanging before it's too late," she said. She had a pencil in her hand and she was folding a piece of paper. She showed no excitement at all. But when I started down the deck toward the crew's gangway she came running after me, and when I looked at her I saw that her face glowed with a wonderful light.

The *Teia Maru* sailed a day ahead of us. The vessel came close as it was turned from the wharf and the Japanese were all out there on deck again, singing and cheering and waving flags and calling out fiercely to us with their hands rolled into fists and their faces grimaced like samurai warriors. And we all watched quietly from our decks with a lazy kind of interest until a group of missionaries who had been standing together on the fantail waving back at them with kerchiefs and towels began to sing "God Be with You Till We Meet Again." Then a counterpoint of catcalls and protest rose. And above it all bellowed the voice of one man who stood behind them, red-faced and swelling with indignation. "Sing that for yourselves, you God-damned Jap lovers," he yelled. "I hope the bastards drown."

PART IV

23.

"Where You Been
All This Time?"

The *Gripsholm* touched at Port Elizabeth in South Africa
and at Rio in South America; we had warm weather and calm
seas all the way; and there seemed to be no hint of war in the
world.

As we neared New York the cold winds of December began
to blow on us and the choppy waters off Cape Hatteras rocked
our gentle ship. We were more than seventy days out of prison
camp and all of us had traveled far along the road to individualism, each of us turning toward his own future.

On the morning of December 1, 1943, we sailed up New
York Bay and watched the spires of Manhattan rising above
the fog. Our welcome that day has now dimmed. I remember it
in a confused way: meeting with officials, then with waiting
family and friends, and with the press. But I remember best
Dmitri Kessel of *Life*, resplendent in war correspondent's uniform, greeting us with a wonderful casualness and saying, as
though we'd never been away, "Better hurry. They're waiting for
you back at the office."

We were home again.

Those who were in America in the years when disorganization,
misjudgment and blunder marred the period in which the great-

est industrial nation in history converted from peace to war may recall the home front in more moderate terms. But the war was more than halfway through when we came home and the national adjustment had been completed and the country's entire war effort was, in an American way, moving along a kind of never-ending conveyer belt. And coming out of another world, we found the United States awesome, dramatically resolved, powerful beyond belief: a homeland inspired.

It was, at the same time, like all home fronts, a guilty one: guilty that it was not itself being bombed and being shot out of planes and abandoning ships at sea and being starved in prison camps.

It was also an impatient one. I caught the quickened pace myself. I seem to remember that I caught it as I stepped off the ship. But if not, I certainly did the day I visited my draft board. My office sent me down there shortly after my return and I found it in a building on Madison Avenue. It was in a big, dark room which looked very much like an unrented store taken over briefly as party headquarters for a local election. There were war-effort posters on the walls and at the farther end there was a long table at which sat an old man, spotlighted by a desk lamp, reading a newspaper spread out flat before him. He wore bifocals part way down his nose and a startlingly white beard which disappeared into an oversized collar as he bent to his reading.

I walked up to the old gentleman and paused. "Good morning," I said.

An arm moved toward me with a printed form. "Fill this out, please," he said without looking up.

I sat at a corner of the table, and using his light, completed the form. I pushed it gently across his newspaper and he began to read it. Then he looked up at me. "Well," he said in a tone of surprise. "Where you been all this time?"

"I've been a prisoner," I replied. "Japanese prisoner. Just returned home." I pointed to the form which he held. "I wrote it all out there."

"I know," he said without glancing back at the form. "I can read, son. But what I want to know is where you've been all this time?"

I began again, louder and coming closer, feeling that his

hearing was impaired. "I've been a prisoner of the Japanese," I shouted, "and I've just been repatriated. Came in on the *Gripsholm* just . . ."

"Yes, yes, I know, son," he repeated patiently. "I can read and I can hear. But the *Gripsholm*'s been here five days and what I want to know is where you've been all this time."

I was so impatient to be back at work again that I accepted my first assignment without question. But when I walked past the guards and felt the gates shut behind me and saw the fences and the barbed wire and the watchtowers, a torrent of old and familiar sounds and smells and scenes rushed me back to more unpleasant days. And I felt, as I stood before the American officer who was greeting me, more a prisoner than a visitor.

I was at the Tule Lake Japanese Segregation Center. "Segregation" was a word dodge, as though a euphemism could in some way blink the fact that it was a prison. My prison in China, too, was called by another name. "Civil Assembly Center" was the Japanese phrase for it. The impulse to use these dissembling words grows out of the same evasion that brings people to say "passed away" for died. For prisons are very much alike, wherever they are, and those who run them feel some sense of guilt. It isn't because they are at a loss to justify their prisons; it is simply because those who punish others are often beset by their own doubts. At Tule Lake there were more than the usual amount of these.

For here, along with the several hundred people who were a danger to the United States, were some eighteen thousand others who were torn between a country in which they lived but which never really wanted them, and a country many of them had never seen but which circumstances and racial pressure led them to dream of as home. These bewildered people refused to declare allegiance to the United States and were listed as disloyal. But more than 70 per cent of them were born Americans, and most of these were young and under the influence of their parents and committed by family pressures.

As a minority group they were overly sensitive people, many

123

of whose hurts had turned them to anger. There was the young farmer I photographed named Yoshitaka Nakai who, in a surge of patriotism, had bought eight thousand dollars' worth of U.S. War Bonds. But when, soon after, he was suddenly picked up off his land for relocation and his crops went bad, he refused in indignant retribution to take an oath of allegiance. And there were many others who were similarly provoked by the disruption of their farming and their commercial and private lives. But more than any other thing, their reaction of disloyalty was a consequence of being treated as disloyal.

"I am an American like everyone else born in this country," a displaced student from the University of California said to me. "And I would fight and die for this country like any other American. But because my eyes are different and my parents come from Japan, everybody looks at me and treats me as though I'm disloyal. And now—I am disloyal. How do you like that?" His eyes were afire and his jaw knotted and he glared at me as though he would knock my block off if I replied.

My story at Tule Lake was intended to provide a thoughtful comparison between American and Japanese standards in the treatment of the enemy. And at Tule Lake I found the prisoners accorded consideration and facilities unknown in Japanese camps. They were provided with food and with medical care on U.S. Army standards. And we, in turn, were often starved and sometimes beaten. Indeed, under the Japanese we were lacking in nearly every material thing provided at Tule Lake. But we had something else: a deep and comforting conviction that we were part of a great national emergency and that we were all playing a part both toward victory and our own salvation.

I knew, soon after entering Tule Lake, how remarkable was the difference. It has lingered with me in the image of a young prisoner I photographed there. He was sitting cross-legged on his army cot, his back to a wall covered with pin-up girls, his face empty. He was strumming slow chords on a guitar and he turned away from me to escape the breath of my comings and goings and my air of fulfillment, so disruptive to peace of mind in a purposeless world. He never spoke to me, but I knew how he felt as I watched him sitting there. For once I had sat just

like him and looked just like him and hoped just like him. And
I knew that his whole mind was possessed, night and day, with
only one thought: deliverance. Only, when I was a prisoner I
had suffered no painful uncertainty as to whether I should be
wishful about it or fearful of it.

I never really had time to identify myself with the home front.
In April I was accredited to the Army once more and author-
ized to work overseas in the European theater. I had long since
replaced the camera outfit I left behind in the Philippines and
now I donned my new uniform, attached the green tabs which
identified me as a war correspondent, and stood by ready to go.
    But I was going alone this time, for Shelley was staying behind
to write a book. We planned that she would join me later, for
she too had been accredited. But for a few months, at least,
the war was separating us as it separated millions of soldiers
and their wives. Now we stood together at Penn Station in
New York to say good-by. I had photographed this scene many
times in many cities. But not until now did I know how it felt
to look from a train as it pulled farther and farther away from
the platform, straining to see that last tiny wave, until, all at once
in the crowded car, you are alone.
    Perhaps I felt it more than most, that soft spring evening. For
I had not yet gotten over the feeling that during my prison
years the world had left me behind, and I was not at all sure
of myself. And that night as I headed back to another front in
another land, I was suddenly aware that so much of the strength
I had always thought was mine, was Shelley's.

24.

The Pipe Line

By the time I left Asia, such war planes as we had based there had long before been flown away or were inglorious wrecks on the ground; our ships were sunken hulks in every harbor of the Philippines; our fighting force was finished, with all its men killed or scattered through the islands in death camps or in Japan as slave labor.

This circumstance gave emphasis, in my eyes, to the might of the Japanese. And over the months, with nothing remaining to provide challenge and contrast, her organization and equipment and men appeared increasingly substantial. It wasn't until I came home and rejoined the armed forces and saw the war equipment that we were producing and the army and navy and air force we were sending into the fight everywhere, and felt the emotional drive and the confidence of the country, that the Japanese military stature fell away to size and I was to see America's role in better perspective. I was never, however, to see it without wonderment. I had been away too long and my view was always to be tinged with a bit of the Rip Van Winkle, and I often found myself exclaiming and being excited over the ingenuity and creativeness of the American mind—of what was produced, and the quantities, and what was planned and imagined—which others seemed to accept as in the natural course of things.

I had my first real look at what America was doing, in the course of things, when I was staging to go overseas again. Indeed, an American staging area in early 1944 was one of my most astonishing experiences in the war. I was processed—that was their word for it—with thousands of others, check-off list in hand and running all the time. Imperative voices sent me here for a helmet, there for web belts, and for shoes and drawers and toothbrush and indoctrination lectures; crying through a tear-gas chamber; fumbling over the side and down a net of a mock-up ship and into a make-believe landing craft; queueing for eye tests where glasses were made for you while you stood there, and for dentists who glanced and pulled a tooth before you could utter "not that one"; down endless pavements from warehouse to warehouse, laboring with arms full of equipment while more and more voices urged me on and hands reached out and turned me this way and that, sending me blindly forward until, finally, I bumped up the ship's gangway, staggered over her decks, and disappeared into her dark hold smelling of men and Cosmoline and new issue clothing. And when, at last, in the fantastic red glow of the ship's battle lamps, I dropped my gear and straightened up, I had been processed and was on my way to war.

This was at Camp Patrick Henry, at Norfolk, Virginia. By then nearly half a million souls going to and from battle regions had been processed through its vast area and the Army knew a thing or two about supply and the movement of men. And the great staging center was in effect a huge American production line with 1984 Orwellian touches. Once in there you were sealed from the world, fed into a pipe line, and disgorged somewhere on a faraway battle field. The process was inexorable. I saw that soon after I arrived there.

I was standing at the end of a medical line. As a war correspondent belonging to no one, I was attached, last man, to a division. We were all naked, save for a pair of newly issued boots, unlaced for quick removal, and an army overcoat. The latter was taken off and carried over the arm as we approached a row of doctors who were spaced along the queue like assembly line inspectors in a factory making men. We were all more aware of our imperfections and shortcomings than were the doctors, and we held our coats over our arms in a modest kind of way until we reached them and they motioned them aside. Perhaps at no time in war is a soldier more abject and defenseless than when he is naked. Even in some of the most frightening moments of combat, soldiers bring forth wisecracks, bursts of inspired humor. This was a line of silent men waiting to get their pants on again.

By the time I reached the doctors they had gathered into a little group, lighted cigarettes, and were enjoying the break. "War correspondent," one of them called out in a friendly tone after looking at my papers. He was a lieutenant colonel. He gave me a cigarette and we were all in a circle, talking, when a sergeant came over to us and waited attentively.

"You want to see me, Sergeant?" the colonel asked.

"Yes, sir, please, sir. There's a soldier out there from the division you've just processed, got something the matter with him. Said he'd like to see a doctor."

"All right. Let's see him, Sergeant," the colonel said.

The soldier came in behind the sergeant, the laces of his boots slapping the floor, his overcoat looking much too big for him and his body not very straight. When the sergeant stepped back and the soldier stood before the colonel, the other doctors stopped chatting and looked. The soldier glanced at them. He appeared frightened and uncertain, as though he wanted to run away. He pulled his overcoat round him like a wrap.

"What's your trouble, soldier?" the colonel asked.

The soldier licked his lips. "It's my back, Doctor," he said. He reached behind him and rubbed his back.

"What's wrong with it?" the doctor asked.

"I don't rightly know, sir. It hurts."

"All right, soldier," the doctor said. "Take off your coat and your shoes."

The soldier looked quickly at the others and hesitated. It was clear he didn't want to take off his coat.

"Come on, soldier," said the colonel. "Take it off and let's have a look."

The soldier put his coat down on the floor behind him and stepped out of his shoes. He folded his hands in front of him, shivering.

"Show me where it hurts," the doctor said.

The soldier put his hand behind his back again, slowly.

128

"Bend over, soldier."

The soldier bent forward and the doctor ran his finger along the curved spine as lightly as the mistress of the house over a window sill.

"O. K., soldier. Put on your coat and shoes again."

The soldier slipped into his shoes and put on his coat, making a face, as though it hurt him.

"All right now," the doctor said. "We'll get that fixed up for you. You just go ahead and rejoin your outfit and as soon as you get overseas, report for sick call. They'll take care of you over there."

The soldier looked dumbly at the colonel, and then he followed the sergeant, his boots sliding noisily and his shoulders more stooped than ever.

We all watched until he was gone. Then the colonel said to me: "He's ill, that lad. But it's not his back. He's got a fever. Here at Patrick Henry we call it gangplank fever."

At Patrick Henry and at staging areas all over the U.S.A., in that year of the Italian and Normandy campaigns, endless columns of Americans were moving up the gangplank and into the pipe line. It was all very American. A goal had been determined and a quota established. And fever or no fever, there was no turning back.

25.

Adaptation of the Species

Camp Patrick Henry's pipe line put me down on North Africa. Soon after I arrived a public relations officer informed me in secrecy that a new and major Allied attack was about to begin in Italy and that arrangements had been made to fly me there at once. This proved to be the May 11 offensive which had as its goal the Liri Valley, the final assault on Cassino, the breakthrough into the Anzio beachhead, and on to Rome. I arrived in Italy just in time to join a push which others had prepared through months of enormous effort and sacrifice, and to roll with it for twenty days, into Rome.

The Allied war machine I saw in Italy was electrifying and incredible. I was accustomed to unpreparedness and undersupply. That morning in the little withering olive grove where we were encamped near the village of Sparanise, I seemed to be the only one who stopped and watched the bombers sail over for their mass attack on nearby Monte Cassino. Everybody else took one glance and then went on with what they were doing. But I stood there transfixed, my head bent back until my neck ached. The sky was full of them, high and moving in slowly from a great arch that curved along the edge of infinity. I had never seen so many planes in the sky and they all appeared to be converging over our encampment. They pounded the air and the earth throbbed with them and men adjusted their bodies to the great vibrations and raised their voices to be heard above the roar. While I was away a change in environment had taken place and already the species had adapted its behavior to it.

"What do you see?" a passing officer stopped to shout at me. There was urgency in his voice, as though I might have noticed something he should know about.

"Planes," I shouted back.

"Yes, lots of them," he replied as he turned away, his mind already back on more important things.

I had arrived in Italy the day before. A transport plane loaded with freight and personnel had carried me across the Mediterranean, the air heavy with traffic skimming under an umbrella of British and American fighters. Late in the afternoon we saw the coast, green and beautiful, with a lacy fringe of ocean. And rising from it in massive grandeur was Vesuvius, trailing a thin line of volcanic ash, like smoke flowing lazily from a weapon after a violent discharge. Below it lay a village in the track of a brown, smoldering outpouring, newly cratered and in ruins. It was as though nature, seeing what men were doing, had greedily grabbed a share before it was too late. And as we flew low toward a landing near Naples, floating over village after village, all leveled and spilled about with rubble, it seemed likely that until Vesuvius took it, that one had been the only village left.

Naples itself was smashed, victor and the defeated alike living in and out of ruins, and everything looking, in the early darkness, like a scene vaguely remembered from an earlier century.

I drew a billet high up in an old building standing strangely alone among the ruins and part way through the night I was awakened by a shattering and shaking. Guns began to fire all around me and I jumped out of bed. We were being bombed. I tore open the great French blinds which had been shut for the blackout and patches of light rushed into the room.

Outside, the city was white with moonlight. I opened the window and the air was brisk and smelled of the ocean. There was no air-raid warning but I could hear the planes and feel the bombs falling nearby. The moon was huge and full and starkly white, lighting the city into a kind of giant stage set. And the sky was filled with long, lovely yellow and orange tails of ground fire running up toward the moon and then falling off into great curves and twinkling themselves out like falling stars.

Below me there was a hissing sound. I looked down. A strange and opaque cloud was rising from the ground all over the city. Smoke machines were sending up a protective curtain. Slowly it rose, obliterating Naples below and boiling up and up until it blotted out the moon. It poured into the room, setting me coughing and groping. The bombs were still falling and the guns still firing. And I was suddenly cold and alone. I grabbed some clothes and felt my way out of the room and ran down the stairs, flight after flight.

They led me into the basement. And there, under the stairs, I found a crowd of officers wearing helmets, some dressed, some with their shirt tails hanging out, and one with no pants at all They were mostly older officers, with big stomachs, and they were all packed in there tight, bent and crouching and waiting, all uncomfortable and a little embarrassed as men always are when they hide in the cellar under the stairs. And I put on my helmet and bent down and pushed in among them and there we all stayed until the all-clear. Then we climbed back upstairs to our rooms without talking very much.

This is how I remember my return to war.

26.

Three More Miles

Lieutenant Colonel Joe Crawford stood beside the mountain trail waiting for his radioman who was kneeling before his portable equipment to make some sense out of the message he was receiving. Past him a single file of soldiers climbed unevenly up the precipitous and steeply humped goat path, appearing one by one over the hummock below him like spokes on a broken wheel. Centuries had worn the path into a rocky trench and as Crawford waited beside it he reached out, from time to time, and gave a helpful push to a spoke that had lost its momentum and seemed poised to roll the wrong way. "Up it is, boys," he muttered encouragingly in the kind of soft tone that carries both understanding and authority. "Keep it moving."

"It's Lieutenant Austin, sir," the radioman broke in. "The Italian drivers say the loads will kill the mules. Too much and too steep, he says, sir."

"Tell him to keep them coming," Crawford replied. "Keep them coming till they drop. After that, tell him, the men will have to carry the stuff themselves."

"Break," the word came panting down the line, and the spokes stopped, folding either side of the pathway, slipping out of their equipment and sitting or lying or leaning wherever the terrain permitted. And Crawford stepped into the trail again and began climbing over and around the men who tried with little tired motions to make way for him.

Down the mountain behind us was Santa Maria Infante, a key strong point all these months in the German "Gustav Line," and now fallen in one of the very first major successes of our spring offensive. Rome was the goal. But the road to Rome was mountainous, with Germans formidably emplaced in a continuous network of defenses. And the plan for breakthrough demanded that initial and local successes be pressed quickly into larger victories. Lieutenant Colonel Crawford was taking his 349th Infantry Regiment straight over the mountains.

Below us our left flank fell gradually away into a valley and through this another regiment was fighting, hill by hill, roadblock by roadblock, toward Formia on the coast. From a distance the sounds of their fighting reached us, dull and impersonal, and now and again we could look down between rugged crests and see the dome of hazy blue smoke which hung above the battle. Sometimes fighter planes curved down into it and reappeared a few minutes later, the belated waspy whines of their power dives chasing behind them.

I had joined the 349th that morning as it came through Santa Maria, its two single columns of infantry winding their way through the battle debris which packed the main street of the town. All the houses had been knocked about into piles of stone and powdery mortar as though they had been built, like primitive dwellings, out of the earth itself and were now simply crumbling back into it. The smell of death was heavy enough to catch the stomach. A quartermaster squad had assembled twenty or thirty American bodies and had them all laid out straight. And across the road German dead had been gathered and tossed into a grotesque heap, some of the clothing torn, exposing expanses of dead flesh, their arms and legs poking disrespectfully at each other, all bereaved of their last earthly dignity.

All this the passing infantry noted subjectively, talking very little and looking right and left with eyes somber and thoughtful and often, when the morning breeze, saturated with death, fluttered along the columns, they retched involuntarily.

Out of Santa Maria we turned up the mountains. The smell of the dead faded away behind us and despite the steep climb the men felt better and began to talk again. Spring had come to Italy and the fig trees were leafing, the little mountain orchards of stunted and twisted fruit trees were flowering, and the daisies and yellowing dandelions, the red and orange poppies, spotted the ground with radiant color wherever they could push their feet into the mountainside.

A mile or so along, three Germans waited in a small emplacement which commanded the trail. It was a well-contrived defense, made of fieldstone and grown with grass and little wildflowers. Above it hung an old bent peach tree, dipping sideways out of a ledge to frame the emplacement with an incredible burst of delicate pink; and just inside it, on the fire shelf, was a row of potato-masher grenades and a long sausage and some green onions. A single red poppy lay among the onions. The three Germans within were sitting on jerry cans, sprawled easily with their backs against the stone walls of their emplacement. Their eyes were open and vacant, as though they had just eaten heavily and were relaxing. But their bodies were drilled and bloody and they were dead. And the column plodded on.

All day we climbed, the spokes of the wheel moving and halting and jerking and tumbling. Once the combat engineers up ahead turned us off the trail altogether when they found it mined. And now and again patrols working on our flanks made contact with small rear-guard units of the enemy and we could hear their guns chattering at each other, shooting it out.

As the day was ending we gained a saddle-top part way along the range and the regiment began to re-form its fighting units in the gathering dusk, placing them in battle positions for the night. The regimental command post was set up in a little stone farmhouse. All about me I could hear the men digging in. At dusk it is a sound that is never forgotten, and a soldier is weary of himself who does not, on hearing it, reach for his own entrenching tool.

I wandered off to our left, over the edge of the saddle, where men were digging foxholes among the trees. Below us spread the valley and the battle for Trivio. The last of the sun's afterglow had colored the smoke and dust of the conflict into a mottled red and pink, and it eddied up like the rosy clouds through which the warriors in ancient paintings gallop their chariots. Instead an American artillery-spotting plane came skipping along just above them. It began to draw ground fire and the men stopped shoveling to watch. Suddenly it was hit and tumbled awkwardly. A parachute broke free. And when we could see a little black speck dangling from it, the men climbed from their trenches cheering and waving their shovels.

We all waited there watching tensely as the pilot fell through arches of tracer fire, and every soldier on that mountainside was that falling speck. Would it land in our own lines or the enemy's? But we could soon see that the wind was carrying him the wrong way, for now that it was almost dark we could make out our positions from the base of fire, and the men's shouts drained off and they stood with their shovels hanging by their sides.

"Maybe he's made it," someone said. But everybody knew he hadn't. And for a moment we all remained withdrawn and silent, feeling deeply about the one man whose danger we had seen and shared—while below him, hidden and seemingly far away, thousands of men were fighting bloodily and being torn and killed.

All the next morning we climbed. The battle still raged on our left flank and we were moving up to join it where the enemy lines spread over the mountain. But the pace and terrain had worn us down, and here and there men dropped out, sitting alongside the trail, still hung with their gear, panting and glassy-eyed. And once I saw a mule, stretched out and dead, its load mercifully gone and its frayed flanks at last stilled and untroubled by the swarms of flies which buzzed around its suppurating saddle sores.

Crawford walked with his men, his eyes darting everywhere. Often he stopped and spoke to a man who had dropped out and was breathing hard. "Sit there a while," he would say.

135

"But don't get left behind. We don't own these mountains yet."

Once he turned back to me as I scrambled up the rocky path behind him. "The trail is clean," he said. "The men are still in good shape. When you begin to see ammunition and equipment abandoned along the way, you know you're getting into trouble."

Late in the morning word came back that we had at last hit the German line. They were dug into the range ahead of us. And Crawford stepped off the trail with his map and his radioman to plan and to rearrange his forces. We were in a tiny mountain orchard of a dozen or so trees which grew like dwarfs in the inhospitable soil. On one side of them an old stone retaining wall kept them from sliding into the ravine below and on the other was a low rocky cliff. Crawford looked at the cliff. "We'll set up the CP there," he said.

In it was a cave, and as he spoke soldiers came out of it with two civilians, an old man and woman, bent and frightened. They blinked in the sunlight and looked at us sideways, as though they were not sure what to make of us or what to expect. The intelligence officer went over to them. "*Americani*," he said. And the Italians began to cry and shout: "*Americani. Viva. Viva. Americani.*" They put their hands together as though they were praying. "*Viva Americani*," they repeated over and over.

"Tell them," Crawford said, looking up from the map he had already spread on the ground, "that we're sorry but we're going to have to take over their home, there." He pointed toward the cave. "*Si. Si. Prego. Prego*," they repeated eagerly, when they understood. They suddenly realized that he was the important man and they both came over to him, bent and halting, their arms outstretched as though in supplication. Colonel Crawford left his map on the ground and rose. The look of the military man vanished. "What is it?" he asked them. He spoke in Italian and in both his face and voice there was compassion.

"God has sent you," they cried, seizing his hands to kiss them. "We have been waiting. Our homes are gone and we live in caves and eat grass. We have been waiting for you to deliver us. Our son is wounded. He is only five years old and his leg is broken. He will die. Please, in the name of God, help us."

They fell on the ground, still babbling, and would have kissed his feet, but he raised them gently. "Our doctor will take care of your boy," he said soothingly. He called over his shoulder and an officer and some men came and led the Italians away. And all the while they kept turning back toward the colonel calling, "*Americani. Americani. Grazie. Grazie.*"

Crawford watched them go, their bodies gnarled and bent as the stunted trees around us. "A five-year-old son," he muttered incredulously. "They look seventy." And then he ran his hand over his own tired and unshaven face. He broke into a little laugh. "I guess we all do, eh, Major?" he said to an officer standing near him.

Then his voice changed and it was the regimental commander speaking again: "Let's move everything but the radios inside the cave," he said. And he sat on the ground with the map in front of him and took the field phone the sergeant was holding out toward him.

I went along the ridge with the wiremen that afternoon. We were now in a new battle. The Germans were emplaced across the crest of the mountain. Down in the valleys on either side we had them under heavy attack and on the heights Crawford had thrown his three battalions at them to try to break their line and pinch them off. Regiment had lost communications with one of the battalions and the wiremen were searching for the break in the line. We followed the wires, sometimes passing troops and supplies going forward and often being passed by littermen carrying back wounded. A few prisoners, unkempt and glancing at us with bloodshot eyes, passed us at the double. Their hands were folded over their heads and their nervous reactions to the guns their captors held, and the alertness of the Americans, indicated that the Germans had just been taken and that neither they nor their captors had yet gotten used to each other.

We found the break the other side of a little ruined hamlet. A shell had ruptured the wires. The wiremen repaired them quickly and we took off as fast as our pride would let us, for the shells were falling near the road again.

Back at the CP an intelligence officer, Lieutenant Bromberg, was leading a prisoner into the orchard. Someone had given the German a can of rations. It was labeled "Bacon and Eggs," and the prisoner, who kept looking about him with apprehension, constantly glanced at the can, trying to understand the meaning of the foreign words.

When Lieutenant Bromberg asked his first question the German bent quickly and placed the can at his feet and shot up straight again, bringing his feet together with a click and drawing himself into stiff attention. And after each reply he relaxed and glanced down at the can. His face was thin and worn and was grown with a short red beard. And when his hands were not stiff at his sides they shook as though he had palsy.

He had been assigned, he said, to a party of twenty men, sent from his company to mine a bridge on the road to Trivio. But they were brought under fire and in their haste they blew it, and it just went "pfft," and nothing happened. He laughed nervously. He got separated from the rest, he said, and was captured.

"I'm taking him down to the POW cage," Bromberg told me. "Want to come along?"

"Where's the cage?" I asked.

"Down the mountain," Bromberg replied.

"No, thanks," I said. "It took me two days to get up here."

"Come on," Bromberg urged. "I'll show you an easy way."

The prisoner and Bromberg started off and I followed down the steep trail. In ten minutes' time we were into a wooded area, a dappled shade closing us in. Then, suddenly, we emerged and looked out upon an incredible scene. The mountainside lay open before us and winding up it was a broad, new highway. It was hung with dust and crowded with moving men and vehicles—trucks and jeeps and tanks rolling bumper to bumper as far as we could see. We stood on the crown of the hill, staring into the dense movement and hearing the roar of motors and the clank of trucks.

"The engineers," Bromberg said at last. There was pride in his voice. "They dozed this road through since daylight."

The German watched with astonishment. He glanced first at Bromberg, then at me, and he looked behind him as though

138

to check his geography. *"Mein Gott!"* he cried.

When we crossed the road into another wooded area the bull-dozers were just finishing a jeep park, all smooth and neat. Soldiers were tying it off with white tape and the first of the vehicles were already turning off the highway into it. *"Mein Gott!"* the German exclaimed again.

We climbed into a jeep and nosed into the heavy traffic down the mountain. It was an absorbing sight: infantry moving up single file on either shoulder of the roadway and in the center an endless chain of vehicles and mobile guns and armor, churn-ing the new road into a yellow fog. Again and again we had to turn off the road to let swelling traffic pass.

The German sat up front beside Bromberg. He had opened his ration can with a key the lieutenant had given him. But the scene so preoccupied him that he wolfed down the food, giving it hardly more than a glance, and all the while he twisted and turned to look about him. At last he faced Bromberg, and spread-ing his arms wide he said: *"Mein Gott.* All this! And we are supposed to win the war!"

It was nearly sundown when I got back to the CP. I was tired and I stretched out on the ground near the old stone fence and fell asleep at once. When I awoke it was night and the sky again was lighted by battle and the fighting was all around us.

I got up and found my way to the headquarters cave. There were old rags hanging in the entrance, left there by the Italians. I pushed through and a light struck me and I waited until my eyes adjusted. It was warm in there and smelled sour, like the inside of a silo. Crawford was shouting into a phone and a few officers and men sat near him in the shadows. When I could see better, I crawled farther into the lair and sat on a pile of reeds.

It is not always easy to reason why one scene of drama remains indelible and so many others dim or fade completely. In this instance, clearly, it was the surroundings which heightened the spectacle that night. The costumes and the appurtenances of the players had changed, but the performance had been given many times through the ages. And it was perhaps this very universality, this realization that the scene was as old as men squatting in caves and as contemporary as men swearing over bad telephone connections, which haunted the lines and made more grotesque the shadows on the walls. In any event, ever since that night the scene has replayed itself to me in detail:

Lieutenant Colonel Crawford sits cross-legged on a sleeping bag on the floor of the cave. Before him, on a little rock shelf a foot off the floor, stands a gasoline lantern. It is bright and makes a steady sound like air escaping from a tire. It lights Crawford from below, making him look bigger and distorting his face, and it casts a huge image behind him which spreads over the cavern roof and walls and sometimes rushes off, disappearing into the rocky labyrinth. If he hunches his back a great giant behind him lurches threateningly. If he bends low over his map the giant races up to peer over his shoulder. The roof is hung with a few bunches of dried herbs and some cabbage leaves and it drips with cobwebs, all casting eerie shadows and sometimes draping the head and shoulders of the giant with uncouth regalia.

A few men sleep fitfully in dark corners of the cave, the sound of their breathing joining with that of the pressure lantern to make a steady hissing in the damp air whenever Crawford's voice is still. And other officers and men are sitting at a distance in the recesses of the rocks, cranking on phones, leaning forward to catch the light on maps they are marking and reports they are writing. They come and go as Crawford directs. But he is the nerve center; and all night his voice rings in the cave.

"Give me the Leather switchboard," he calls into one of the field phones. "Leather? Is that you, leather? Give me leather-white-six." The lines are always faulty. "Leather-white-six . . . Are you on your objective yet? . . . Well, get up there. Be there before dawn. That's an order. An absolute order . . . You've got what? Repeat that. . . . You've got what? . . . Well, we'll try to get plasma through to you. But you keep pushing. Keep killing Krauts. . . . Before daylight. That's an order."

He bends over his map for minutes. Then he cranks away again and he's through to another battalion: "Fine. Good. But what I want to know is are you killing any Krauts? . . . You're what? . . . All right. Good. But don't forget. It's Krauts we want."

Someone in the background reaches over with another phone.

"Leather-blue-six has come through, sir." Crawford takes the phone quickly. It's almost a snatch. He's electrified. "Wonderful!" he exclaims. "Wonderful! Can you stay? . . . Can you hold?" He shouts louder. His face swells. But he's lost the connection. He's frustrated, but he's elated too. He turns to the others: "Colonel Yeager's taken his objective. He's up on the hill now. But he's in a real fight; he's under heavy fire."

He beckons toward an officer who comes forward into the light. "Captain Sawyer," Crawford calls, and raising his map a little he runs a pencil over a small area. "Here's where Yeager is now. Just this side of the phase line. Don't get short of it with your artillery, but I want you to give him support with everything you've got."

"Yes, sir," the captain says, and he stoops and marks his own map, checking very carefully, and turns and walks bent toward the entrance and goes out.

Another phone is offered Crawford. He begins to reach for it and stops. "Is it Walter Yeager?" he asks. "That's what I want now. News of Walter Yeager."

"No, sir," the voice answers. "But I think you'd better take it."

Crawford takes the phone. "I know your mules are tired," he shouts. "Every man and animal in this outfit's tired. God-damned tired. But we've got to get those supplies up there. They've been calling for ammunition all night. They're in trouble. Can you hear me? They're in trouble."

For a moment after he has hung up Crawford sits looking at the phone, whether in disgust with the lagging company, or at that very moment holding desperately up on the hill with Yeager, he gives no indication. But all the while—and it seems a long time—everybody else sits motionless and the sound of the sleeping men and the lamp fill the cave, getting louder and louder until, suddenly, abruptly, Crawford begins to grind at a telephone and to shout impatiently into it, and his voice again takes over the cave.

After that I fall asleep on the reeds. But throughout the night I hear Crawford's voice yelling. Sometimes it's about Krauts and sometimes it's about Yeager and heavy enemy fire and litter bearers and mules.

Close upon that, it seems, I become slowly conscious that the lantern still flares and that men near me still sleep. But the cave is empty. I lie there for a while, slowly coming awake and trying to think back to when Crawford was an actuality and when he became a dream. Then I leave the cave.

Outside, morning had come and the sun was just beginning to touch the little orchard. Men were sitting about eating out of cans and there was a good smell of coffee and bacon. Crawford was in his undershirt, bent over a helmet full of water, shaving. He looked refreshed and smiled when he saw me. He straightened up. "Yeager held last night," he said. "He had a bad time for a while. The Krauts threw everything they had at him. But he held."

He wiped away the last of the lather, and when his face emerged from the towel it glowed and was suddenly younger. His smile broadened. "We made almost three miles last night," he said.

27.

Along the Tracks

A long way back that morning we had dismounted from the jeep when we ran out of road. Now we labored up the mountain in the early mist of an Italian summer day, hauling on scrub for support and wetting ourselves with cascades of little silver balls of dew.

We could hear the firing as we climbed and we avoided the open areas, keeping to the cover of the brush. When we reached the railroad tracks which cut a narrow swath around the mountain we found some of our troops resting and preparing breakfast. "They're fighting farther up the tracks," said one of them, pointing with his mess cup. The hillside echoed with a persistent, business-like rattle of small arms that sounded like a forest of woodpeckers.

The soldier stooped over a little basin formed of sand in which gasoline was burning and with his bayonet forked out a blackened can of rations. He rolled it about with his foot. Pausing, he glanced up the track and said: "The Krauts are holed up there in the railroad tunnel and we've been waiting for a seventy-five to get up here to work them over."

The soldiers were relaxed and methodical in their breakfast. "Coffee," one said, handing us a steaming cup. Another slid over an open box of ten-in-one rations. "Help yourself," he muttered from a full mouth and watched us with eyes absorbed by the contentment of satisfying food. At our feet two men in green fatigues, yellowed with sweat and dirt, played gin rummy.

We thanked them and started up the tracks. The sun was now high and hot. In the distance, straight ahead, we could see a tiny black circle. This was the tunnel entrance. We passed foxholes dug alongside the roadbed. They were empty except for one up ahead of us. When we walked by it we saw a medic feeding a wounded soldier who had been shot in the head. The wounded man surprised us by giving us a half-wave with a dirty hand. The medic just looked.

Then we began to see dead on the tracks. First there was one body, then another, and then twos and threes. We came down off the roadway and walked in the ditch for cover. When we reached the shelter of a lonely pine, we stopped. We were hot and our gear was heavy and we rested in the long cool shadow. There was a single dead German lying there on the tracks. We smoked, watching the tunnel and sometimes looking at the dead soldier.

He was sprawled at full length before us, lying almost on his back, a small man with his head pointing down the tracks away from the tunnel. We could see no wound, but the rocks of the track bed near him were stained with blood. Beside him was his rifle, a new shiny weapon with the breech bolt open. His helmet hung above his forehead like a huge jaw, the weight of his head propping it there against the ground. It was a black-lacquered

143

helmet without a scratch or blemish. A white swastika outline in red looked as though it were embossed on its side.

His face was young and girlish. It was pretty. Death had already colored it a waxy yellow. A hand still lay on the rifle, the fingers in repose, delicate and slightly bent, as if its owner were resting momentarily. It was as though a Queen's Guardsman had fainted on parade and gone down in full kit. And as we sat watching I almost expected the yellow eyelids to open, the bloom to come back to the face, and then, as he slowly sat up, to see on it the embarrassed look of the Guardsman who has fallen in the Mall.

A squad of Americans was coming back from the tunnel, their voices loud and echoing in the mountain air and their weapons clanking like a tinker's wagon. They were walking single file in the ditch by the tracks. We could see them clamber onto the roadway at a pile of German dead and stoop over them. They were searching them. Then they came on down the ditch toward us. When they reached our dead German they climbed onto the tracks again and stood looking at him for a moment.

"The son-of-a-bitch was running for it," one said. "Got it in the back, the bastard." Someone picked up the rifle and the German's fingers seemed to quiver. "It's hardly been fired," he said and he pulled on the bolt that was already open, holding his hand like a mirror at the breech as he peered down the barrel. "Yeah," said another reflectively as he touched the boy gently with his foot. "He's got all his points now. He's got it made."

One of the soldiers pulled the helmet away and the boy's head dropped back an inch in an almost lifelike motion. It gave the American a jar and he looked at the German with a kind of surprised sidewise glance. "Son-of-a-bitch," he said involuntarily, and somebody laughed.

A soldier had taken off the boy's belt and while he was strapping it around his own waist another was unbuttoning the German's tunic. He slipped his hand into its inside pockets and came out with a wallet. At this everybody crowded around. It was a fat wallet. "Kraut money," the soldier said as he produced some currency and passed it out to the men around him. "Shortsnorter money." He dug farther into the wallet. It was filled with

144

letters. Each one he opened and dropped to the ground. "They're all in Kraut," he said disparagingly, and tossed the empty wallet at his feet. Then they stepped down into the ditch again and waved to us and went on.

And we went on too, leaving the German in his scattering of letters, for we heard the first heavy rounds echoing down the tracks, and we knew they were now shooting into the tunnel.

28.

Major Collins

When we first saw Major Collins he was walking along like an Indian scout, a small pack on his back, his body bent to a slight crouch, his step catlike, and a forty-five in his hand. He heard us coming a long way back for our jeep was laboring in low gear, its engine clamoring loudly in the mountain air; and without taking his eyes off the trees or vines he waved an arm for us to come on, as though he were bringing troops up after him.

We were in terraced vineyards in the mountains, pushing a jeep where no mechanized vehicle had ever been before, and we were in the middle of a battle. Behind and above us was Velletri, still in the hands of the enemy, and we were fighting up the rear slope. The Germans were all around us in the vineyards and there was shooting everywhere.

When we came abreast of Collins he gave us only a brief look. "Where you going?" he shouted, his eyes back on the trees.

"Up with the advance units," we yelled at him.

"So am I," he answered, keeping up with our roaring jeep. No one wanted to stop there.

"Come on," we urged. And with his head still turned outward, he hunched his body, pulled his backside up over the edge of the jeep, and was suddenly sitting in it with our driver's carbine in his hands, looking as though he'd been there all the time.

"Thanks," he said. And he reached an arm over and shook hands with Eric Sevareid, another correspondent, and with me. "John Collins's my name," he said, seemingly talking to the vineyards. "I'm on my way to join my new outfit, Third Battalion, hundred-forty-third of the Texas Division." He had been in the Pacific, a paratrooper, and had just arrived in Italy. "The battalion's up ahead of us somewhere," he said. "I know a lot of the boys in it and it sure will be good seeing them again."

He gave us the quickest look. "War correspondents," he said in a friendly tone, and that settled that. He was a handsome man, built as a paratrooper should be. He wore a confident smile. "Sounds like everybody's shooting everybody," he said pleasantly.

We had gotten onto a winding mountain pathway, two wheels on and two making the best of it, bumping and jumping over whatever obstacles they met, and the going was slow. At last we stopped. All the men around us were now dug in. "Can we get through?" our driver asked a soldier who was crouched in his hole by the roadside looking up at us.

"You can get through all right," he said, still keeping low. "They just killed our BAR-man by that tree up yonder, but you can get through sure enough."

Our driver gunned the engine, but he hesitated. He turned back toward Collins. "Go ahead," Collins said. "You heard the man. He said we can get through." And he smiled and held his carbine a little more firmly and sat up a little more alert. And Eric and I slumped lower and lower in the jeep.

"How far is Highway Six? Sevareid shouted to a soldier who was hiding behind a tree.

"Straight ahead," he yelled. "You're almost on it."

We bounced out of the vineyards and through a gully and up onto the highway. There were tanks rolling along it, all buttoned up and flushing us with heat as they passed, showering us with black-top and gravel torn up by their tracks. The fighting was heavier up there and all the men were either side of the road, low and in cover. We slowed down. "How's the road?" Collins asked a lieutenant who was lying with some men along the ditch. Near them was a dead German and a couple of American casualties. Now that the tanks had passed we could hear the small-arms fire all around us.

The lieutenant sat up. "It's under fire," he said in an easy voice. "Another jeep made it up there a little bit ago. But when he went by us he wasn't wasting much time, and if you're going I wouldn't linger much either."

"All right," Collins said to the driver, touching him on the shoulder. "This is no place to think it over. Let's go."

We could see them fighting on both sides of the road, now, and the jeep fairly flew along the highway. Then suddenly we all saw someone standing clean out in the middle of it, waving. He was flagging us down. The jeep slithered and stopped.

It was a soldier. We had skidded past him and he walked up to us slowly, his rifle hung on his shoulder as though he were off duty. He walked stiff-legged and his body shook and his teeth chattered.

"What is it, soldier?" Collins asked impatiently.

"Can you tell me, sir, where there's a first aid station?" We could hear the bullets and we all bent lower.

"Are you hit?" Collins asked.

The soldier stood shaking and chattering, his mouth open and his tongue going quickly out and in like a lizard's. "Are you hit?" Collins asked again, his tone imperative.

"No, sir," the soldier stuttered slowly, "I don't . . . think so. It's nerves . . . I think."

"Well, get down off the crown of the road," Collins said. "Get over there in the cover with those men. You're a duck up here. A sitting duck."

"Yes, sir," the soldier chattered again. But he hardly moved. Our driver gunned the engine nervously. But the soldier just shivered and chattered and his tongue snapped in and out.

"Go ahead," Collins said to the driver. And as we pulled away he raised himself in the jeep, shouting at the soldier. "Get down," he urged. "Get off the road." And we could see the soldier nodding obediently. But he couldn't move. He was frozen there. And as far back as I could see, as we dashed along the highway, he was standing right there where we left him, in the middle of the fight.

We came up with the tanks as they were turning into a narrow dirt road and a combat MP jumped out and stopped us as we turned to follow. "Let the tanks through first," he said, sweating and anxious. "They're calling for them up there."

We left the jeep and went on by foot. The road was a deep gully-like passageway, some of it hedgerow, and it was strangely quieter than the highway, the only firing nearby from isolated snipers. Infantrymen had joined the engineers, shoveling frantically to cut the embankments wider wherever they stopped the tanks and laying out by-passes so that jeeps coming back with the wounded could make their way rearward by dodging around the oncoming traffic. Almost all the jeeps were filled with wounded, some lying on stretchers strapped across the hoods. And while the jeeps bounced and rocked along, the aidmen, kneeling and balancing and clinging miraculously with one arm, raised the other high, as one would a torch, holding a bottle of plasma, pouring life back into a broken body. I think I have never seen a soldier kneeling thus who was not in some way shrouded with a godlike grace and who did not seem sculptured and destined for immortality.

Collins led us. Sometimes we climbed up to walk along the embankment, looking down at the traffic that snaked by our feet, and sometimes, when we heard shooting near us, we scrambled down into the ditch again, falling in with a line of infantry and dodging the tanks as they roared and clattered by.

There were Italian refugees down there too, passing us singly and in little groups, panting and frightened, carrying improvised stretchers with their wounded and infirm, and bent under enormous bundles and baskets which they carried on their heads and backs. They seemed shattered by what had happened to them, poised to run this way or that as ordered, like slaves before the whip. Surely no human being is ever more forsaken and lonely than a civilian who finds himself in the midst of a battle, for the soldiers around him are preoccupied with fighting and at such a time have very little compassion for the innocent man or woman who in any way hampers its progress.

The road began to flatten and the embankments to fall away and soon we were in the vineyards again—and the fighting. The sound of firing was loud and the troops fanned out away from us. The tanks turned off the road and went thrashing through the scrub, ungainly monsters firing their fifty-calibers, and the men followed along behind like chicks running after a mother hen.

Major Collins had been asking for his unit along the way. Now he got directions from an infantry officer who passed us, and he turned up the slope and Eric and I followed him through the vines and up into a forest. Here the men were moving from tree to tree, firing and taking cover Indian fashion. We kept on moving behind Collins until a voice stopped us. It came from behind one of the trees. "Hello there, Major," it called.

Collins looked over and waved. "Hi," he called, as one might to a friend who had hailed him as he walked through Times Square. We followed him over to a young officer, a lieutenant, who came from behind his tree to shake hands. He was crouching and keeping a sharp lookout around him as we talked, and so were we.

"Heard you were coming," the lieutenant said.

"Sure glad to be here," Collins replied. Then he looked about him with a confident and appraising eye. "What have we got here?" he asked.

"A clean-up, right here," said the lieutenant. "And a real good fire fight just up ahead." He waved up the hillside. "We're taking the hill right now. But this place here's loaded with Germans." He glanced behind him again. "We've pushed through them, but they're all through these vines, so watch yourself."

"How's your company doing?" Collins asked.

"Just fine," the lieutenant replied. "They're soldiers now. I think you'll be proud of them, Major."

"Lose any?"

"Yes, we've lost some. Just lost one a minute or two ago down there in the scrub." He pointed. "Jergens. You knew him. And Johnson got hit too. You remember the little corporal, Johnson? But he just got it through the elbow and the boys have started

149

him down the hill already. He'll be all right."

"Jergens," Collins muttered. "Sorry I won't be seeing him."

He turned to us and his face brightened again. "Thanks for the ride," he said. We shook hands. Then he glanced up the hill. "Looks like the boys are working up there," he said. "Maybe they could use another body." And we waved good-by to each other and he disappeared into the foliage.

29.

The Wedding Procession

At ten o'clock on June 4, the muted cackle of hens scratching in the sun, the caw of crows, and the gentle cadence of a church bell tolling filled the air with the unmistakable sounds of a Sunday morning. A wedding procession of eight Italians came round the bend of the old Roman highway, Via Casilina. They were young and fresh and carefully groomed, walking that day with a notable leisure and carrying themselves with the manner of impertinent aloofness which is so often the fashion of a youthful wedding party.

They came in twos, the girls on the men's arms and the newly married couple leading. The bride carried a gathering of roses and green leaves and the groom held a pair of yellow gloves in his hand. Under a large blue sign reading "ROMA" posted above the eight-kilometer mark, they passed a man standing by a stone fence. He was decked out too, with sprigs of the olive tree in his hat. The couples were close enough to touch him, but they neither looked at him nor in any way indicated that they saw him. And he in turn looked straight ahead—indeed, straight

150

through them—silently holding in his impatience until they passed. Then he bent again over his bazooka which was supported on the top of a gate pillar, sighting along it, waiting tensely, while behind him, down the road, the wedding party slowed up at a mess of several dead Germans strewn there by an earlier shell hit. But though the party lost a little of its order, it lost none of its manner, the couples simply holding hands and leading each other on tiptoe around the carnage. Then they formed up again and continued their aloof and leisurely procession along the highway.

Moments later, an explosion blew debris and gravel over the road and sent up a cloud of smoke and dust, and the man with the camouflage of olive leaves ducked behind the fence. We watched as he rose slowly, sighting his bazooka again, and then a blast of flame flared over his shoulder as he shot his weapon. He disappeared quickly for cover, and the rest of us, lying in a ditch across the highway, waited for the counterfire.

Earlier that morning I had come bowling down the ancient highway in a jeep with Ed Morgan, another correspondent. We were both sitting up there urging the driver on like jockeys on horses, for Rome was falling at last and we had just been told that the road was open. But soon after that, men had come up out of the ditch yelling at us and frantically waving, and our driver's reflexes were so sharp that he screeched to a stop only a little way beyond them. "Come back!" they all shouted and beckoned. "Come back! There's a Tiger and some eighty-eights around that bend. They just got a tank and the jeep ahead of you."

We pulled the vehicle back to the roadside. In the ditch were some soldiers and some war correspondents.

A Sherman tank had come up the road and was pulling in alongside the ditch, near us. A lieutenant stood on it, looking through binoculars. He told the correspondents that there were elements of a Hermann Göring Battalion with guns around the bend and that he had just had a radio message to stand by for supporting troops before he attacked.

Italians had miraculously appeared and had circled the tank calling, "*Caramella, cigarette, viva Americani.*" And the tankmen were delighted with them, handing down cans of rations and packets of coffee and cigarettes. And one of them, a sergeant, helped quite a pretty girl onto the vehicle, and in their brief encounter they were already holding hands and exchanging names and plans for a later rendezvous.

Across the street the bazookaman was still watching for his target. He was now protected by a soldier who sat a little distance from him, covering him with a Browning automatic rifle. And still another figure had entered the scene. His shoulders were stooped and he wore an old felt hat and his faded blue jacket and baggy trousers were both too long for him. He stopped and stood with his hands behind his back watching the soldier and his bazooka as a stroller coming down the street might pause to watch a construction riveter with a jackhammer. When the soldier bent alert over his sights, the man bent too, looking very much like an umpire crouched behind a catcher. And during the moments when the bazookaman, triggered by something he heard or just by some combat instinct, ducked for cover, the man waited there, standing with his hands behind him, until the American had had enough of that nonsense and once more took his position over his weapon. Then the man moved up behind him again, looking.

When the troops came down the highway they turned off into the fields before they reached the bend, to begin a flanking movement around the Germans holding the road. The land was deep with ripening wheat and the men waded out into it, disappearing up to their shoulders, their helmets glistening in the sun like turtles swimming through a lake of waving grain. The Germans were dug into the low hills skirting the wheat, and the fight to open the road began.

I had chosen a bit of high ground near an old farmhouse, just off the road, to photograph the infantrymen going into the wheat, and when I finished I started in after them, wading through an area which offered a short cut. But as the sound of firing swept through the grain, I soon felt the folly of continuing through the tall grass alone, and I hesitated. And when I did I became aware of something moving a little to my right. I crouched quickly and tried to look up through the bending wheat heads. But I could see nothing and my muscles grew rigid and the hot sun suddenly felt icy cold. I wished I had a weapon.

Then I saw something moving, tied with an old rag. It was a woman's head, and it was coming right at me. When she saw me she jumped a little. Neither of us uttered a sound. Her back was round as a bowl and she leaned on a stick. Her face was hung with creases and her hands were red and very thin and the fingers all looked as though they had been broken and set wrong. One hand gripped the walking stick and the other gently felt the grain. She went slowly on, her body bent over the stick and her hand passing lovingly from grain head to grain head. When she disappeared I went on through the wheat as quickly as I could, falling in at last with a column of infantry.

Later, when I got back to the highway, the scene had changed and the mood had passed and I found myself feeling a little sad that it was gone forever. The roadblock had been broken and the Germans had pulled back, leaving some lying in the fields and ditches dead, some to be marched along the highway with their hands on their heads. And now U.S. infantry was moving along the road past the point where we had stopped that morning. The bazookaman and the Browning automatic man were gone. And so was the sign reading "ROMA." General Clark, someone said, had come by and taken it as a memento. I looked for the old man but he too was gone. And there was no longer anything distinctive about that bit of highway except, like thousands of other bits along the road to Rome, what lingered on in memories.

30.

Villa Tasso

Rome fell as it had fallen many times before, the aftermath fluttering over the city and touching its people in various ways. To those who sat in candlelight that first night with their grievously wounded, unable to find a doctor or a priest, and to those who gathered in grief around their shattered dead, this turn in the long history of the Eternal City was felt as a remorseless point in time. For others it was something less.

That first night in Rome I came up the Via Veneto, feeling the city's twenty-seven centuries looking down upon me. I was soiled from the field and carrying on one shoulder my cameras and all the gear I had lived with for almost two months and trying to whistle to keep my emotions under control. It was more than history that stirred within me; it was like the deep thrill of coming home after a long absence. And I had come back the hard way, sometimes wondering if I would ever make it.

I chose the Majestic Hotel where I had lived when I was last in Rome in 1940. The porter who took me to my room remembered me and we hugged each other and rejoiced. He told me how good God had been to have at last sent the Americans to Rome, and I gave him two packs of cigarettes. He was overcome with thanks and gave me in return the Fascist salute. Then he felt awful because he had, snapping the erring hand as though he would like to shake it off for its indiscretion. "A habit of twenty years," he said to me, begging me to understand.

A few days after I arrived, I had word that a German Gestapo prison and torture chamber had been found and I went over to see it. It was in the center of the city and was called Villa Tasso. From the street it looked rather more like a modern apartment house than a villa. Its main entrance, however, led me through a corridor into a large and lovely Roman garden with stately trees and clipped hedges and a spraying fountain, all touched with color from carefully tended flower beds.

A little gravel pathway wandered through the grounds, curving around the fountain and following along the flower beds to the back of another building which shared the garden. This was Villa Angeolotti, a seventeenth-century Italian mansion. Villa Tasso, it developed, was the prison, and Villa Angeolotti the torture chamber. And I sat by the fountain a long time trying to imagine the manner and bearing of both the warder and the prisoner as each day they walked that little distance from a dark cell in the basement of one building across that lovely garden to the other, where an ordeal of mutilation and perversion and savagery awaited the prisoner.

Did the prisoner see the garden as he passed along the pathway? Did he smell the flowers? And the warder. Could he deliver a man to the rack like a postman a letter to the box? And did he sometimes find himself exclaiming as they walked along the flowers and round the fountain: "Look at those rosebuds! I would not be at all surprised this evening when we come back this way, if you are alive and conscious, that we shall see many of them in bloom."

I walked along the path to Villa Angeolotti. Its windows had already been boarded over and I waited for some time for someone to answer my knock. At last a very stout man let me in. He did not welcome me. He just opened the door. He had done that, I had already learned, when the Germans were there; and I felt sure that if he wanted to talk he could have helped me with some of the things I had been pondering in the garden. He made it a point, however, to say nothing, except that he did not like my taking his picture.

The walls and ceilings were all painted with frescoes, many of them frightening scenes from Dante's *Inferno*, showing Satan and a lot of lesser devils torturing the damned; and if one managed that trip through the garden without seeing the flowers, he would have been blessed indeed not to have seen the graphic display of horror which decorated the entry into that house of terror.

These thoughts were interrupted by footsteps coming down the stairs and in a moment a young man, accompanied by a seven- or eight-year-old boy, reached the landing. Seeing me, the man exclaimed and came toward me as though we were old friends. He led the boy by the hand and he spat at the doorkeeper as he passed him. Then, taking me aside, he raised both his trouser legs so that I could see the distressing scars and still-festering wounds all over his legs.

"Beasts," he said, making the same kind of noise with his lips that he had made when he spat. "You are in the house of beasts."

This was his nephew, he told me, putting his arm affectionately round the boy's shoulders. He had brought him there that morning to show him the room in which he had been tortured. But all the implements had been taken away, he declared, looking with suspicion at the doorkeeper. The room now, he said in disappointment, was empty.

They were examining the frescoes when I left them to go back through the garden to Villa Tasso.

There I met a man named Mario Giuntini who had also come back for a visit. He had been a prisoner of the Germans for two and a half years and finally released when the Germans thought he had tuberculosis. It was, however, only a self-induced illness, he told me, brought on by smoking cigarettes dipped in machine oil. "It is well worth remembering," he said to me, lowering his voice and giving me the look of a comrade, for I had already told him that I too had been a prisoner, and there is no quicker bond. After his release he worked with the French and Italian undergrounds until he was captured and sent to Villa Tasso.

He took me down to the cells and into the tiny room which he had shared with fifteen others. "We could not move," he said to me. "We had to sit, just so, day after day." And he sat quickly upon the floor of the cell, crossing his ankles and putting a hand around each knee. "Like this," he said. "Seventy days like this.

And when we moved they beat us."

I took his picture as he squatted and then I stood over him, waiting quietly. But he just sat there with his hands holding his knees, saying nothing and not moving. A distant look had come into his eyes and he seemed to have forgotten all about me. When I thanked him, he got up and shook hands. But he stayed on when I left, all alone in that cell where he had sat for seventy days.

I was already outside Villa Tasso and preparing to get into my jeep when still another man arrived. He was broken and stumbling, leaning almost helplessly on a young woman and a man who flanked him. When they entered Villa Tasso, I went back in again.

They started down to the cells also. They had a dreadful time of it, for the broken man had lost almost all control of his limbs. I met him down there. He was Angelo Ioppi who had returned with his daughter and a friend to see the dark room where he had lain so long, the last fifty-two days with his hands and feet tied behind his back. Now, at the door, he let go the arms of his daughter and his friend and, stumbling like a spastic, crossed to the farthest wall. There he felt slowly along until his fluttering fingers met something upon it. And when they did, he cried out and jerked into convulsions, and his daughter and friend ran over and took hold of him and half-dragged him out of the cell.

After they had gone I went over to the wall and found what he had felt. It was a name scratched into the plaster. It was *Angelo Ioppi.*

31.

A Man of
Experience

When the van door opened, Pietro Caruso stood there uncertain
and off balance as he favored his broken leg. He was a heavy
man and he leaned forward cautiously into the many arms
which were reaching up to him. He had a little smile of thanks
on his face when they helped him gently to the ground and he
looked gratefully toward a soldier who was coming into the
circle with two crutches. They were simple things: sticks with
crosspieces. But the crosspieces had been freshly wrapped with
white gauze for the occasion.

The soldier placed a crutch under each of Signor Caruso's arms,
attentive to their fit and heedful of the first steps, moving along
beside him with his hands spread out as though he were fearful
of a mishap.

He need not have been. There were too many others there, all
solicitous and considerate and attentive, holding him gently by
an arm as he hobbled along the gravel roadway, or alert and
ready to assist if he stumbled or faltered.

Nearby was a chair and the limping man saw it and moved
slowly and willfully toward it without direction, taking with
him the little shuffling circle. It was a rather sleazy chair, crudely
put together, as though its maker cared little for his craft.
It was standing with its back to a great grass-covered embankment, its legs tied to stakes which had been driven into the
ground, and a cord hanging in a loop from its back.

When they all reached the chair, Caruso handed his crutches

to those near him and slowly and awkwardly stooped to get onto it, facing its back. It was a painful operation, straddling the seat with a broken leg, and as he did so they all bent over him, suffering with him, helping him with gentle hands and muttering soothing words.

He aided them as the cords which were to bind him to the chair were wound around him, holding them helpfully until the knots were tied. The circle opened to make way for a priest. Then they all gave him one last look, as though to be sure that he was comfortable, for no one would cause him pain. And with a kind of tiptoe step they backed away from him, looking, however, with even more care to be sure that they themselves were safe from the volley of the firing squad. And he was left alone with the priest.

The embankment, which was to be Pietro Caruso's last worldly sight, must have been for him a monstrous mockery. It was within Fort Bravetta, a medieval bastion which stands on a little hill a few miles from Rome, and for many years it has been the place of execution of countless men. Signor Caruso himself had arranged the death of many and had sometimes come there to watch them die as they faced that same embankment. And indeed, when the moment moved him, he had himself shot the *coup de grâce.* For until that last ignoble day when he tried to flee Rome before the oncoming Allied forces and was wrecked in his car on a German mine, smashing both his leg and his chance for escape, he was the Police Chief of Rome, the *Questore,* a position of power and terror which was felt in almost all Italian hearts to be the most hateful in Fascism.

I had seen him a few weeks before. He was then lying in a prison bed, holding in one hand a crucifix and in the other a history of Roman society under Nero, and declaring his innocence to Colonel Charles Poletti, then Allied Regional Commissioner of Rome. "What do you find of interest in Nero's Rome?" Colonel Poletti asked him, glancing at the book.

"At least nothing that can be charged against me," he replied, showing how one's fears can chase one like a shadow.

Now, at the embankment, he was answering for those charges which could be made against him. The *carabiniere* officer signaled the priest to withdraw. Caruso knew every move. He also knew the unpleasantness of waiting for the *coup de grâce*. He turned his head toward the *carabinieri*. "*Mirate bene*," he cried. "Aim well." And the sword flashed and the volley resounded.

They were putting the body in a box and someone was carrying away the chair when an Italian officer came over toward us waving down our cameras. "Enough," he exclaimed. "It is all over." He paused and looked over the scene. "It is never good," he muttered. "But it is always easier when they help, and this one knew how."

32.

Off Limits
to All Troops

The day after Leghorn fell, Sergeant Slim Aarons of *Yank* and George Silk of *Life* and I drove into the coastal town. And finding the great port area so heavily mined and booby-trapped that we could not enter it, we were easily tempted—as indeed were many others in that town that day—to look into a report that somewhere in the city a German brewery had been captured.

We found it by the simple expedient of driving up and down the narrow streets until we spotted a crowd. When we rolled up to it we saw that the combat MPs had encircled the front of the building and that they stood there with their backs to the door and their guns at their hips facing an assortment of jeering soldiers who called them unpleasant names and shouted at them asking who in hell they thought took this lousy town and who in hell that God-damned beer was for anyway, the guys who fought for it or the guys who come in with the rear echelon?

The combat MPs accepted all these questions as rhetorical, standing with their feet apart, chewing gum and watching stolidly. But as we sat in our jeep on the edge of the crowd one of them, a sergeant, and the biggest of the lot, was goaded into a reply. "This brewery's off limits," he said with unmistakable finality. "Those are orders. And any son-of-a-bitch who gets any beer while we're on duty's gonna have to shoot for it." And he pushed his Thompson forward and moved his finger on the trigger so that everyone could see what he meant.

But the gathered soldiers were determined and they were also armed. A few of them held their weapons threateningly to show they were combat men too and not that easily intimidated.

It was at this moment of crisis that Slim rolled our jeep around the crowd and in toward the MPs. They turned and covered us at once, and the big sergeant came over with his weapon on us.

"Where the hell are you going?" he asked in a pained voice as he glanced at our jeep and then at our insignia. "War correspondents," he read aloud in a way that made it plain he saw no aura of privilege hovering around us.

"Yes," said Slim brightly. "We've been sent up here from Rome to photograph this German brewery that you fellows have captured."

"It's off limits," said the sergeant. "No one goes down there."

"We only need a couple of minutes," said Slim, who had earned a reputation long ago of knowing his way around in the army. "We just want to make one picture of the brewery and a couple of you MPs who are guarding it. They'll be in *Yank* and *Life* and all the papers back home. How about you, Sergeant, and say two others from your outfit posing for us?"

The sergeant's face came alight with that look that tells a photographer he's won his point. "Maybe the boys would like that," he said. He walked over to several of the other MPs and talked for a moment and then came back.

"O.K.," he said to us, signaling us to come on. And then turning to the crowd he said: "They're official. They've come to photograph the joint." And the soldiers replied with catcalls and vulgar suggestions as we followed the sergeant.

When we got in there it smelled like the inside of an empty beer bottle. We went down two flights of stairs and found ourselves in a huge whitewashed room with two great wooden vats. Slim posed the MPs in front of one of them, making a great thing of getting them just so, and after a couple of pictures, someone—I can't now be sure whether it was one of the MPs or one of us—said: "How about one beer before we go up?"

And after a while a couple more MPs came down to see what was taking us so long, and then more and more.

It was the sergeant himself who suggested that we fill our two five-gallon water cans which we had strapped to our jeep, and he was still sober enough to send one of the MPs up to fetch them rather than have one of us appear before the crowd.

We were all singing down there with George Silk leading us in Australian songs and passing a helmet as a loving cup when the sergeant, in some way, fell into one of the vats, and we had to grab him and pull him out. And by then the great white brewery room was jampacked with soldiers all drinking and singing, and a camaraderie had grown between the MPs and the troops that would warm your heart, everybody standing with arms about each other's shoulders and passing helmets slopping with beer and not a gun threatening anyone.

"See," said Slim proudly. "If it hadn't been for us they would have been killing each other. Look at them now. Friends. Real friends."

We had trouble lugging the ten gallons of beer up those stairs. And when we got out on the street it looked like an ant run with soldiers hurrying in both directions carrying water cans and sloshing helmets and wine bottles. And as we drove through the town the word was in full cry: "Beer! Beer!"

"See," said Slim with great satisfaction. "See what we've done?"

We found a chow line that had just been set up in the remains of a hospital building and got our dinner and a place to bunk down for the night. The beer had already found its way there

and almost every jeep that pulled up added to the supply; and by
the time it got dark there was a very jolly crowd in that newly
taken town. The mess belonged to the 442nd Combat Team,
mostly Japanse-Americans from Hawaii, and several banjos and
guitars appeared and the patio of that broken hospital, brightened
by a couple of lanterns, looked like a tourist scene of a Hawaiian
party.

Somebody came in with two trailers loaded with hats and
swords. They had gotten into a theatrical supply shop. And
soon everybody was wearing straw hats and fancy tweed caps
and silk toppers and strutting around with glittering swords
strapped to them.

About ten o'clock the Germans began to shell the town. They
knew every building in it and their earliest salvos hit the hospital. They worked the whole city over methodically, always coming back to the hospital where they knew very well there would
be troops. The boys put out the lanterns, but not very much
could be done about dimming their spirits. Some, to be sure,
were already sacked out, twitching in their sleep when shells
hit nearby. But many more were still out on the town, roaming
about in the moonlight, dressed in ridiculous hats and swords
and not caring very much about the shells.

On the street in front of the hospital I saw two soldiers,
both in top hats, engaged in a playful duel. They were not
very steady on their feet and they had trouble keeping their hats
on their heads. A shell hit on the road nearby and several of
us watching threw ourselves to the ground. The duelers did too;
but it was plainly a reflex action of training and experience,
for as soon as the flying debris came to earth they were up
again and at each other.

"Come out of there, you crazy bastards," someone yelled at
them. "Get under cover." But they just raised their hats to the
voice and kept ambling about like two stags in the moonlight.

By then Slim and George were asleep and I sacked out too.
The Germans shelled us all night, and in the morning there
was a singular lack of spirit all through the encampment. And
while we were packing the jeep to go, an officer gathered some
noncoms around him, giving them the order of the day in a

voice that was not very friendly. "And you pass the word to everybody," we heard him say, "that the brewery is off limits to all troops. Those are orders from Division."

We were climbing into the jeep to drive away and Slim stood up there looking into the group of noncoms with an expression of withering judgment. "Off limits," he repeated with scorn. "You wait," he said to us. "Before the day is over they'll change their minds again—just like they did yesterday. It's always that way in the army."

33.

Food for a
Berber Warrior

When I first joined the Goumiers in the fighting before Siena their French General, Joseph de Goislard de Monsabert, told me that in all the world there is no more ferocious fighting man than these bearded and fierce-eyed Berbers who go into battle with Allah on their lips and a plaited pigtail on their heads so that he can more handily pull them into heaven when they are killed.

The Goumiers were very good to me, accepting me as still another prodigy of the curious world they had seen since they had left their tribal homes in the Atlas Mountains of Africa. And in our very first combat together I became the subject of some interest as I lay upon a knoll photographing a tank encounter below us. The Goumier soldiers near me were not in any way familiar with the camera, and after a while I held one out to them. They looked through it and passed it along and discussed it in their Berber dialect. Then one of them, returning it to me, holding it forth with two hands to show his thanks and respect, said to a French noncom: "In this war we have seen many things; but this soldier here is the first we have seen going into battle with only a looking glass."

This brought forth an explosion of laughter from the soldiers around me and a number of them patted the *koumias* which were thrust into their belts to show a preference for their ten-inch mountain knives to a looking glass.

These Goumier knives are renowned throughout history and their wielders noted for the daring and savagery with which they make their attacks. But though I was with the Goumiers in battle in Italy and France and later in Indo-China, the only time I saw them raise one threateningly to a man, a little boy with great blue eyes made them feel the shame of it; and later, when they did cut a throat, it was with little of the assurance and remorselessness expected of a Berber fighting man.

We were in Tuscania, encamped near some old peasant farmhouses. Around us were gardens and pasture lands rolling up and down the little hills. The Goumiers had set up a field kitchen in an olive grove and were preparing dinner, cooking in great pots on open fires. Much of their issued food came from American rations which they ate grudgingly, for they were Moslems and feared the taint of the pig and had very little taste for Western cooking.

Their chief cook was a great specimen of a soldier with a brown, bare chest, a large turbaned head, and a beard combed carefully into two sharp points like saw teeth. I watched him supervising the preparation of American baked beans. They came in gallon cans, specially cooked and marked for Moslems, but the expression on the cook's face as he told his men how to prepare them left no doubt but that this was a food of war and not of choice. The men slashed the cans open and poured the contents into an old wooden wine press they had found nearby, and then pumped water over the whole mess from an ancient Tuscanian well, washing away everything but the beans. These the cook used to start all over again.

Some of his men were coming in now, armed with rifles and with knives, parties of twos and threes, carrying chickens and eggs and tomatoes and squash. And when they came through the grove, everybody working in the field kitchen paused to see what luck and a quick hand had brought them. Each carried his plunder to the chief cook and received a grunt or something more favorable, according to how much his contribution would add to the dinner that night.

Then I heard excited talk and laughter and the cook shouted with enthusiasm, slapping his sides with his hands. I looked and saw some Goumiers walking toward us through the grove leading a sheep.

The sheep was a young and fat one and he was not at all sure that he wanted to come; and each time he hesitated, the Goumiers nudged him and he jerked forward and I heard cries of delight all through the grove. For of all the foods in the world, nothing is more delicious to a Goumier than a sheep nor, in the Italian campaign, more difficult to get. The farmers soon learned how much the Moslem soldiers prized these animals and in some way managed to hide most of them whenever the Goumiers came through their area. But today the soldiers were more fortunate than usual and the cook was lavish with his compliments to the laughing men who provided this one.

Already someone had a rope tied to an olive tree and the cook was running a honing stone over the blade of his *koumias*. He looked at me with a grin. "*Bon appétit,*" he said with satisfaction.

At the outer edge of the trees I saw a small man coming into the grove. He was walking warily, putting each foot forward as one might walk on ice that was not quite safe. And behind him came a little fellow with lovely black hair which fell round his forehead like an inverted bowl, and little bare feet which kicked up tiny puffs of yellow dust. One miniature fist was squeezed round a piece of the man's trousers and the other pressed to his breast with a little coil of rope. They were clearly father and son.

The Goumier cook saw them too, but with a quick glance, as though it was something to be remembered and looked into later. And the sheep saw them and stretched at the end of his tether, pulling and pulling until his little hoofs left grooves in the soil.

When the man reached the fringe of the kitchen activities he stopped timidly and the boy stood close to him, his eyes fixed on the sheep and his little fist still rolled into his father's trousers, sometimes tugging on them like a tram conductor on a bellpull.

Slowly they edged closer to the sheep. The cook had been watching them slyly as they neared the animal and now he twirled, his face contorted fiercely and his mouth open, yelling savagely at the man and boy, motioning them to get out.

It was plain, watching it, that this was a tactic that had been used before and that its timing and expression and strategy had been evolved through a series of such experiences. The man turned almost involuntarily to run, but the little boy, holding on, was in his way and he stumbled. When he recovered, the little fellow was standing out in front of him and, though still reaching a hand behind secured to a new hold on his father's trousers, he was now stretching out the other, holding the coiled rope toward the sheep.

The cook walked toward them. He was annoyed and he waved for them to go away and shouted at them again. But this time neither his wave nor his voice was nearly as imperative.

By now, all the Goumiers in the olive grove had ceased their kitchen tasks and were watching.

The little boy let go his father's trousers and ran over and put his arms round the sheep's neck. His father looked at him and then turning to the cook, spread his arms wide. How universal is such a language.

The Goumier muttered something and put his hand into his pocket and drew out some money. It was French currency and the Italian had never seen anything like it before; it meant nothing to him. He shrugged and shook his head.

At this the Goumier roared with anger and grabbed for his knife. He raged toward the Italian farmer so suddenly and with such a frightening action that I felt my stomach tighten. The Italian's mouth fell open and I heard him gasp, and he threw his arms up, convulsed with terror as the Goumier rushed at him with the *koumias*. But the little boy stood there without a quiver, his face which reached only to the Goumier's knees turned up and his eyes, startlingly big and blue as the sky,

167

looking straight into the bearded face of the warrior. The Goumier looked down on the little fellow and then turned, muttering something, and stalked away. I watched him go into the trees and sit down on a box and light a cigarette.

Another Goumier went to the Italian. This one was smiling and uttering friendly sounds and he curled a finger under the boy's chin and gave the farmer a roll of money. It was lira. And while the farmer stood there counting it, still another came, carrying a two-kilo tin of coffee and a box of biscuits. And the boy held the rope in his hands and looked.

In the end the Italian stopped counting and shrugged. It was now evident that the final settlement had been made and that he could not hope for more; and he opened the box and took out a biscuit and gave it to the boy. The boy ran with it to the sheep and put his arms around its neck again and the animal nuzzled against him and gently nibbled the biscuit. And everybody stood there watching and there was not a sound in the grove except for the birds.

After a while, the father took the boy by the hand and they walked away, the boy with his head turned back watching, and the sheep straining on his tether to follow them.

Everybody waited until they were gone. Then the cook again put the hone to the knife and a couple of soldiers untied the sheep and each seized a hind leg and flung the animal over so that its haunches rested upon their knees and its neck lay upon the ground. Two more soldiers knelt by the neck and, looking up through the trees at the setting sun, moved the throat this way and that for just the right position for the kill. There was a disagreement and the cook came with his big knife and, having a look at the sun himself, settled the difference by moving the neck once more. Then quickly he slashed the animal's throat.

When he arose to avoid the gushing blood his eyes caught something that made him start. We all looked. It was the boy. In some way he had slipped back into the grove and had seen it all; and now he stood there crying quietly, his eyes riveted on the dying animal. The Goumier swore fiercely and threw his knife to the ground. He looked helplessly at the boy. Then, wiping his hands on the sides of his trousers, he walked over to him and, with a swing through the air, sat him on his great shoulders. And the little boy, grasping for something to hold on to, found the end of the pigtail and his little hand closed round it.

And so together they left the grove, neither that great Berber warrior nor the little boy having been very brave that day about the cutting of a throat.

34.

Boulevard Madeleine

Boulevard Madeleine was a lovely French street. It was wide and cobbled and lined with sycamore trees. Its buildings were all joined and rose three and four stories with pubs and bistros and little shops on the street level and flats above. The street stretched gently downhill. Beyond it, in the bright morning sun, was the harbor of Marseilles. And straight across that lay the forts of Saint Jean and Saint Nicolas.

We had come into Marseilles just eight days after the landings at Saint-Tropez that brought the French Army back into southern France, and we were not sure which parts of the city were really free. There were six of us correspondents in the jeep and we drove cautiously along the streets, some crowded with happy people and some empty and silent, until we came to the Boulevard Madeleine.

We saw a line of vehicles with French Army markings parked along the curb ahead and across the street a group of men standing in the doorway of a pub. They cheered us as we approached and we cheered back and pulled our jeep up in the line. Madame the proprietress joined the men in the doorway.

She held up a bottle to us. *"Vive la France,"* she called. *"Vive l'Amérique."*

As we strolled across it, the street gave off such a deserted feeling that I paused in the middle of it to make a picture—the look of the city at that hour of liberation. Then as I stepped onto the sidewalk something glowing orange zoomed past me, bouncing along the cobbles, throwing sparks and spraying chipped stone in my face. It disappeared swiftly up the street like a dart. I ran into the entry of the pub and shouted. The rest of the correspondents filled the doorway to look, the proprietress with them. Another shot came up the road, floating just above the cobbles like steel coming out of a rolling mill. We all stared.

"All morning it has been like this," the proprietress said. "The Germans are in the forts." She pointed down the street toward the harbor. Then with a sweep of her hand she showed how their guns looked straight up the Boulevard Madeleine. "That is why there is no one on the street," she explained, "and why the soldiers have left their cars. They drove here without knowing; now they cannot move." She shrugged, not unhappily.

After a little while the shooting stopped and I looked down the street again. I was surprised to see a large body of people coming right up the middle of the road. It was a column of German prisoners, perhaps twenty of them, being marched up the boulevard by some half a dozen French soldiers. I could see civilians running out to shake their fists at them and I decided, too, that while the Germans were in the boulevard the forts would hold their fire. So I ran down the road and made pictures of the oncoming column and the civilians shouting at them. Then, wanting some height, I ran back and climbed on the weapons carrier which was parked ahead of our jeep.

A mass of red swished by my face. I clutched my camera, and in the instants that followed I saw other shots come tearing through the column. One drove through the back of a prisoner and came out his chest, blowing off the arm of the man in front of him. A French civilian lay split open on the pavement and German dead and wounded were sprawled all over the boulevard.

170

I jumped for the nearest doorway and stood there all alone while many of the bodies on the road began to uncoil and to rise and run for cover. Some of them came into my entryway, pushing me farther and farther back into the dim hall. Soon there were eight of us in there, and slowly I realized that seven of us were German.

No one spoke a word. Most of them were hit, one of them through the foot. He was in great agony and leaned against the wall, his fingernails scraping it as though he would tear a piece out. The man next to me was shot through the arm and bleeding profusely, trying to stem the flow by twisting his torn sleeve above the wound. I tied him tight with a bandage from my first-aid kit.

A French soldier came stumbling through the doorway. He was in bad shape, shot in the stomach. A German helped me lower him to the floor and everyone squeezed back to make room for him. He died as we watched him, desperately trying to say something none of us could understand. As we stood over him, looking at each other with wordless compassion and humility, a group of French soldiers and FFI men appeared with guns, crouching close to the doorway. They ordered the Germans to leave. The shells were still sweeping the street and the dead still lay twisted on the road and the Germans tried to stay where they were. But the French grabbed them, wounded or not, and pulled them out. I watched them go, admiring the way they moved up the street, both the French and the wounded Germans, taking cover from door to door with great skill as they went.

A partisan slipped into the hallway—a young man with a green arm band. "The Germans are counterattacking up the road," he said. We peered down the boulevard and saw the Germans cross the street and start up toward us, throwing grenades and firing into doorways. The boy ran out and up the street and I followed him, running close to the buildings until I reached the corner and slid round it into a side street.

The other correspondents had got there too. We gathered and counted heads. All made it and none of us was hurt. There was another pub just across the street and another Madame the proprietress came out into the doorway when she saw us, holding up another bottle. "*Vive la France,* she called. "*Vive l'Amérique.*"

We walked across and joined her. And all the while we drank we could hear the fire fight going on around the corner on the Boulevard Madeleine.

35.

Between
Surrender and
Stockade

One of the most harrowing experiences a soldier can have comes during that period between the time it takes him to raise his arms to the enemy in surrender, and the moment he has completed the trip somewhere rearward and is delivered alive into the hands of higher authority. This does not guarantee him life. But it guarantees him that much life. For he has just passed from the point where the law of war makes killing right, through that terrifying zone of anarchy where men, brutal with the impulses of battle, decide the law for themselves. And he has entered again into an area where codes of justice—sometimes feeble, to be sure—begin once more to operate.

The U.S. Marines were burdened with few prison cages in the Pacific. It was said that the Japanese just did not surrender. But when they were needed for interrogation, there were always some who were found to give themselves up. This usually followed the order: "Bring them in alive."

When we were fighting for Velletri in Italy, a U.S. infantryman showed me the body of a German he had just taken and shot. "Look!" he said to me. "The son-of-a-bitch is wearing GI boots. He boasted that he killed four Americans and he yelled *'Heil Hitler!'* We gave him a fair break. We let him run for it—a little ways."

I don't know how he would feel about it now. But he must be judged according to the times in which he acted. We were at war, and we were killing and being killed. And circumstances had suddenly put him into that singular area of civilization where one man's judgment is the law. So it is with nations. There is a moment for them too, between the battle and the safety of the stockade, when men create the law to suit the circumstances. When the Germans retreated from southern France, loosening the grip under which they held the French, there was a period before the laws of an established government could rule the people when each man's opinion, sparked by his long-pent emotions, counted as law. Frenchmen roamed the streets and broke down doors looking for other Frenchmen who they thought deserved to die.

Informal conclaves of embittered or vindictive men took the place of courts of justice and their punishments were swift. Women who had fraternized too openly with the Germans or who were accused of doing so, were taken to the street amid taunting laughter, cursed and spit upon and their heads shaved for shame. Men who served the enemy—some of them wicked men who acted as informers and contributed to the deaths of many of their countrymen, and some merely stupid—were found and beaten by the crowds. A few of them were killed right there. The rest sat waiting in the jails of southern France for French justice.

It was because of those in jail and, ironically, because France is a nation devoted to law and justice, that I was to witness a scene in Grenoble reminiscent of the days of Robespierre.

Grenoble had just been liberated. The jails were packed with those charged with treason and now the Maquis, having wandered the streets shaving heads and bloodying faces, demanded that the authorities open the cells to them so that they might pass judgment and administer justice.

To forestall this danger, a public trial was announced at

173

once. It was the first court of law to try a traitor in southern France since the liberation. Ten men stood before the court. In a short session six were found guilty of bearing arms against France and sentenced to die.

"The sentence will be carried out before the day is over," the authorities advised a small group of American correspondents. They were acting fast because they were under dangerous pressure from the angry citizens of Grenoble. All the defendants were guilty as charged, they assured us, but these men were, quite frankly, a quick sacrifice, made so that the 440 others awaiting trial might be judged and sentenced after more temperate deliberation.

It had just turned September and it was suddenly cold; that day it seemed that summer had ended. It began to rain and the mountain clouds came lower and lower over the city, darkening it early into a dreary dusk.

Late in the afternoon, however, the people of Grenoble, untouched by the cheerlessness of the day, filled the sidewalks and the roadways and, buttoned into raincoats and sheltered under umbrellas, streamed along in a festive mood, calling to each other and laughing and hurrying with that same sense of happy urgency which crowds have as they near the circus tent and press on for seats.

Their destination, however, offered neither seats nor cover. It was a great cinder lot, dismal in the dripping rain, beside a brick factory on the southern outskirts of the city. It was a melancholy spot—a half-acre of Grenoble one could easily pass without noticing. But everybody knew its location. For here, only a month earlier, the Germans had tied twenty-three French patriots to stakes and shot them. All of Grenoble heard the volley; and every day after that, fresh flowers appeared in the lot.

Now six more stakes stood waiting. These were for traitors.

It was nearly seven o'clock and the crowds continued to grow and press upon the police. The Maquis sent their soldiers in to help hold the lines. Men and boys and even women shinnied up trees and lamp posts, hanging there dripping wet. They crowded all the windows and roofs which afforded views, and from wherever they were they called out in shrill voices demanding vengeance. For France had fallen ignominiously and for four years had lived under alien domination and every man and woman in the crowd felt the shame of it. Now, at last, there was retribution.

The victims were all young. One was only fourteen years old when the war began. Now he was nineteen. The oldest was twenty-six. They were all part of the collaborationist militia, the hated "Milice," though none of them was much more than a lackey in the movement. One was a plumber who cared for the toilets in the Milice headquarters. But under the law of the hasty tribunal, they had borne arms against France and by their own confessions had betrayed patriots of their country—some, indeed, who died only a month earlier on that very lot.

Now, only a few hours after their trial, they stepped out of the black van and into the doom of a dark storm, surrounded by an ocean of tossing faces all contorted with hatred and filling the air with screams and hoots of derision. Before them stood the Maquis firing squad, quiet and controlled, wearing old French helmets and odd bits of uniform and holding German, French and American rifles.

The boys' eyes darted and their bodies tensed. It was as though all had been too swiftly done and there had been no time for them to realize how short the road from court to stake. They looked confused, and pitifully frightened.

They were led to the stakes, their laceless shoes flopping and scraping. Two were bare to the waist under their ill-fitting jackets and their necks looked thin and white.

I followed them to the stakes as the cries of the crowds rose higher and higher. The boys' hands were shaking. And I saw that mine were also. What, among men, is more frightening than the cry for death which rises from the crowd? And who can stand, as I stood that day, and not, for an instant, feel his own wrists being bound?

I tried to hold my camera steady as I stepped up to them one by one. I was not in good control. But each in his turn surprised me: for as each saw the camera coming in toward him, his body straightened and he threw back his shoulders and

175

a look of courage came into his face. Inexplicably, that last picture gave strength to the condemned men.

The captain of the firing squad shouted at me and I ran back. Without signal they fired and the boys slid slowly down the stakes. The crowd roared and broke through the police. The Maquis held them back as the bodies were dumped into boxes and hastily loaded into the van and driven away.

It was still raining and now almost dark. The crowds turned slowly and began to stream home again along the wet streets. They were quiet now, as though they were thinking, and the festive spirit was gone.

Somewhere in the cells of that city were 440 more Frenchmen charged with crimes against their country. And now, perhaps, as the men who were bringing France back to the zone of law and honor prayed, vengeance had been appeased and the slow course of justice might once more proceed in dignity.

PART V

PART V

36.

Luzon Landing

In the middle of September a message came from my editors suggesting that I return at once to the Far East. I knew what they meant: the attack on the Philippines was about to begin. I wanted to be there when the Army retook Manila.

I left France the next day, flying to Rome and then on to the United States. Shelley had finished her book by the time I reached New York and she was ready to go to Asia with me. But women war correspondents were not yet admitted into MacArthur's theater and, with the invasion already under way, I left her behind to be accredited to the Navy and to follow out as soon as she could. I flew on across America and the Pacific— from Pearl Harbor to Johnson Island to Kwajalein to Saipan: island airdromes which themselves told the progress of the war since I had left the Far East. I was at last put down on Leyte's Tacloban field, an inadequate Japanese strip of gray, mud-splashed coral cut from the jungle at the water's edge, and now the only operational airfield we had in the Philippines. As soon as I stepped from my plane I recognized in the soldiers around me the feeling that fighting men give when they are still unsure of victory, and before I had a chance to move, there was an air-raid warning. I ran for the trenches alongside the strip. The one I got into held a forty-millimeter rifle, its gunners browned and stripped to the waist waiting beside their weapon for their targets to come in. And they came, even before I could settle comfortably in the trench: four Japanese fighters swooping low over the field, strafing a line of parked planes amid a clatter of antiaircraft guns, and curving off untouched into the sky. Almost before they disappeared we all clambered out of the trenches again.

A tall, personable young man walked up to me as I stood there staring. Bill Chickering of *Time* had come to meet me. "Nice welcome," he grinned, nodding at the planes. Then, as we carried my gear across the battle-pocked field to his jeep, he said: "I've got a sack for you at Sixth Army for tonight. But first let's check in with PRO."

The road to Tacloban had broken down. Trucks and jeeps slithered through deep mud-filled ruts, their whining gears setting up an overtone along the whole road. And as our jeep labored between palm trees and jungle growth, the pastelike slop of the road sometimes rose to the floorboards. Troops we passed sank to their knees in the quagmire and all kinds of military vehicles stood bogged down and canted where Philippine mud had at last won over Detroit engineering.

"I hear it was all dust in Italy," Bill said. "None over here. Just mud." He laughed, pointing down at his trousers and shoes. They looked like great candy bars dipped in chocolate.

When we reached the Tacloban post office building where GHQ had set up its public relations office, we left the jeep in a back alley and stepped into the muck and waded across a couple of neighboring back yards. "We don't use the road out front any more," he said. "It's full of holes."

The post office was a shabby little two-story structure of wood. It had a tin roof and great, open, porchlike windows. As we climbed the stairs to the second floor I heard the familiar pounding of typewriters and I followed Bill into a large room scattered with cots and tables and mosquito bars and cans of food and bottles of whisky. Fifteen or twenty correspondents worked at makeshift desks of boxes and chairs and boards all propped higgledy-piggledy.

There were some old friends among the correspondents. Frank Hewlett was there, and we sat talking until someone who was looking out of the window called back into the room: "Here's another one coming up the road."

"Let's see this," Frank said. And I noticed that many of the others had left their typewriters and had gone over and were hanging out of the windows. I joined them and looked out too.

The road was filled with muddy water and looked like a canal. Along it a jeep was making its way slowly toward us, dipping and pitching and splashing and often sinking below the floorboards. Just before it reached our building it suddenly fell into a hole and disappeared completely, the two soldiers in it sitting there in mud up to their shoulders, their faces full of surprise.

At this point laughter and a general comment of satisfaction came from the men around me and they all turned and sauntered back to their typewriters and picked up their work where they had left off.

"They'll never learn, those crazy bastards," someone near me muttered happily.

"Learn what?" I asked.

"Learn there's a hole in that road," he replied.

"Why didn't someone shout and warn him?" I asked.

He looked at me in surprise. "You new here or something?"

"Just got in," I told him.

His face relaxed and he nodded knowingly. "After you've been here a few days you'll sit and wait for jeeps to fall in that God-damn hole too. That's all there is to do in Tacloban."

Bill and I waded back to the jeep and started off again for Sixth Army headquarters in the town of Palo. Palo had been taken after a costly fight and its torn and cluttered streets were filled with homeless Filipinos who had come through the Japanese lines. In the central square the great cathedral still stood. It had been turned into a hospital and was crowded with both worshipers and wounded. We went in to make pictures and there we met a Filipino doctor who stopped to talk to us.

"When you write about this cathedral," he said, "you ought to point out that this is where the Japanese suffered their greatest defeat on Leyte."

"You mean in the fighting for Palo?" Bill asked him.

"No," the doctor said, "long before that . . . In fact, the first day the Japanese arrived. It was after Bataan and Corregidor had fallen and General Wainwright's order to surrender had been sent out to all our forces in the Philippines. Just one small unit of Japanese came to Palo. There was no resistance to them, no shooting. They were the first Japanese we had seen in all those months of war. And they were very correct, very polite. The occupation couldn't have started better for them.

"They said we were all to assemble in the cathedral and when it was crowded full a Japanese colonel came and stood before the altar and started to talk. He spoke in English and many of us could follow him. He was precise and very clear. He said that the Japanese had come to Leyte as brothers and that we were all Asiatics together, with the same destinies shaped by the same hopes and prayers. He spoke of the Greater East Asia Co-Prosperity Sphere and promised that within its framework we should all prosper, sharing together our goods and our related cultures and that we would soon see how little the nations of the West had given us, materially and spiritually.

"It was hot in the cathedral that morning and the colonel unbuttoned his jacket and took it off. He turned around for a place to put it and chose the nearest object. It was the image of the Virgin.

"And in the few seconds it took him to hang it there," the Filipino smiled, "Japan lost the island of Leyte."

As the year closed, our forces drove up the steaming valleys of Leyte and converged on the last strongholds of the enemy until their remnants were divided and pinched off. The Japanese had thrown one-fifth of their total Philippines forces and the last of their great fleet into the fight for Leyte—and they had lost. By Christmas there remained of them but a few thousand men, cut off from reinforcements, starving in the mountains. Leyte was securely in our hands.

The new year came, hot and muggy. It was January, 1945, and

we were ready for the attack on Luzon. We correspondents drew lots for positions in the invasion fleet and I drew the one photographer's spot on MacArthur's flagship, the cruiser *Boise*. Bill Chickering drew the battleship *New Mexico*. Four days later, during the prelanding shelling of Lingayen Gulf, the *New Mexico* and her escort came under one of the first fierce Kamikaze attacks of the war. Bill was on the bridge when a Japanese plane crash-dived into it. He was killed instantly.

General MacArthur told me this, calling me to the quarter-deck that day to break it to me gently. Then he paused and leaned against the rail. It was the last day before the landing and we were sailing close to the Luzon coast so that we could just pick out the line of haze along the horizon that was Bataan.

At last he spoke again, not about Bill but about those Americans who were waiting for us behind the barbed wire of Japanese prison camps. "We land tomorrow," he said, "and there'll be no opposition. We'll walk in. . . .

"But after that we must move fast. We must fight hard and fast. As soon as we have a foothold on those shores my aim is to push south before they know what's hitting them. I want to save as many of those prisoners as we can."

37.

The End of a Death March

There were no prisoners to save in the first camp we liberated. And yet, in a strange kind of nonexistence, they were all there —those thousands lying under the overgrown hummocks and even those others who had long ago been taken away.

The weight of our offensive on Luzon had carried us swiftly southward. In two weeks' time we had come more than fifty miles toward Manila, fighting all the way, but moving so fast that the Japanese were always off balance.

On the day our fluid front pushed on past Capas, a weapons carrier in which I was riding with several other correspondents turned out of the central Luzon town and headed up a yellow dirt track. It was a desolate road. Once it had been crowded with men, stumbling, dazed and dying. For we were traveling the last leg of the Bataan Death March into Camp O'Donnell.

The camp was empty when we got there. It had been abandoned more than a year before, the survivors marched away and the thousands of others left there in the ground. A piece of old rope was tied across the entrance to the camp. Our driver stopped in front of it and for a moment we all sat looking at it. Then he started the carrier and slowly drove right through as though, on second thought, the rope wasn't there at all.

A few crows rose into the air as we dismounted. In the distance, along a blue fringe of foothills, we could see hazy white puffs of smoke and hear the muffled explosions of fighting. But where we were it was silent, with only the sound of our boots pushing through the wiry cogon grass.

In other prisons we would enter, flaccid men would come toward us with impoverished bodies and sluggish minds and talk and talk about what had happened to them. But here no one moved. Here we heard no words. There was no need. In its lonely desolation, Camp O'Donnell told its story silently, in the long rows of empty prison shacks with crumbling roofs of nipa leaves, the empty sentry boxes standing awry, the broken fences with barbed wire falling away and trailing along the ground like vines.

Thick grass had grown up around the last reminders of the men of Bataan who had lived and died there: a canteen, worn to a pearly finish by those who had held and shared it through those months of fighting and of starvation; a tin dinner plate, dented and discolored; an army mess pan still embossed with its U.S.Q.C.; piles of rusting tin cans, heaps of rags; bits of frayed rope ends; a worn and broken wooden leg with

184

decaying straw fastenings; a pile of fire-stained rocks cradling a charred and rusted helmet where dying men once cooked weeds and grass. All over the grounds and in the tumbling shacks they lay, talking to us wherever we found them.

And all about, stretching off into the quiet fields, were the graves: mass graves under unmarked mounds and hillocks of earth; acres of others marked with crosses made of sticks, overgrown, all but obliterated, some with dog tags nailed to them, some with names carved lovingly by comrades. I knelt before one to read an inscription. "Good-by," someone had carved upon it. "We will always remember you."

By the time we liberated Camp O'Donnell that was the most we could do: remember.

38.

The Liberation of Santo Tomas

At Cabanatuan, where men still lived, we did more than remember. There the Sixth Rangers slipped twenty-five miles behind the Japanese lines, destroyed the prison garrison, put pistols into the hands of every prisoner who could hold one, and led or carried them all to safety.

The success of this bold operation decided General MacArthur to risk an even more daring one: a lightning thrust sixty miles through Japanese strength into the heart of Manila to deliver from Camp Santo Tomas the four thousand civilians who had been held prisoner for more than three years. It was to be the liberation of my own prison camp.

It was just three weeks since we had come over the beaches of

185

Lingayen. The Second Squadron of the Eighth Cavalry Regiment had been chosen to make the thrust. I joined them in a sugar-cane field where they had assembled a few miles south of Ca-banatuan. It was dusk and the great field, flattened by the tires and tracks of jeeps and trucks and tanks, stretched around us in the growing darkness as flat as a lake. Smoke tails and small glowing fires and red-dotted cigarette ends showed faintly all over the area. The sounds of metal upon metal, the cough and roar of engines, and the voices of men talking rose over the field, and the restless movement of vehicles and men shuttling and shifting seemed in great disorder.

Yet as soon as the jeep which I was sharing with four other correspondents turned into the confusion a second lieutenant appeared and greeted us. He knew at once who we were and what to do with us. "Your jeep will be the fourth vehicle after the tanks," he said. "The colonel thinks you'll see more up there. Just pull in as near as you can to that jeep and fall in behind it when it moves out."

Thus we became part of the special task force. Its strength was about seven hundred men and it was commanded by Lieutenant Colonel Haskett Conner. Our mission was to be in Manila on February 3, which meant getting through sixty miles of enemy territory in two days. Colonel Conner briefed us. "We're travel-ing light," he said. "When we hit the enemy we're going to cut right through him and get into Manila before he knows what's happening. The rest of the division will be coming along after us and we'll let them worry about what we leave behind."

It was midnight when the word was passed that the column was moving; the jumble of men and vehicles in the field untan-gled into perfect order as the task force turned up onto a road and headed south. The tanks loomed ahead of us, their exhausts flashing and barking in the quiet night; and behind stretched the rest of the column, all bulging with men and weapons and all black except for a faint glint on helmets and guns from a cloud-dimmed moon and the glow of burning cigarettes flicking along the column like fireflies.

Morning came and we kept rolling. Sometimes we rode on highways and sometimes we bounced and trundled along in

fields and carabao trails. When the terrain stopped us, the bull-
dozers clattered up ahead and cut a clearing while some of the
men set up a perimeter either side of the column and the rest ate
out of cans and cat-napped in the vehicles or on the ground.

Almost all the bridges were out and we forded the rivers, the
men holding their weapons high and often wading up to their
chests in the water while the trucks and the lumbering tanks
pushed and pulled each other with engines screaming and water
flying.

We were almost always a surprise to the enemy when we ran
into him. On his first volley we would jump clear of the vehicles
and crawl out into whatever cover we could find and shoot him
up with a racketing fire of nearly everything we had in the train;
then on a word yelled along the column and the signal of a
rolled fist jerked up and down in the air, we would throw ourselves back into the vehicles and take off before the Japanese
could muster strength again for another attack, the tanks at the
end of the column running and shooting until we were clear and
away, and our medics changing from vehicle to vehicle to care
for the wounded.

In some villages the Filipinos ran out of their little houses to
greet us, holding up their naked children and crying "*Mabuhai*,"
and "God bless you," and thrusting things into the hands of
soldiers: eggs and fruit and whatever else they could grab
quickly as we passed.

Night came, and dawn, and we kept rolling. As we climbed up
out of another river onto another road, Colonel Conner stood
on the embankment watching and jerking his arm up and down.
"Let's go," he kept calling. "Let's go. We've got to be in Manila
today."

All day we ran into ambushes and fights, pushing through
and rolling on. Near Novaliches a recon car raced back to us to
report that the vital bridge there was still intact. When we got
there the bridge was mined and the fuses burning. An officer ran
up and kicked them out and the tanks went on through the town
and plastered the Japanese who were waiting there for us. Now
we were on our last leg.

A great red ball of sun was setting over the city as we turned into the outskirts. Hysterically cheering people came out to run along the column. Suddenly they disappeared. We were driving by the Grace Park Airfield and the hangars were burning brightly and we could see Japanese soldiers running and getting into their trucks. We passed them by, going fast and hard; time was now desperately short and we wouldn't fight the enemy unless he stood directly in our path.

Near Great China University we paused to get our bearings and were immediately brought under fire. We dismounted and threw ourselves on the pavement, the men shooting from where they lay, while the lead tanks returned the fire. One of my jeep companions was Frank Hewlett. He had come a long way since he met our exchange ship at Goa and learned that his wife was still a prisoner. We had not mentioned her since then. But now as we lay in the roadway he suddenly grabbed my arm. "Tell me you think she's there," he demanded.

Just then Colonel Conner gave a signal and we leaped into our vehicles again and turned into a side road. I recognized where we were—just a few streets from Santo Tomas. "We're there," I muttered to Frank. "We're almost there." But he said nothing. I saw the wall of the compound and gripped his arm. Slowly and cautiously we rolled through the darkness till the lead tank came to the gate. Then we all dismounted and ran crouching along the black woven sawali fence. Near the gate I stopped and lay down alongside it with the others. Behind it was my old prison.

There was not a sound from within. I cut a hole in the fence with my knife. But I could see nothing. The main gate was ajar and the earth-bunkered guardhouse which stood outside it looked deserted. Everywhere it was black and silent.

"Maybe they've gone," someone said in a low voice. "Maybe they've taken them all away."

Frank was lying near me. I heard his strained whisper. "No," he said. "They're in there. It's only the Japs are gone." We listened. It was terribly silent. "There are no Japs in there," he repeated hoarsely.

After a while I said: "What are we waiting for? Let's go in."

Frank rose with me and we went forward slowly, bending

188

low, and looked through the open gate. It was totally black. We straightened up and suddenly something loomed from behind the bunker and fired at us point-blank. We both hit the ground. "You all right?" Frank whispered to me. "O.K.," I said. "You O.K.?"

A voice was shouting: "I want two men to go in and get that son-of-a-bitch." Frank and I were crawling away. Other voices were yelling. I heard the word "grenade!" and seconds later there was an explosion and men went down. Among them was Colonel Conner. I crawled over. He had been hit in the leg. He swore and waved up at the tank standing nearby. "Go ahead in!" he yelled. And the engine shattered the air around us and the tank started through, and I remember how astonished I was to see that gate and fence, which had stood so long between me and freedom, fall over like a painted illusion.

Crouching behind the tank ran the cavalrymen, and Frank and I picked ourselves up and ran with them. Behind us more troops poured in and flares were shot into the air, brightening the compound and buildings with phantom moonbeams. A man came from behind a tree. Twenty guns were on him. "I'm an American," he gasped. The guns went down.

"There's a Jap machine gun at the corner of that building," he said, pointing a shaking arm.

"Thanks, Mac," a soldier said.

The tank turned and headed for the gun and the soldiers ran behind it. I stopped Frank and pointed straight ahead. "That's the main building," I told him. We ran for the entrance. I could see a feeble light as we neared it. The big doors were open.

Inside a few candles flickered miserably on the balustrade of the main staircase, illuminating the area just enough for me to see that the lobby and the great stairway were filled with people. When we stepped in, bodies moved away from us.

"Who are you?" a voice called out, loud and unfriendly.

"Americans," we answered.

There was a whispered murmur. Still no one moved.

"If you *are* Americans," somebody shouted, "put that flashlight on yourself."

I turned the light on myself and said, "I'm Carl Mydans."

There were murmurs, and after a moment yells and screams. A woman threw her arms about me. It was Betty Wellborn, one of Shelley's prison roommates. "We thought you were Japs," she exclaimed. She was laughing. "We thought you were Japs." She began to sob.

Hands grabbed me and lifted me and carried me, equipment and all, onto the stairs. More candles and some lanterns were lighted and names and greetings were shouted back and forth. When I could I started out after Frank, who had disappeared. But it was a long time before I could get through the people in the lobby, many crowding around and asking for Shelley and telling me bits of news.

A child stopped me. Perhaps he was six. The only world he had ever really known was within the walls of that prison. "Mister soldier," he said, "what's that on your head?"

"An American helmet," I told him, handing it down to him.

"Gee," he exclaimed, hefting it. "Do all Americans on the outside wear these?"

For a moment I stopped and listened to some officers questioning a prisoner. Someone had just put a lantern in their circle and I could see one of the officers writing something and the prisoner's skinny arms shaking nervously. It was Earl Carroll, chairman of the prisoners' executive committee. He had a hand over his forehead as though he were shading his eyes from the light. "Just a minute," I heard him saying as the officers fired questions at him. "Hold on now for just a minute. I want to help you all I can, and it's all up here somewhere," he said, tapping his forehead. "But I'm not thinking very fast these days."

At the doorway a group of my old roommates were waiting. I could scarcely see them, but as I passed from thin hand to thin hand, each voice had a strangely familiar sound and each unlocked a flurry of memory fragments from long ago.

Outside in the night, the compound was full. Cavalry vehicles and great monsters of tanks were pulled up all over the area. Artillery units were setting up guns. And everywhere prisoners were eating—some not moving a step from the spot where soldiers had given them a box or a can of rations, some hurrying this way and that, calling out names. A little boy came galloping

190

by with his arms locked around two or three tins. "Mother, mother," he called. "See what I've got."

Then I saw Frank. He had found Virginia and they came toward me, hand in hand, smiling, looking at each other and smiling again. "She's just fine," Frank kept repeating. "She's completely recovered and she's just fine."

Suddenly we heard shooting in the compound. We stopped and listened. A sergeant came hurrying past us and I asked him what had happened. 'They've just found Jap soldiers holding out in that next building," he said as he ran on.

I started after him. The internees were being hurried back into the main building. There was more shooting and I heard orders being shouted to clear the compound.

When I got through the crowds in the doorway, I saw soldiers lying on the ground around the Education Building, firing into doors and lower windows. Others were digging foxholes. The Education Building was a men's dormitory and in the upper-floor windows I could faintly see faces peering out into the night.

"What's happened?" I asked an officer who was standing by a forty-millimeter gun crew which had been firing into a side door.

"Well, the God-damnedest thing has happened," he answered. "We've been in this place for more than two hours, walking around these buildings like they were ours. And all the while, in this one here there's fifty or sixty Jap soldiers holding the prisoners hostage."

39.

Strange Column
at Dawn

When it grew light the prisoners on the upper floors of the Education Building hung out of the windows and waved and called messages to little groups, some including wives and children, who had gathered at some distance behind the cavalrymen dug in around the dormitory. No Japanese could be seen and the shooting had stopped. A bucket line had already been organized by the prisoners who had learned long ago to meet new situations quickly, and a continuous hoist of water and coffee and food was going up into one of the top windows by rope and basket. This operation was not challenged by the Japanese who were themselves recipients of the prisoners' resourcefulness. But any other movement between the building and the line of infantry was likely to bring Japanese fire.

Elsewhere in the prison the remarkable plight of a perimeter within a perimeter and the threat of more than two hundred internees being held before the sword did not noticeably dishearten the thousands of others. Too many years of crisis had conditioned them to accept such a juncture as normal. And they crowded the other side of the compound, looking at tanks and equipment and soldiers with the curiosity one might imagine a community on earth would show as it wandered among friendly Martians who had come in the night, dressed oddly and equipped with machinery of another planet.

There was nothing Martian, though, about the men under their uniforms; and as these muscular young Adonises filled the compound with their presence, shaving and bathing by their jeeps, digging trenches, setting up weapons, or just sitting and talking with the prisoners, an almost forgotten feeling of what they too had been came over that community of shrunken bodies. The men prisoners looked at them with envy and the women, often, with unconcealed passion. "I can't resist touching them," one woman confided to me that morning. "I'd forgotten that men looked this way."

As the day progressed, however, the uneasiness of the troops dug in around the Education Building spread to the prisoners. For it was becoming clear to them also that the Japanese could not be extricated from the dormitory without a fight within the prison compound.

Late in the afternoon I joined Lieutenant Colonel "Todd" Brady, who with a group of officers was standing some distance behind his men, waiting for orders. Brady was famous in his division not only for his bravery but also for his mustache, which he kept meticulously trimmed and waxed into dagger points. Now, as he stood looking at the Education Building, his fingers felt along the points as though to make sure they were in proper form.

There was a stir behind us and I saw General William Chase getting out of a jeep. Chase commanded the First Brigade of the First Cavalry Division which had taken Santo Tomas. He began talking as soon as he reached us. "We're going to let those Japs go," he said without introduction. "Our mission is to save these prisoners, not get them killed. And it's a good trade, two hundred Americans for less than half that number of Japs. Good—if we can make it.

"There's a Jap lieutenant colonel in there, named Hayashi," he continued. "We know enough about him not to trust him very much. But we've got to try it. We're going to offer him and his men safe conduct out of this prison into an area somewhere out there in the city near their own lines. That means we're not going to have to take them very far.

"Somebody's got to go in there and talk to him." He stopped and looked at Brady for a moment. "And, Todd," he said at last, "you're the one who's going to do it."

Brady's face wrinkled into a smile and his hand reached up and turned the points of his mustache. "Hayashi," he said, his eyes seemingly judging something beyond his general. "A lieutenant colonel." He nodded, and with the easy half-salute often thrown in combat, he turned and walked through the line of soldiers in their shallow trenches and toward the door we had blackened with our firing.

I had been with Colonel Brady in combat before. He was cut just about the right size for a fighting man, spare, with a thin face that frequently rippled with humor. He had been a cavalryman all his army life and in combat he carried himself a little bent and alert as though he was just about to throw himself on a horse. And though horses in the cavalry had long since been replaced by chargers of steel and wheel and track, Brady, twisting his mustache, hoisting his pistol belt with the insides of his elbows, swinging one leg into a jeep and shouting "Mount up!" seemed no anachronism. This, he made you feel, is the way the cavalry had always done it. He walked, now, relaxed and direct, on through the blackened doorway as though he lived there.

Word was passed down the line to hold the fire but to be alert. And we all stood watching and waiting. It was almost dusk. He was not in there very long; maybe a quarter of an hour. But I remember looking at my watch, thinking it had stopped. None of us spoke, the others, perhaps, straining, as I was, to listen for the shooting.

When he came out he walked immediately to General Chase. "I saw the man," he said with the flick of a smile.

"How did it go?" the general asked.

"Pretty well, sir. There are 65 Japs in there," he said, "holding 220 prisoners. Hayashi wants safe conduct with honor—and he says to a Japanese that means full arms and ammunition. I agreed to side arms and rifles. But no grenades or machine guns. He finally accepted. I told him to come out at dawn with rifles on the shoulder and form up into a column of threes and we would see him into an area between the lines. And I think he'll do it."

"Good," said General Chase. "You take him out in the morning."

We still crowded around Brady. "What was he like, this Hayashi?" I asked.

"He's big for a Jap; about my height. And a rough customer. He came up to me wearing two pistols on his hips and stood with his feet apart and his hands on his guns, raising them up out of the holsters and dropping them back in while I talked."

"What did you do?" we asked him.

A little grin rippled his face again. "My hand twitched so, watching that son-of-a-bitch," he said, "that I had to twirl my mustache to keep it steady."

There was a tropic chill in the air next day when Hayashi and his men formed up at the blackened doorway, rifles on the shoulder. Brady's cavalry troops, automatic weapons and rifles in their hands, were waiting just outside. It was still dark. Most of the camp was asleep, and the sounds of fighting in the city had lapsed into a few intermittent explosions.

As the Japanese emerged, a column of Americans fell in on either side of them. Colonel Brady took the lead; just behind him marched Colonel Hayashi. Beside him walked a grotesque figure in a floppy white shirt, Ernest Stanley, the British missionary prisoner who was accompanying the column as an interpreter. Brady shouted over his shoulder: "Let's go." Stanley whispered to Hayashi; Hayashi yelled an order to his troops; and one of the strangest columns of the war moved forward across the compound and out of the main gate of Santo Tomas. The few prisoners who were about stopped in their tracks and stared.

Outside the gate the veteran American troops, their weapons poised, eyed the Japanese beside them. Not before had they been that close to an enemy soldier without either shooting or being shot at. But the Japanese marched confidently, singing cadence, heads erect, seemingly without thought of fear.

In the silent, empty streets the column moved swiftly through the brightening dawn. Here and there a few Filipinos peering out of their houses in the besieged town witnessed the incredible sight and either ducked to safety or stood transfixed and silent. Several I noticed started to make the V-for-Victory sign but then, seeing armed Japanese as part of the column, froze in their motion.

Brady suddenly called for a halt and said to Mr. Stanley: "Tell the colonel that this is as far as we take them." Hayashi shook his head. "He asks you to conduct him farther," Stanley said. "He says we are still within American lines."

Brady thought a second and then nodded. The column moved on. It was much lighter when he halted again, and a few more people were coming out of their houses as we passed. "He requests that you take him farther," Stanley said again. Brady listened. The sound of fighting was heavier and closer, and when he waved the column on this time his troops began to take the slightly crouched position of soldiers moving into a combat zone.

At a major crossroads Brady again stopped the column. "Tell him," he said to Stanley, "that this is where we leave him." Brady's men stepped back a pace, their weapons turned slightly inward toward the stiffly erect Japanese soldiers. Hayashi still held his position. He glanced behind him at his men. Then again he asked for further safe conduct "Tell him no," said Brady. His tone was decisive. "He's walking right into his own troops. Their lines are only a few blocks away. Tell him this is as far as we go."

Across the wide intersection little groups of Filipinos were gathering on the street corners. Some began to shout: "V for Victory! Americans! *Mabuhai!*" The cry was picked up and more of them poured out into the street, waving and cheering. Brady raised his arms toward them for silence. He was misunderstood. The shouts of welcome increased and more people came running toward the street corner.

Brady called an order and his men moved out another pace. Hayashi glanced once at Brady and then, raising his sword, he yelped an order in a high voice. The Japanese stepped forward smartly, heading across the intersection toward their own lines. The Filipinos were stunned and their shouts of welcome froze into silence as they saw the armed column of Japanese bearing down on them. Then a wave of panic struck them and they turned, running, shouting, crying, falling and tripping over each other in frantic flight.

Under orders to make a show of bravery, the Japanese could

not look back. They could see only the terrified Filipinos scrambling for cover in front of them; and they knew only that the Americans stood behind them with guns at the ready. Their uncertainty mounted as the Filipinos ran screaming from their path. Their column wavered. Then infectious fear overwhelmed them. They broke ranks and scrambled in terror after the fleeing Filipinos, throwing themselves into gutters and doorways. And behind them, screaming like a madman, ran Hayashi, grabbing at them, shoving them, beating them over the shoulders and rumps in a futile effort to re-form them into a dignified unit of soldiers.

And all the while Colonel Brady stood before his men, one hand supporting his elbow while the other gently twirled his mustache, until the last of the running Japanese had disappeared down the street.

40.

Some Who Survived

From the moment our troops broke into Santo Tomas, liberators and liberated were drawn together with a magnetic force, the troopers feeling a kind of deep, paternal love for these abused and blighted and unnerved people, giving them of their own short rations until they themselves were without food, helping in strong and easy motions with prison household tasks, and listening by the hour to painful stories of injury and longing and starvation.

The prisoners returned a different kind of love, adoring and worshipful. For to them these soldiers were the fulfillment of every single romantic fantasy they had dreamed every single prison night of that momentous hour when their own people, brave and unbelievably strong against this puny enemy, would come knocking down the gate, shooting their way in, cutting down those who had so long oppressed them and showering them at last with love and compassion for all they had suffered.

But quick and deep as this relationship was, it nonetheless had to reach across an imperceptible barrier. For one who has long been shut away cannot easily walk into the open, even if the gates are down.

That first morning as I worked through the compound, one little group I stopped to photograph sat under a tree. There were a man and woman, terribly thin, their ankles swollen with beriberi, and two young healthy lieutenants. The man held an unopened carton of cigarettes in one hand and in the other a K-ration chocolate bar which he was eating, and the woman sat sewing the fatigue shirt of one of the officers who was bare and brown to the waist. They gave me a little look of welcome when they saw me and went on talking.

"Tell me honestly," I heard the man say, "what's it like out there?"

"Oh, it's going to be all right," one of the officers said reassuringly. "Our outfit got across the river at Novaliches this morning and they're fighting on the outskirts of the city right now. Don't you worry. They'll be in here today, and it won't be long before we have this city."

The man said nothing for a moment and the woman stopped sewing and looked at him.

"I didn't really mean Manila," the man said.

"He means the outside," the woman spoke up.

"It's going to be fine out there," the other officer said gently. "Don't you concern yourself with that. All you've got to do is to get your strength back. That's what you need now: food and strength."

The man did not reply for a while. Then with his face perplexed as a child's, he said: "It's hard . . . it's awfully hard after all this while . . . to explain what I mean."

As soon as our spearhead had entered the city the Japanese blew up all the bridges and dug in across the Pasig River, a few blocks from Santo Tomas. As the fight for Manila progressed they began to shell us in the prison and we shelled them from the prison. And the almost five thousand civilians and fighting men, who were all there because they had survived other crises and learned to adjust, adjusted once more. And life went on.

I queued up in the same food line, shared the same mirror with the same men in my old room, saw the same people sitting in the same chairs in the same corridors. But it was when I used the showers that I most had the uncanny feeling that nothing at all had changed and that I was still a prisoner, for there we were, crowded under the same shower heads, placing our soap and towels in the same little personal niches chosen years ago, and bumping and crawling over each other with a kind of reptilian unawareness of the bodies next to us. The voices, even the points of view, seemed the same. And so did the rumors. "You know those sixty-five Japs they took out of the Education Building?" someone said. "Well, I just heard that they walked them right into an American-led Filipino ambush and killed every God-damn one of them right there on the street." Nothing had changed; and even some of my own prison self remained, for I knew enough not to inject fact into prison fancy and went right on showering.

That afternoon I saw Spike Heyward. He was distinctly familiar but I was not at all certain who he was. He was so wasted and feeble that when, at last, I was sure it was he, my stomach tightened. His arms were thinned to the bone, his chest was a skeleton stretched with skin, and like so many others I saw around me, his legs and ankles had swollen with beriberi into clublike appendages. When he walked he was clearly in pain.

Before the war Spike had been the managing director for the largest sugar company in the Philippine Islands. In Santo Tomas he was one of the soundest and most thoughtful men I knew, living above the despondency and the rumor-mongering of prison life. Now, despite his distress, he was examining each

199

little detail of the new scene about him with his old curiosity. I heard him asking bantering questions of the soldiers with his usual detachment and equanimity, and I walked up to him.

"Spike," I said.

Turning slowly about, he saw me. "Well, indeed!" he said. "I see you came in with more this time than you did the last." And he sat down stiffly on some ammo boxes and painfully moved his legs out in front of him.

"I've been looking for you," I said at last, pointing up toward the window of our old room.

"I haven't lived there for a long time," he said. "About two years ago I got some bamboo and things, along with John Benton, and built a shanty out there back of the main building. Since then John and I have shared the shanty and my wife Grace comes down and joins us in the daytime." He seemed to be thinking over this life in the shanty and I waited a bit.

At last I said: "How was it, Spike, when you saw that tank and those troops coming in through the gate last night? Did it look like we always said it would?"

"You know," Spike said with a quizzical look, "I didn't see any of it last night. After all those years of waiting, I never left my shanty." He paused.

"It seems odd this morning," he admitted, "now that I've felt the strength to move around and have a look. But last night I just lay there and listened to it. . . .

"Last night," he repeated. "It was around twilight. Grace was cooking up our congee for the morning. Our rations have gone down considerably since you left us. Especially in the last few months. We've been getting a daily allotment of rice—about enough to fill the palm of your hand—and the three of us have been pooling ours. Grace always cooked it up with salt water just before she left us for the night and we saved it for morning. And it's not always easy," he said, "to lie there and let that congee be, sitting up there on the shelf. . . .

"Last night," he repeated, "John and I were lying in our bunks and Grace was stirring the congee and we heard some shooting out beyond the back fence. We didn't get up. There's been a lot of guerrilla activity in the last few weeks and we thought it was the Filipinos. And besides, I haven't been getting around very much in the last month or so. Legs are too swollen and we've just been spending more and more time lying down." He waited. "So last night, when we heard the firing, we just lay there listening.

"But then the shooting got louder and there was a lot more of it. More than we'd ever heard before. And suddenly John said: 'I think the Americans are out there.'

"Grace went right on stirring the congee, and I didn't say anything. We just lay there.

"Then we heard something that sounded like tanks, and a hell of a lot of firing, and it seemed to come closer and closer. And John got up on his elbow. 'Spike,' he said, 'it *is* Americans!'

"'Maybe,' I said.

"'Then what are we waiting for?' he said. 'Let's eat the congee!'

"'And have nothing for the morning?' Grace said. It was time for her to leave for the main building or the guards would be down on us. So she put the congee on the shelf and left. And after she had gone we lay there listening. After a while we heard the shooting in the front compound—and then the cheering. John sat up in bed and shouted, 'It *is* the Americans!' And I said, 'By God, it *is!*' And we both got up and ate the congee."

He smiled. "Then we lay back and listened to you fellows. It wasn't till this morning I felt I could walk out here and have a look. And you know, Carl, it looks just as I thought it would when I pictured it last night—and all those other nights."

tales of crawly things that happened in that silent, blackened skeleton after we had gone for the night. They heard noises after dark, they said, and when they yelled challenges they got no reply; food and water and ammunition, carefully arranged, showed signs in the morning of having been disturbed; sometimes supplies were unaccountably missing. In the daytime they would search the building, grenades in hand, sure that after a bad night they would find someone. But they never did. And although the telling of these stories seemed to us at first to be a lark, the humor with which they were told grew noticeably less each day, and at last one of the correspondents, plainly uncomfortable, challenged them: "All right," he said one morning. "You say you've searched all through this place. Where the hell could they hide?" A second lieutenant shrugged. "Maybe," he said, "these aren't the kind you see."

Whatever it was that shared the building at night with those American troops we never knew. But we ourselves had an adventure there in the daytime which adds to the tale if not to the solution.

It was a day or two before we finally sent the infantry across the river in assault boats to climb over the crumbling wall and at last take Intramuros. I had made the trip to the OP with John Leonard of Reuter's. We spent part of it discussing and admiring the new hand-tooled leather shoulder holster which John wore with such pride that I couldn't help feeling he hoped for an occasion before we reached the OP that would give him reason to reach into it and snap out the forty-five that nested there. But in the contrary way of war our walk that sunny morning was an uneventful one.

We found the top floor of the building busier than usual with the artillery concentrating on several points along the wall, trying to breach it so that the tanks could roll in at the hour of assault. From time to time we could see the Japanese moving in and out of trenches and spider holes, dragging away their wounded and bringing in supplies.

After a while I decided that I would go up on the roof where I could work with a wider angle of view, and John came up with me. The roof was a great big area, full of holes and

204

covered with chunks of masonry and sheet metal blown into odd shapes, and the little house which had stood over the stair exit lay uprooted on its side.

John watched for a time while I worked near the edge of the roof, the whole panorama of the prebattle scene spread at our feet. Then he walked back to the stairs and leisurely took off his cap and his holster and forty-five, and then his shirt. He put them on the roof and sat down beside them, leaning against the side of the stair-well house, and relaxed in the sun.

He was still there, watching the war in luxury, when I started back toward him, ready to go down again. He saw me coming and got up and put on his shirt and hat. Then he started turning round and round, looking for something near his feet.

"Hey," he said. "What did you do with my holster?"

"I didn't take it," I answered, beginning to help him look.

We spread out a bit, searching in wider and wider circles. Then he stopped. "Come on," he said, annoyed and glancing at his watch. "Let's have it and let's get out of here. It's getting late."

"But I haven't got it," I protested. "I haven't been near you since you took that thing off and sat down here."

He began to laugh in exasperation. "*Somebody's* got it . . ." he said. Then he stopped and the laughter died and his face took on a sickly expression.

We both looked round, sweeping our eyes across the wide rooftop. It was plain that there was no one up there with us. John looked at me again. "Oh, the hell with it," he said.

Suddenly we were both hurrying toward the stairs. As we started down we both took one more quick look. But it was gone.

Neither of us ever saw it again.

42.

A Mental Attitude

During the battle for the Philippines Shelley was reporting the naval and air war from Guam, and after Manila was taken I flew there to join her. For us the war had come full circle and I carried with me an air of optimism won in the Philippines campaign. But I was not prepared for Shelley's confident assurance that the war was in its last months and that futility and defeat were openly sweeping the Japanese homeland. For I had not been privileged, as she had been, to attend the briefings of the B–29 crews which were then fire-raiding Japan, or to read the Navy's daily intercepts of the Japanese radio. Shelley soon introduced me to both of these.

In the briefing room of the oversized Quonset a neat, slender, pedantic young colonel, the intelligence officer, stood before rows of backless wooden benches on which the airmen sat chewing gum, smoking, some with mugs of coffee in their hands. Their commanding officer had just told them their target for the night: Tokyo again. It was another maximum effort strike—a low one at six thousand feet. There would be 570 aircraft concentrating on the drop area.

"Here's your target," the intelligence officer said, picking up a pointer and turning around to face a huge photo-mosaic which covered the entire wall. Before us, showing in detail every street and every surviving building in that great urban complex of Tokyo-Kawasaki-Yokohama, was the industrial heart of Japan. Already more than half of it had been burned into great black patches.

High on the map was a section in Tokyo not yet stricken by the black blight and it glistened white under the great room lights. The pointer reached up and tapped it with the touch of doom. "This is the area we're taking out tonight," he said. He turned and faced us again. "Light industrial and residential, small aircraft engine plants, some food-processing establishments, small shops. Most of the housing is wooden. The population density is about thirty thousand per square mile . . ."

He picked up a dispatch board. "Weather officer reports a minimum ground wind over the target tonight—not more than fifteen knots. In this section of the city buildings have been torn down to widen the fire-breaks. Your pattern for the drop therefore has been planned so that the fires will increase the wind velocity up to sixty knots. Where we don't straddle the breaks with our initial drops, the fires should jump them.

"You will be carrying the usual 500-pound incendiary clusters, but since there's been some pretty effective firefighting recently, we are interspersing a few antipersonnel explosives with each fire cluster. . . ."

While he talked, phrases came to my mind from the file of Japanese home radio broadcasts I had been reading: "The conflagration has practically laid waste the world's third largest metropolis. . . . Tokyo is literally scorched to the ground. . . . It must be admitted the Americans have not yet exhausted themselves. . . . The foe is attempting to pound us into unconditional surrender . . . however . . . of course . . . it would be impossible for us to conform to such a foolish demand. . . ."

That night as we followed the B–29 crews down to their planes I remembered another phrase which was used in Japanese radio broadcasts to condition the nation against the frightful fire-bombings: "Enemy planes are on the way," the warning went. "Prepare your mental attitude."

As Shelley and I stood watching the continuous line of planes roar down the runways and lift into the darkening sky, I too knew that we were coming to the end of the war and that for the Japanese there was, indeed, little left except to prepare their mental attitude.

It was soon after this that the news Shelley had been waiting for so long arrived. The ban against women correspondents in the Philippines was to be lifted and General MacArthur, remembering his promise, included Shelley among the first to be invited. We flew there together as soon as we could wind up our naval assignments.

Almost three years and one of the bitterest battles of the war had passed since she had left Manila on the prison ship and she was eager to see the city. The morning we arrived we drove together to the old places we had known. Things had changed even in the few weeks that I had been away. The streets were filled with the people and the aimless look of the refugee was gone. A thin covering of grass and tiny vines was creeping over the ruins.

Everywhere we saw things framed in the outlines of our memories. The shell of the Bay View Hotel stood in ruins, our window empty and blackened by the fire. The yacht harbor where I had photographed the demolition of our sailboats was now filled with landing craft and the fine green lawns we once knew around the High Commissioner's office was a broken sun-baked plot.

At Santo Tomas the guardhouse door was open and the bunker beside it which hid the Japanese who shot at me that night was covered with grass and morning glories. The liberated prisoners had all been sent home by now and the main building had become an Army hospital. We walked up to our old prison quarters. The wall between Shelley's room and mine had been torn down and twenty-six American soldiers were lying on white beds where sixty-five of us once lived. A soldier, bright yellow with jaundice, was reading in a bed in the far corner where my cot had been. We went over to him.

"This is where my husband slept when we were prisoners here," Shelley said to him. But he just stared at us with a curious expression.

After we had left him and were walking out of the main gate again, I suddenly remembered Villa Tasso. The soldier had been looking at us the way I had looked at Angelo Ioppi.

43.

The Rocking Horse

By the time the Americans took Manila the back of the Japanese Army was already broken. The remnants of the Imperial Forces were scattered in the mountains of central Luzon, starving, bug-ridden, sick and bewildered. For the most part their spirit was gone and the Americans were taking them as they advanced, in individual little skirmishes or sometimes even without gunshot, and bringing them back to tiny improvised stockades in the Filipino villages. Here the Japanese learned from looking at each other the impact of their defeat. Utterly tired, dejected, dirt-covered little men, they lay or squatted within their temporary wire-bound prisons and waited to learn what their conquerors would do with them.

The morning patrol had returned, wet to the waist, their faces red with perspiration in the sticky tropic heat. The men stood about smoking, their rifles slung on their shoulders, watching their prisoners file before them and then slump to the ground.

Most of the prisoners were already seated or spread out exhausted on the grass when he staggered into the assembly point, each arm over another prisoner's shoulder. His head wobbled loosely and his dragging feet made erratic lines on the ground. When they let him down at the edge of the circle he breathed in gasps and his glassy eyes in his sunken face looked nowhere.

An American medical officer was making a quick survey of the sick and wounded, poking under filthy bandages with a bright pair of scissors. An enlisted man followed him with a medical kit, redressing wounds that needed immediate attention. Behind him walked a lean young captain, Austin Bach.

The exhausted man was sleeping when the Americans reached him at the fringe of the prisoners, and the medic woke him by tapping him on the head with his scissors. The prisoner sat up quickly, bowing and forcing little smiles. The doctor stopped a little longer over him and then turned to Bach and said: "Let's get him out of here tonight. He looks like he's in an advanced stage of tuberculosis."

The Japanese stared uncomprehending, bowed again and tried to arrange his torn, filthy shirt and pull his trouser legs down over his bare, scaly feet.

Bach called for a Nisei sergeant. "Tag this fellow. The doctor wants to get him out of here quickly." The sergeant knelt before the wasted prisoner who now sat at attention. Bach questioned the prisoner in Japanese and the sergeant converted his name into English letters on the POW tag.

"Where do you come from?" asked the captain.

"Kumamoto," whispered the prisoner.

"Kumamoto," said Captain Bach to the sergeant. Then he turned to the prisoner and in a more personal tone: "Kumamoto? Whereabouts in Kumamoto?"

"Kumamoto City," answered the Japanese.

"What street did you live on?"

"Hoita Street."

Bach was now kneeling before him. "Hoita Street! That's a very short street. Do you remember the primary school there? The primary school in Hoita Street?"

The prisoner, sitting uncomfortably, kept smoothing the front of his foul shirt with his hands. Some of the glassiness in his eyes had gone. Yes, he remembered well the primary school there; he had gone there as a boy.

The captain persisted: "Do you remember the big foreign house at the end of the street?"

At first the prisoner did not answer. He was bewildered. Then he said, "Yes, I remember. I used to play there."

"Do you remember the name of the people who used to live in the big foreign house?"

The Japanese concentrated for a moment, shook his head, and then, slowly: "Yes, I remember now. It was a long time ago. It was Bakku."

The captain sat down beside him. His hands shook as he handed the prisoner a cigarette and lighted it. "Bach," he said. "And do you remember the children?"

The prisoner's mind was years back now. "Yes," he said, "and the big rocking horse."

"That rocking horse was ours, and one of the kids you played with was me," the captain said.

The prisoner closed his eyes slowly and breathed hard. Then he opened them and gazed at Bach. "You," he muttered. "Yes. Many years ago in Japan. And the rocking horse."

He looked down at himself, at his patched and torn pants, at his feet, at the scaly backs of his hands. Slowly he turned to the captain and whispered: "This is certainly sad. And I am so dirty." Then he lay back and put his arms over his face and wept.

PART VI

44.

Colored Perspective

The end came quickly. On August 7 we dropped an atomic bomb on Hiroshima. On August 9 the Russians declared war on Japan and we dropped a second bomb on Nagasaki. At noon on August 10, Radio Tokyo broadcast that there would soon be "an important announcement from the citizenry of Japan that the whole world has been waiting for."

The war in the Pacific was over.

It took us almost three weeks to arrange the surrender, but at last, on the thirtieth of August, we loaded, the largest single-operation airlift in history, and took off into the morning darkness.

For me that day, sliding down the sky at dawn toward the shore of Japan, it was a kind of fantasy, like something remembered from a legend. For the scene before me seemed too real to be real. A thin white mist hung low in the sky, falling in great cottony heaps over the land, and piled in clusters around the foot of Fujiyama. And behind the great mountain, as it towered alone, climbed a faint orange sun.

Yamaga was a little man who viewed the first sweep of the morning sun across the airfield through thick eyeglasses. He had been standing there with his back to the ruined hangars and smashed planes in the chill of an August dawn, shivering a little and watching the skies. He was dressed in his best: a dark blue suit cut a little too short at the trousers and wrists, a pair of patched but carefully polished black shoes and a striped necktie of red, white and blue.

The fearful air war over Japan was now finished. This was the day the Americans were coming in with troop-laden airplanes to seize the country and claim the victor's rights over a prostrate and burned-out nation. The shivers which fluttered Yamaga's body as he watched for the enemy continued even though the rising sun warmed his back.

Near him were hundreds of others, dressed immaculately, some in civilian clothes, some in the uniforms of the Imperial Japanese Army and Navy. All faced the skies.

As soon as we landed and taxied off the strip, we set ourselves upon Japan with headlong haste. Some of the soldiers stopped to put a hand to the ground as a personal symbol of accomplishment. But all of them moved quickly into defensive positions, the metallic clanking of weapons spreading and resounding across the field as machine guns and equipment were assembled. The roar of emptied, departing planes merged with the coughing, throttled-back reports of the endless chain of newly landing transports. And into this organized confusion wandered sword-clanking Japanese officers wearing fixed smiles and uttering painfully memorized English words of greeting.

As stipulated in the terms of the American landing, transportation, guides and interpreters were waiting. A long line of assorted charcoal-burning trucks and limousines were parked at one end of the strip, a cloud of dense white smoke filling the area as Japanese soldiers furiously cranked the odd apparatus on each to keep the fires burning. The carefully dressed interpreters fanned out among us, moving into each unit with stiff bows and a variety of English.

Out of one C–54 came a jeep and after it a husky major, Tom Mesereau. "Hey, you!" he barked at a young Japanese who was studiously examining his jeep, his hands carefully locked behind his back. "Speak English?"

"Yes, sir," said Yamaga, awkwardly straightening to attention with an air more academic than military. "I am an overseas Japanese." He blinked through his thick glasses and held a half-smile on his frightened face.

The major relaxed. "O.K., Professor," he said. "Get up into that back seat. You're going for a ride."

Yamaga started. "Going for a ride?" he repeated hoarsely. He had sensed an almost-forgotten American meaning. The major caught it. "Get up in there, Professor," he said more gently. "We're not going to hurt you."

Yamaga followed the major's thumb and climbed clumsily over the tail end of the jeep. Then, finding it piled in disorder with combat gear, rations, clothing and other oddments of field living, he stood nervously before a mounted fifty-caliber machine gun which all but filled the rear of the vehicle.

The driver, who had been resting with his hands on the wheel and his chin on his hands, looked around. "Sit down, make yourself easy," he drawled, pointing to the heap on the back seat, on top of which was a yellow Mae West. Yamaga sat uneasily on this, his hands by his sides for balance. I squeezed in beside him. A sergeant took over the machine gun and the major slipped into the front seat.

We pulled off the strip and found a convoy waiting for us. It was unorthodox in any U.S. military manual. We rode the only American vehicle. Ahead of us was a big black gasoline-burning limousine crammed with gendarmerie officers. Behind us was a collection of broken-down, charcoal-burning trucks, some of them still carrying the Imperial Army crest. These were loaded with American troops.

"We're going to Yokohama," the major said over his shoulder. "And we want no funny business."

"Yes, sir," whispered Yamaga as the sergeant noisily slammed a round into his heavy weapon as if to give emphasis to the major's words.

The convoy wove its way through the confused jumble of the field, leaving behind a trail of white smoke, and headed out a winding yellow road. It was deserted except for Japanese soldiers who stood singly, a hundred yards apart, with their backs to the highway. Each snapped to a stiff present-arms as the gendarmerie limousine approached them and held it through the dust and smoke of the convoy until the last vehicle had passed. The paper doors of the little farmhouses along the road were closed and the fields were vacant. Over this empty scene leaned the American soldiers in the Japanese trucks, their rifles poked outward.

The jeep's windshield was down, combat fashion, and the major stood holding to the gun mount for support. He was alert and troubled. "Those soldiers with their backs toward us," he asked, turning to the teetering Yamaga. "Is this their way of showing disdain?"

"Oh, no, sir," said Yamaga, rising a little as though to stand up and then bouncing back onto his seat. "This is the Emperor tradition. They are honor guard for your protection."

The major was examining his map board. He was puzzled. "Is this the right road?" he asked.

"I don't know," said Yamaga, looking around and blinking furiously.

"You don't know!" challenged the major harshly.

"I don't know, sir," answered Yamaga uncomfortably. "I am overseas Japanese. We have been suspected during the war. All of us. We have never been permitted to leave our section of Tokyo and so we have never known where the airfields were." During this speech he tried again to rise respectfully, only to plop back as the jeep bounced. Suddenly he jumped as though he had been stung by an insect and began turning in mad circles like a puppy trying to see its tail. The seat of his blue pants was stained a bright sticky yellow. The survival-at-sea dye package attached to the Mae West had burst.

"Sah!" said Yamaga involuntarily as he surveyed the damage. "What is this please?"

"It's dye," the machine gunner said as he looked around, and he reached behind Yamaga and picked up the messy Mae West and hurled it out of the jeep.

"My suit," whispered Yamaga, "my only suit. I have saved it all through the fire raids. I wore it today for you."

The Americans watched the road. We had just turned onto black-top and were driving through little villages which ran end to end along the highway. There were more and more people about, most of them taking off at a run when we approached. The major signaled with his map board for the lead vehicle to stop and the convoy came to a halt.

"Go up and ask those fellows the name of this village," the major ordered Yamaga.

"Yes, sir," said Yamaga, again examining his bottom. And then, as he got on the ground: "Will it come out, sir?"

"Will what come out?" snapped the major, swinging about with an apprehensive look.

"This," said Yamaga, slapping his bottom with a hand which was now also yellow.

"What in the hell . . . !" started the major. And then he stopped with the beginnings of a smile. "Get on up there, Professor," he repeated, pointing to the black limousine, "and talk with those men with the swords."

"Maybe it will come out?" repeated Yamaga as he started off, first walking backward and then running at a little trot that looked unnatural and uncomfortable.

As the door of the limousine opened and two gendarmerie officers stepped out we could see him talking, gesticulating, pointing at us, pointing at his pants. Then suddenly one of the officers who had his sword and scabbard in his hand made a sudden, threatening motion at Yamaga who ducked and came running back to us. "It is the village of Akasaka," panted Yamaga when he returned. And he climbed stiff-legged into the jeep and the convoy rolled again.

When we came into the outskirts of Yokohama with its utter devastation the major said, "Not much left here." Only the Bund was intact and the Grand Hotel overlooking the great harbor was miraculously unscathed. As the convoy pulled up before it, white-coated waiters ran out carrying lacquer trays and brightly colored dishes heaped with big blue grapes.

The troops dismounted from the trucks and began to dig holes in the grassy parkway under the cool trees across from the hotel. The major sat on the hood of his jeep writing a message. A red-lacquered tray heaped with blue grapes moved slowly into his vision. It was held by two yellow-stained hands. The major looked up. "Thanks, Professor," he said.

The machine gunner slipped up behind Yamaga and tucked a pair of GI trousers under the interpreter's arm. Yamaga turned about but the machine gunner was gone. The major took his pencil from the message board and carefully disentangled a bunch of grapes from the heap.

Then he looked kindly into the face of the little Japanese who continued to hold the tray before him. "I don't know, Professor," he said. "Maybe the stain will come out. But only time will tell."

45.

Occupation
in the Night

With Major Mesereau's reconnaissance into Yokohama peacefully accomplished, General MacArthur and his staff followed that very afternoon, and the occupation of Japan was begun.

And that first evening, standing on the tiny balcony of my hotel room which hung over the harbor, I saw one of the loveliest sights of the war—as imponderable and insubstantial as the mystical kingdom of Japan. Darkness had just come. The great harbor was empty except for some sunken ships. Below me the Bund was deserted and in the quiet I could hear the ocean lapping at the sea wall.

At a distance along the edge of the ocean my eye suddenly found some moving lights. They came steadily nearer, growing in size and jogging up and down. Then I saw three glowing figures running along the Bund, one behind the other. Each carried a large Japanese paper lantern.

There was an incredible sameness about the runners. Each wore something bound round his forehead; jumper-like coats flapped at their knees and large, white characters showed on their backs in the lantern light. They were running steadily in step when they passed under my balcony making no sound at all, as though their feet were not in contact with anything of substance.

They ran on down the Bund, getting smaller again. Then I heard an American voice cry, "Halt! Who are you?" The lights went out.

"Who are you?" the voice yelled again. It sounded frightened. There was no reply.

After that it was dark again, and quiet. And the first night of the surrender settled over Japan.

Our delay in getting to Japan after the first declaration of surrender, we now knew, was because there were still many Japanese Army officers who favored a suicidal fight to the finish. The military authorities who were in contact with us after our entry warned us not to spread out too fast. "Give us time to disarm the troops in the Tokyo area," they pleaded. And Mac-Arthur threw a perimeter around Yokohama and placed Tokyo out of bounds.

The order was openly ignored. Intelligence reports and top-level negotiations were not available down the line; as far as the troops were concerned the war was over and to hell with the consequences. For correspondents, of course, Tokyo was now the story. It was only thirty miles away and each of us knew that all the others were set on getting there first.

The jeep I was sharing with two Eleventh Airborne officers was turned back at roadblocks set up on every road leading north from Yokohama. We tried circuitous and devious routes but each time we were stopped at American outposts. In the end I left the jeep and walked over to the Yokohama railroad station and took a regular commuting train to Tokyo. The car was fire-charred and shabby and it was filled with straphangers packing the aisles, their arms and backs loaded with smelly bundles. The odor of fish and the unwashed was strong. I joined them and we stood, enemy by enemy, packed together all the way to Tokyo, trying not to look into each other's eyes.

In Tokyo I wandered off by myself, making pictures in the ruins. Only a few Japanese were about and when they saw me they turned and made off. It was late in the day when I reached the Imperial Palace. Outwardly it was unscathed. Eyes observed me from peepholes in the big gates and peered down upon me from under the curved roofs of the watchtowers, keeping me under surveillance as I photographed the scene, concerned, no doubt, with what I was going to do next. For how could they know that I was simply the first of an inordinate number of Americans, all inveterate tourists, who were to stand before those very gates and walls and watchtowers and make the same pictures over and over with no more consequence to the Emperor and no less satisfaction to themselves?

I crossed the Imperial Plaza and stood before the Imperial Hotel. I had planned to try to spend the night there. And as I walked up the driveway I noted that other Americans had planned the same thing, for several jeeps were already parked before the entrance.

There were some GIs in the lobby as I entered. It was darkening and damp in there and it smelled moldy. Someone called my name and I was greeted by a signal corps captain and four of his enlisted men who made up a photographic team I had worked with in combat. They were all sitting with their feet up on the thickly upholstered chairs passing a bottle among them. They were glad to see me and pretty soon we all decided to register at the hotel. We walked over and stood in a row at the desk while the young clerk there watched us apprehensively from behind his glasses.

"We want rooms and hot baths," the captain said loudly, hoping by volume to make his English understandable.

"Yes, sir," said the clerk. He reached under the desk and then handed each of us a pink card. They were registration forms printed in English and in the fading light we could make out a list of searching questions. They were obviously intended

222

for a different era. "What is the purpose of your visit to Japan?" they asked. "By what mode of transport did you come?"

The captain looked at his card and laughed. Then he pushed it back across the desk.

"You must fill in the card, sir." The clerk was smiling nervously. "It is a Japanese police order."

"We do not fill in the card," the captain mocked him. "We just take room and bath. It is *my* order." And he reached into his shoulder holster and laid his forty-five on the desk.

An hour later we all met again in the lobby, fresh from hot baths and ready to see the town.

The captain had taken his bottle of bourbon into the bath with him and the world was warm and fuzzy. He wanted to see a geisha house.

The clerk shook his head in dismay. The geisha houses had all been closed. He could not leave the desk. All of Tokyo was burned down. There were no geisha any more.

In the end, though, he sat in the front of the jeep, still protesting faintly but guiding us through the flat acres of the burned-out city. "There are no landmarks," he complained. "I have lived here many years but now I am lost."

Sometimes when we stopped to find our bearings, dark figures would approach us cautiously in the blackness. They were policemen who peered at us warily, trying to get their first look at the evil presence brought them by defeat. The clerk would jump out and they would talk, pointing and exclaiming in guttural sounds. And then he would climb back into the jeep and we would turn about and go elsewhere.

Finally, far out in the eastern outskirts of the city we saw lights. They were faint and tiny, like bulbs on a Christmas tree. But the clerk pointed quickly, saying, "There! Maybe there!" And the jeep bounced on toward them over the broken streets.

We could soon see little houses and we drove up to them and rolled into a tiny alley so narrow the jeep could just get in. It was paved with round, graded beach stones. "Stop here," the clerk said, and we all got out and he went into one of the houses. Each doorway was lighted with small paper lanterns that threw patches of orange bloom and cherry and cardinal and

223

vermilion on the house fronts and glimmering road stones. And the whole delicately lighted alleyway was spotlessly clean, an oasis in a wilderness of cinders.

The clerk came out of the house with a fat woman who put her hands together like an old-fashioned diver when she came up to us and bowed and bowed.

"She is frightened," he told us, "and she says, please understand that if the girls run away it is not because they are bad. It is only because they are afraid."

She turned reluctantly, as though she were not at all sure that what she was doing was right, and led the way with little running, rocking steps, her wooden geta clacking on the stones. We followed and she ushered us into one of the largest houses on the alley.

A pattern of seashells was inlaid on the entry floor. Moss and green plants and a miniature pine tree grew out of carved bamboo vessels. And on a shelf of polished redwood knelt a girl in a flowered kimono. She was motionless, with her head bent low, and seemingly as miniature and inanimate and as carefully placed as everything else in that little entryway. We could not see her face, but her neck was powdered white and looked like alabaster. And as she slid forward on her knees to unlace our combat boots she bent her head still lower as though to be sure we could not see her face and to hide her hands which were shaking.

We stepped beyond her into a narrow passageway and were directed up some twisting bamboo stairs. They were pleasantly slippery and led us into a surprisingly large room for such a tiny house. It was delightful in its sparseness. Underfoot was smooth cool matting, thick and springy and luxurious to our shoeless feet. We slid them soothingly back and forth over its surface. The ceiling was of white woven-wood staves. Sliding paper panels formed the walls. Across them, through long blades of yellow sea grass, stalked golden cranes. In that frail and immaculate room we suddenly felt uncomfortable in our slovenly field-soiled clothing, hung with guns and knives, and we sat dumbly on the cushions the fat woman had spread for us.

We could hear whispering behind the paper walls and then

224

one of the panels opened and six girls stepped into the room, each picking up her spotlessly white cotton-clad feet as though she were walking on eggs. They kept their heads bent with their faces turned away from us, and their oily black hair, piled in identical traditional forms, glistened in the light of the kerosene lamps which hung from the ceiling.

For a long time they stood there in their bright kimonos, still as flowers, their faces hidden, and we sat, large and dirty, watching them. Finally one of the soldiers made a move. He took a package of cigarettes from his pocket and, slipping slightly in his stocking feet, went to each of the girls in turn. But they would neither turn their heads nor move their hands and after pushing a cigarette between the fingers of each girl he gave up and returned.

The fat lady could stand it no longer. She rose and shuffled from the room and returned with a musical instrument, a samisen, which she thrust at one of the girls. To each of the others she gave a little shove, scolding and hissing at them, till they raised their heads a little and came alive. The samisen player lifted her arm and her fingers began to pluck the strings. As she played she swayed slightly and the others stepped apart and began to move their feet and arms. The tone was mournful, incomprehensible to us, and the girls' mouths opened at last and they began to sing with little chirping cries and odd descending whines. All but the samisen player still held the cigarettes between their fingers.

When the song was finished we clapped and cried out with delight. It was not because we had enjoyed the music. We had no appreciation of it at all. It was simply that the girls had moved and that the impasse had been broken. Now one of the girls walked with tiny mincing steps to the captain. Bowing and putting her hands on her knees, she then offered him the cigarette that had been given her. When he took it she withdrew a match from her obi sash and put the flame to his cigarette. The tension was going and everybody began laughing.

Someone brought an old Victor phonograph and a pile of records into the room and the girls began picking over the records, discussing them in high voices. Finally they agreed on

225

one and put it on the machine and waited for our reaction while it played first in squeaks and scratches. Then the music came. It was "Yes, We Have No Bananas," and the girls cried out "American! American!" and soon we were all dancing.

As the night progressed we drank Japanese beer and ate from little heaps of cold Japanese beans; and the girls had their first American K rations and began reaching freely into our cigarettes.

Sometime past midnight I saw the girl who was dancing with the captain stop and bend over a pile of pistol belts and forty-fives and sheath knives which we had taken off and cast into a heap. She gathered them all up and carried them across the room and pushed them into a corner out of the way. And as I watched her turn about with her arms held out toward the captain, I realized suddenly how far we had come that night.

46.

Defeat Comes
to an
Old Man

The sentries at the gate of the Yasukuni Shrine had changed. For three-quarters of a century an unbroken detail of soldiers had guarded the entrance to the holy sanctuary where the god-spirits of comrades killed in battle hovered over the hallowed grounds. Now some American soldiers, at ease and unawed, were standing in their places. The words of the sergeant of the guard, however, showed that although there was no communion with the hovering spirits, the asylum was still inviolable. "The joint's out of bounds," he said to us when we got out of the jeep. We were four Allied correspondents and a Japanese reporter coming there for a secret and important interview. We showed him our military press credentials and persuaded him to let us in.

Inside there was a feeling of hush. On the immaculate pebbled grounds, raked to the smoothness of a carpet, a dozen women in brown *mompei* overalls, their heads tied in kerchiefs and their feet in white cotton *tabi*, stepped about on tiptoe, picking up the few leaves which had fallen in the night, placing them in baskets as though each leaf were a soul.

At the top of the steps of the shrine a young man in a Western suit appeared. He came down to meet us. He was Hajime Suzuki, son of Admiral Kantaro Suzuki, who had been, until two weeks before, Premier of Japan.

"Only you have come?" he asked anxiously. We said yes. But he looked beyond us as though to make sure. Then, bowing politely, he led us up the stairs into the shrine. We entered a little room swathed in golden drapes. A splash of blue hung on the wall. It was a painting of a Japanese artillery battery firing blue smoke over a range of blue mountains. The scene was clearly China, a representation of prouder days.

We waited for the Premier, but when a sliding panel opened and a man entered it was not he. It was a priest dressed in an exquisitely colored kimono, flashing white to the waist and the skirt darkening into purple. He had a white walrus mustache and a hairless head the color and texture of cordovan leather. It shone like a polished boot when he bowed. He was General Takeo Suzuki, chief priest of the Yasukuni Shrine and brother of the ex-Premier.

"Admiral Suzuki is not here," he said when he straightened from his bows. "He could not come. It is too dangerous." We showed our disappointment but he just spread his arms in a gesture of helplessness. He had the same apprehensive manner of his nephew and he too kept looking beyond us as though the golden drapes were not there and he could see into the compound.

We had made the rendezvous with him through the Japanese member of our party, Masaru Fujimoto, once interpreter for

Ambassador Grew. For two weeks—almost since the day we occupied Japan—we had been searching for Admiral Suzuki. So had many others. For he had disappeared the day he resigned as Premier—which was the day the Emperor made the recording of his broadcast to the people of Japan announcing the surrender and asking them to lay down their arms. We had already learned something of that night—and of the country we were occupying. A band of terrorists within the army, determined to destroy the recording and carry on the war, had shot their way into the palace, killing the chief of the Imperial Guard, kidnaping the Radio Tokyo technicians who had cut the record, and spreading terror throughout the royal sanctuary. They failed to find the recording and the next day it was broadcast and the war was stopped. But before that both of the Premier's houses had been burned to the ground and he had disappeared. Some said he was dead, killed in a bloody shooting at the palace gate, some that he had been slaughtered in his home as his wife pleaded for his life, others that he had escaped and was in hiding.

The admiral's brother appealed to us. "My brother is old and tired," he said. "They hunt him night and day. In 1936 he was shot by terrorists and lived only by a miracle. Now extremists are again determined to kill him. He can stay only a few hours, sometimes only a few minutes, in one place. Every night he sleeps in a different bed. There are still many who do not yet understand that the war is lost. It would not be safe to see him now."

We left. But that night Fujimoto brought us a secret message that the admiral would see us, that he wanted to see us. And the next morning we drove out to the western suburbs of Tokyo. And there, in a small, modest dwelling, we were led into a dark room cluttered in un-Japanese fashion with commonplace Western furnishings. The old admiral was sitting at a table. He rose when we entered. He was a tall and distinguished Japanese with a careful military bearing. His hair had receded leaving a great bare patch above his forehead as brown and glistening as his brother's, and his widespread, white mustache was cropped close. His eyes were clear and they were set in turn upon each of us as though to measure at a glance the kind of people who had brought his nation to its knees —for we were the first he had seen at such close quarters. And I realized as I caught his glance that there was little about us, in our designedly nonmilitary and rather ostentatious shabbiness, that would give a beaten admiral the consolation that defeat at least came from a superior people.

Behind him stood his son, Hajime, pale and frail-looking, and beside him, a dramatic contrast, a huge Japanese with a barrel chest. He was not armed but clearly his strength and his body were there to defend the admiral. He scarcely moved during the interview. Opposite the admiral sat Dr. Hiroshi Shimomura, Minister of State and President of the Board of Information in Suzuki's Cabinet. He too was marked for death by the terrorists.

"I must tell you," Admiral Suzuki said, "that outside of the group of top militarists and most of the Cabinet, the people of Japan were ignorant of the state of the war. And even the top militarists and Cabinet members were not always informed of important developments. Sadly enough, the greatest cry for continuing the war came from the uneducated people. This was because they were told almost nothing of the truth and were kept in ignorance during the whole period. They did not know our losses. Until the Emperor's radio broadcast, they did not know that we were beaten. Even today they do not yet know why."

The whole war had been one of deceit and secrecy between the various cliques of Japan's rulers, Dr. Shimomura told us. "It was as though not only you were the enemy, but that those in our various uniforms were enemies of each other. Tojo and the army leaders did not know for weeks afterward that the Battle of Midway had been fought and lost. I did not know anything about it myself for more than a year. Not until a month ago did I learn of the Battle of the Coral Sea. And I was a member of the government!"

Admiral Suzuki kept looking at his watch. He rose. "If you are to understand what has happened to us you must understand that for years we have been living a lie. And those who have refused to believe the lie are killed by those who are themselves still ignorant." He picked up his maple cane which had been lying across the table. "I must leave now," he said. "I have already been here too long." He bowed and then he shook hands with each of us.

We all stood there quietly in the little flagstoned courtyard as he went away, out through the back garden, epitomizing in his forlorn person the end of an epoch in Japan. Seventy-seven years before, when his life began, Japan was a mysterious, isolated land, hidden away from the rest of the world. Ten days after his birth the most dramatic change in the history of modern Japan occurred: the old Tokugawa shogunate was overthrown and Emperor Meiji placed upon the throne. The Meiji Restoration had begun, and as Suzuki grew into manhood, so did the industrialization of his country and the spread of Western civilization, both making their way irrevocably and often bloodily against the older feudalistic society. In the process, Suzuki served in the war against the Chinese Empire in 1894. He commanded a ship in 1905 which helped to destroy the Russian fleet and establish his country as a modern world power. And then, in a matter of a few years, he saw the Japanese march toward military eminence: they annexed Korea; they took over the former German possessions in the Pacific after the First World War; they made the famous Twenty-One Demands on China and began their military conquest of its vast areas. Then they attacked the West—all in his lifetime. Finally, he not only saw his country lose everything, but he himself prepared the way for its unconditional surrender.

And now, at the end of his days, he was fleeing through back yards. We watched him go, with that great hulk of a Japanese guard leading the way, crouching like an alerted samurai, and his son following, flashing frightened looks left and right. Between them walked the old man, leaning heavily on his cane, picking his way through a vegetable patch and finally disappearing behind a war-frayed family wash which hung from a line tied to two naked cherry trees.

47.

Something from Mars

In those early occupation days the Japanese avoided their conquerors. They shared the same streets, crowded the same railroad platforms, worked as servants in American billets and provided labor for the Army of Occupation. But mostly they looked away and tended to their own business. Their fine sense of curiosity, however, and their secret admiration for things American frequently overcame their fear and shame. This was especially true if, by chance, they witnessed American machinery at work or indeed any American innovation or labor-saving device. Then it was that their stoic avoidance would for moments be forgotten and their deadpan faces come alight with a charming and infectious friendliness.

Dressed in their shabby wartime clothing and carrying their day's food of rice balls and fish in little metal boxes wrapped in bright scarves, they would be scurrying along with every air of being late. Then suddenly they would see something and stop. It might be a young American soldier sitting on a massive bulldozer, an Atlas with a scrubbed baby face dangling a cigarette, moving a mountain of debris, or they would be pinned in their hurrying footsteps to watch a strange machine moving slowly down a street, leaving behind it a beautifully smooth and glistening black ribbon of finished road surface. It was at such moments that they respected their conquerors.

One crisp, frosty morning the American Army had set itself the task of undoing a mistake. Several days earlier it had deposited four huge crates of machinery in a narrow roadway in the heart of Tokyo. The address was wrong and the crates blocked the alley. A monster of a truck with a low-slung platform, striking twentieth-century industrial lines, and shiny new olive-drab paint, backed slowly down the alley. A bright-faced lad with a green fatigue cap on the back of his head maneuvered it neatly, with his face out of the cab door and one hand on the wheel. Hurrying footsteps hesitated and the gathering crowd paced the backing vehicle. As it stopped a few feet from the crates, hands of the watching Japanese touched its sleek cab as one would the fur of a kitten and then moved on to caress the giant tires.

At the other end of the alley a small and oddly shaped vehicle appeared, bouncing along, another youngster at the wheel and two more walking beside it. It was a fork lift on a small-wheeled tractor. When it arrived its driver spun the vehicle around with a swish and a swerve, threw it out of gear, knocked his fatigue cap to the back of his neck and was down on the ground tapping out a cigarette from a transparent plastic case in a sequence of such quick, adroitly co-ordinated actions that, to the eye, the human and the machine moved as one. The two soldiers coming down the alley on foot arrived and the truck driver came out of his cab and joined them. There was the plastic case again, a chrome lighter, a flip, and they were all smoking.

Relaxed and neatly attired in starched field greens and combat boots polished to a dark mahogany, they looked and moved very much like their apparatus—slick and newly turned out. The two drivers had a chevron each on their pressed sleeves. Their two companions wore all the stripes and rockers the Army could pin on a sergeant. They glanced at the gathered Japanese. Then they sauntered over to have a look at the crates.

Each box weighed perhaps a couple of tons and the first had been partly dismantled, apparently for inspection. One of the sergeants removed the loose boards and made a quick appraisal. "Looks like something from Mars," he said over his shoulder, and the others joined him. The crowd swayed a little as they peered forward. They were restrained and polite. But it was something to see, this business from Mars. They stood their distance, bending as far forward as gravity would permit, some looking as though their feet had been nailed to the pavement. In the crate was an elaborate and incomprehensible piece of machinery. One Japanese who knew some English could not contain himself and read aloud and haltingly a stencil marking on the end of the crate: "International Business Machine Corporation. For U.S. Signal Corps, APO 500." The sergeant toyed testingly at the corner of the crate for weight. "The sons-of-bitches are heavy," he muttered. Then the soldiers withdrew a few paces and stood finishing their cigarettes.

The Japanese crowded around the open crate, bending, pointing, talking, but not touching. Theirs was admiration. They backed away again when the Americans approached. The soldiers put the boards back in place and the truck driver hammered in a couple of nails. "Let's put the sons-of-bitches aboard," said the sergeant. The fork-lift driver slipped into the seat of his machine and made the purling engine growl. Then he swung the lift around and rolled it up to the first crate, lowered the two forks, moved the vehicle forward and slipped the forks under the crate. He pulled a lever and up went the forks with the crate as high as the crowd's heads. There was a murmur from the gathered Japanese. He wheeled the vehicle around and rolled up to the tail of the truck, lowering the crate to proper level, placing it aboard, withdrawing the forks and backing away with infinite finesse. The Japanese hung on each other's shoulders and their earlier whispers grew to excited talk.

"The next one," the sergeant said out of the corner of his mouth. With a flicker of a glance past the crowd, he snapped his fingers and muttered, "Let's go, Mac." The fork lift repeated its performance, only this time when it reached the truck it had to shove the combined weight of both crates in order to make room for the second. It took a little longer. "Let's go. Let's go," the sergeant said, pointing to the third. "Let's get the next one." The third crate slid onto the truck with more difficulty, the weight of the first two making quite a heavy job of it.

The alley was packed by the time the fork lift reached for the fourth crate. It picked it up handily and hoisted it smoothly to the level of the truck. Then it forced it part way onto the tail platform. But it would go no farther. The wheels of the fork lift spun in a screech, the motor roared and the alley smelled of burning rubber. The driver pulled levers, he changed gears, but the crate stuck. There it was, half on, half off the truck. The driver backed up gingerly, leaving the crate poised and insecure. He climbed down and the soldiers lighted another round of cigarettes. Then they walked up the length of the truck, looking carefully at each crate, and came back into a little huddle. The Japanese watched the end crate and they watched the huddle.

The sergeant pointed to the fork lift. "Back the son-of-a-bitch up, put the son-of-a-bitch in low, and come at it running," he said. He flicked the cigarette off the end of his finger and gave the crowd a quick look. The lad with the single stripe hesitated a moment. Then he turned and looked at the truck as a pitcher sometimes looks at a batter before the throw. He climbed into his machine, shifted into reverse, and bounded swiftly backward down the alley. He stopped, changed gears again, and waved the crowd clear of the truck with a motion right and left. Then, looking straight at his target, he gunned his engine and came roaring up the alley. The forks of his lift hit the crate high, drove right through the wood covering and stopped with a crash and a jingle of smashed metal. The crate did not move.

The driver, thrown forward, slid back into his seat and idled his engine. After a few moments he alighted and joined the three soldiers on the road. Again he reached for his plastic cigarette case. This time when it was passed, however, their backs were to the crowd.

48.

A Disarming World

Those of us who entered Japan in 1945, flushed with victory and touched with varying degrees of vindictiveness, found a world that was often disarming and filled with wonder.

"Sah!" is a Japanese expression of surprise. It is often used to indicate surprise at one's own stupidity. In such circumstances, the word is an outburst and trails off into a whisper, sometimes accompanied by a resounding self-slap at the forehead with the open palm of the hand.

I remember it sounding the loudest the first week of the occupation. An American officer, one of the very many who were to comb Japan for the answers to the multitude of questions which the war had shrouded, was conferring with a Japanese. The Japanese was eagerly co-operating, for each had discovered that the other was a chemical engineer and a mutual background is a basis for friendship in any land.

During the war the Japanese had unleashed into the upper jet stream paper balloons carrying fire bombs. These ingenious devices were blown across the Pacific and landed over a wide area in northwestern United States. They set a few small fires and killed one family who unwisely tampered with the strange apparatus which had landed on their farm. But otherwise no harm was done—primarily because almost all the bombs landed in snow-covered forest regions and harmlessly burned themselves out. However, their possibilities were so much more frightening than the mere threat of fire alone that the U.S. War Department immediately tagged them top secret and persuaded the publishers in that area not to mention any fire of unknown origin or the finding of any mysterious instrument of destruction. Thus, apart from the very few who saw them coming down or lying dead in the snow, no one outside the War Department ever heard of or even imagined such things as ocean-hopping fire balloons.

The Japanese scientist, in his academic way, took delight in describing the contrivance which so effectively bridged the Pacific for it was indeed an imaginative accomplishment. The balloons, weighing more than a hundred pounds, were filled with hydrogen which carried them into the high reaches of the rarefied jet stream. There they were swept along at better than two hundred miles an hour. When they rose too high the heat of the sun, expanding the gas, opened a valve which lowered the balloon. At this point sandbags were dropped and it went up again. Thus it alternated within a chosen altitude across the ocean.

"What did you hope to gain by this?" the American asked.

"We were hoping," the Japanese replied, "to read in the newspapers, which we monitored in neutral cities like Lisbon, that large and unexplained fires were being set in the northwestern part of America. Then we would know that our calculations were correct and that the balloons were getting there."

"But was it really to set fires in the United States?" the American pressed him.

"That was our job," the Japanese replied. "But if it worked, I learned later, the army had a plan to use the balloons to deliver disease to America—possibly anthrax. But of course they never got that far because when we received no reports of great fires the whole project was dropped."

"Tell me," the American said after a while, "did any of the balloons ever fail to rise into the upper currents and get turned back to Japan?"

"A few."

"Did they start any fires here?"

"No. It was in the wintertime and they fell in the snow."

The American paused for a moment, watching the Japanese. Then he said: "Didn't you know that it also snowed in America?"

The Japanese's eyes spread wide and the open palm of his hand reached slowly toward his forehead.

"Sah!" he exclaimed.

I called on Mr. Matsuoka one afternoon after an American occupation officer had arranged the interview. I was involved on a story on public health and Mr. Matsuoka was a highly placed public health officer who had earned the respect of the Americans. He received me formally and rather coldly, and all during the lengthy discussion maintained a stiff and impersonal manner. But when I took him to dinner that night he changed suddenly, as though we had put aside the official mask and could now bring ourselves into the great flood of events which earlier in the day had been portrayed by a series of figures and percentage signs and climbing curves on charts.

His home, he said, was in a small village near Ichikawa, some ten miles from Tokyo, and he and his family had lived there through the fire raids which, night after night, slowly burned away the surrounding areas until at last only his village stood in miles of destruction.

I exclaimed how fortunate this was. But he shook his head slowly.

"Five days before the surrender," he continued sadly, "a single plane came over in the night and dropped fire on us. We all ran into the fields and in the morning not one house in the village remained."

"Five days before the end!" I said with feeling, for the mask had been put aside and we could both now share the tragedy. "How unfortunate!" I exclaimed.

"Oh, please!" he cried quickly. "Do not feel bad. There is a little river which runs along the edge of our village and all night my family sat with me on the embankment watching the reflection of the flames in the water, and it was truly a beautiful thing."

Because few American correspondents in Japan could read Japanese, a number of press translating services sprang up around us, flooding our newly established offices with almost hourly English conversions of what was appearing in each edition of the Japanese newspapers. There were too many of them right from the start and soon they grew highly aggressive in their efforts to outsell each other. They not only translated, but in their enterprise they reported too. No service, however, could long boast an exclusive, for it would simply be copied by the others and ground out on their own mimeograph machines.

One day a fine story from one of the services came over my desk. In an hour's time it was carried by most of the others.

Every night, it read, a beggar appeared at a tiny noodle shop. The shop was one of the many flimsy boarded lean-tos jammed among a jungle of shacks that had mushroomed along the destroyed Ginza.

"Honorable Oba-san," he would call humbly, his hands together beggar fashion, "please give some noodles to a starving man." And the proprietress, a kindly woman, always had something for the beggar.

One night a fire which started somewhere in the jumble of shacks swept through the area and put the little noodle shop to flames. The proprietress was helpless before the fury of the fire and she stood apart, wringing her hands, as her shop crumbled into glowing embers.

Suddenly she saw the beggar arriving. "Begone!" she screamed at him in anguish. "Can't you see that I am ruined and that I have no noodles?"

"Ah, honorable Oba-san," the beggar replied. "It is not noodles I have come for tonight, but only a little heat from your fire to warm myself."

The story had such a fine human quality and such a universal touch that I chose it at once as one to be sent to New York. Of course it had to be checked and some facts added. Where on the Ginza? I recalled no fire there that week. Who was the proprietress? And the beggar—perhaps he was a soldier returned from the wars.

For two days my Japanese assistants searched for the man

who wrote it. At last we found him. He was a frail man in a
worn-out coat. A shock of black hair fell across his forehead,
and he could easily have been claimed by any of the arts. Reluctantly he told us the circumstances of the story. He was on his
way home a few nights before, he said. He had just finished
a long day's work and it was very cold. And as he waited on a
street corner for a tram, standing there underfed and dreaming
about warmth and food, he looked longingly across the street at
a line of noodle shacks and the scene just came to him. It seemed
so real, he said, that that night he could not resist the urge
to write it. And after that, he explained, it *was* real, and there
was therefore no good reason why he should not offer it to his
office. They took it without question, he said, and now he was
sorry for all the trouble it had caused us.

I remember how disappointed I was then, after all our work,
to find that it was a pure fabrication. But now I know that it
was worth it. For in some strange way it has become a reality
to me also, recapturing the mood of the early occupation days.
And sometimes I find myself, like its author, unable to resist the
urge to tell it.

49.

A Look That
Comrades Share

When I visited Nagasaki in 1946, my companion, a marine
officer whose unit had been the first to enter the city after the
surrender, took me to the edge of town to find an old lady
whom he had known in those earliest days just after the bomb.
She and a son, he told me as we walked through the little alleys,

were the only survivors of a large family and had lived in the
shelter of a remaining wall of their home, cooking for his
men and hauling water.

More than a year had passed since then and the whole face
of the city had changed, with miles of cheap bare-boarded
shacks spread thinly over the clinkered land, and he had to
study the geography to place the exact point where she had lived.
Finally, narrowing his search, he went from door to door of
the almost indistinguishable shanties until at last she came out
of one of them shouting her greetings with such vigor that the
neighbors came running to see.

"Mama-san!" the marine cried, throwing his arms around
her.

"Ah! Ah! Ah!" she cried back, taking his hand in both of
hers and patting it and looking up into his face with the love
of a mother seeing a long-absent son come home.

Her own son came out and stood behind her, laughing and
exclaiming too. What his mother said in Japanese he echoed,
sometimes in English. In the midst of her exclamations a question came repeatedly. "My mother asks," the boy said eagerly,
" 'Please, when are the old men coming back?' "

"The old men?" the marine asked, wondering.

"Yes," the boy said, nodding. "The old men. She wants to
know when they are coming back, like you."

Suddenly we both understood. The "old men" were the weather-
beaten youngsters who had survived the bloody fighting to
Japan and, aged beyond their years, had come into Nagasaki in
those first days to garrison the city. Now, more than a year after
they had gone, this old lady and her son and their nodding
neighbors were remembering them nostalgically and asking
hopefully when they would return. For in this time the character of the occupation had changed. The men who had fought
the war were gone and their replacements were for the most
part peacetime soldiers untouched by the bloody battles which
had put them into a strange and afflicted land. Ironically, the
bond between them and the Japanese was very much more tenu-
ous than that between the defeated enemy and the men who
had defeated them. This was not because the replacements were

so very different but rather because two people who have lived
through a great and terrifying ordeal—even though they are
enemies—are so often drawn together by a softening of memory
and a growing sympathy for the pain each has felt.

The meeting of the marine and the old lady at Nagasaki made
but a momentary impact upon them and the gathering in that
little alley. Such profound changes in national attitudes are
subtle and almost imperceptible unless viewed from a distance
in time. I saw it from such a distance. For I had just returned
to Japan after nearly a year's absence. I saw it also at a juncture
when my own life had changed dramatically too: while Shelley
and I were home our first child was born. We named him Seth,
and in his fifth month we brought him to live in a country
which had so fatefully become part of his family history. He
arrived as so many other Americans had arrived before him—
aboard a U.S. Navy assault transport. But even that was a
symbol of the changing times. For now it had been put to
the duty of carrying American dependent families into Japan
and had been redesignated "the diaper transport service."

As a correspondent accredited to the U.S. Army, I was allowed to draw a house for my family from the Army's "Dependent Housing" list, the size and opulence of it to be based
on my simulated military rank (colonel) and the number of
stripes I had earned in combat areas during the war. Since the
Army kindly threw in my unproductive months as a prisoner,
I had a most favorable position on the list and could look
forward to quite a mansion. This seemed important to me. It
was to be Shelley's and my first home of any permanence, the
first house we had ever had together, and of course it would
form the background for my son's earliest memories.

I studied the list and went to see the houses on it but none of
them seemed even remotely suitable. At last I went to see an
old friend, a colonel with whose regiment I had been in combat
and who was now assigned to the Dependent Housing section.
He was glad to see me. He said he was tired of playing real
estate agent for a bunch of God-damn officers who never left
the U.S. till the shooting was over, but for me it was different,

for me he'd find a God-damn house.

But it wasn't that easy. We drove, map and lists in hand, and stopped and hunted and drove again, searching section after section with such unrewarding results that by late afternoon the colonel's hopeful spirits had vanished. In fact, we had given up and were on our way back when he made the find. It was on one of those little dirt roads so strangely rural in the heart of Tokyo. He had chosen it on the map as a short cut home and we were not really looking any more when we passed a high concrete wall lined with thin pines. "Once, I suppose, there was a damn good house behind that," the colonel said. "Now all these fences hide is ruins." The fence followed us a little more and then we passed a great black wood gate shut across a pebble driveway. The colonel, looking back, slowed down. Then he stopped. He backed up. "Let's see what's over that fence," he said idly.

He was a tall man and his chin went nicely over the top of the gate. I was climbing up when I heard him exclaim. "Good God," he said. "How did our search teams miss this one?"

On the other side of the fence was a large house of Western design. It was surrounded by an extensive overgrown garden. A Japanese torii of faded red stood on its own reflection in an old lily pond and beyond was a stone lantern covered with lichen. The house was shuttered and seemingly closed, but blue smoke trailed up from its rear and a few hens scratched in an old flower bed. We both shouted but no one came, and after a while we climbed over the gate and walked up the pebble driveway to the door. The colonel rapped and we waited. He rapped again and we waited again. Then he tried the door; it slid back easily and we found ourselves standing in a tiled entryway, silent and not looking at each other until we saw someone coming down a long corridor. It was a woman in a soft kimono, her feet noiseless in white cotton *tabi*. Her walk was direct and she reached us smiling. Her hair was in Western coiffure. She wore lipstick and her cheeks were brushed with rouge. She was wondrously petite and her face delicate and lovely. A suggestion of French perfume seemed to float in with her.

"Good afternoon," she said in the musical scale Japanese

242

women use to greet people. Her English was excellent with just a touch of something British. Her confidence and manner were superior to ours. She had reversed the roles. We stood there, hats in hand.

"We were passing and saw this house," the colonel began uneasily.

"So you climbed over the gate and came right in." She laughed in just the kind of way that would not take the reproach out of the jest.

"We're, eh . . . we're visiting houses to be chosen for occupation personnel. I wonder . . . I hope you won't mind our looking at this house." The colonel had lost some of his command presence. I felt equally off balance.

"Of course," the woman said with bright eagerness. "Please come in." And she motioned us forward and led us down a shining corridor where sliding glass windows looked out upon the garden on one side. Several of the shoji on the other side were open and as we passed I looked into well-ordered rooms, partly Japanese and partly Western in design and furnishings. It was a fine house. What a fortunate impulse the colonel had in looking over that fence! I thought.

We entered a large room. Two walls were paneled with soft rice-paper shoji. Otherwise it was Western in architecture and appointments.

"Please sit down," she said. "I am Mrs. Sugiyama." We introduced ourselves. "I'm sorry everything is so untidy," she went on. "This house, before the war, you know . . ." She stopped, turning to the colonel with a charming smile. "But I needn't apologize to you." She made it sound familiar and personal. "I can see . . . well, it's quite apparent that you know what war is, that you have felt its hardships and tragedy yourself." It was clear to her which of us had the rank and she scarcely addressed herself to me.

The colonel relaxed. "Well," he said, "I guess there are a few of us still around who came in here the hard way." He gave each of us a look that comrades share.

"I'm sure it has been trying for you," she answered. "But for you, at least it is over. For us, what can I say? And for my

husband, what can anybody say—or what will anybody say?"
She gestured gently, opening the palms of her hands. They were
so lovely that I found myself nodding as I repeatedly looked
from hands to face, not wanting to miss either. I caught the
colonel doing the same.

"Your husband?" the colonel asked.

"Yes," she replied. "Missing in action. That's all I know.
Perhaps that's all I will ever know.'

The colonel's command manner returned. "What theater was
he in? When did you last hear from him? Maybe I can help."

Her hands flashed. "So many have already tried," she said.
There was the sound of defeat in her voice. "I have had no
direct word from him since your landing in the Philippines—
since your landing on the island of Luzon. He was last seen in
the mountains there at a place called Balete Pass."

"Balete Pass," the colonel repeated with feeling. He sat forward in his chair. "I fought a regiment there myself."

Mrs. Sugiyama was sitting alert, just like the colonel. "You
were there too!" she exclaimed. "Perhaps you can . . . But of
course that would be asking too much."

"No, no," the colonel protested. "Tell me all you know. Do
you know his outfit—his command?"

"He was a colonel too," she answered. Both now were absorbed
with each other. "He was in command of the Shimbashi Group.
And when last seen he was on the left sector of the defense line.
That is all I have been able to learn."

The colonel scratched a note on the back of the housing list.

"You were there," she repeated in a tone that made it seem
that she was talking to herself. She was leaning forward with
her elbows in her lap, staring at the colonel.

Neither of them, I think, saw me when I arose. "May I have
a look around?" I asked. My voice seemed to intrude and
sounded embarrassingly out of place.

"Oh! Yes." She looked at me suddenly as though she had
forgotten I was there. "Please do. Please help yourself." She
motioned me vaguely toward a door at the far end of the
room.

Despite the impression of neglect that the shutters and unkempt garden gave to the house from the outside, it was in good condition within; far better than anything I had seen in my search. The more I saw of it, the more attractive and livable it seemed.

They were still intent on each other's war experiences when I returned. It had gotten quite late, and when I could I broke in. "Perhaps," I said to the colonel, "before it gets too dark we might have a look."

"A look?" he replied, turning to me.

"Yes," I said. "We might have a quick look at the rooms and the facilities here."

"Oh," the colonel said in an offhand way, waving his hand gently at me, "I've already discussed the house with Mrs. Sugiyama. There have already been two other officers out here from Dependent Housing to see it—and it doesn't make it. It's lacking in almost all the requirements. It's already been on the list twice, Mrs. Sugiyama says, and has been taken off each time."

"Well," I said, pressed on by a terrible disappointment, "it . . . it looks pretty good to me."

The colonel waved at me again. "No," he repeated with authority, "this one really won't make it." He saw my face. "But don't you worry," he exclaimed, breaking into a kind of good-fellowship laugh. "I said I'd find you a house, and by God, I'll find you one." She was laughing too and I was suddenly struck by how nearly alike their expressions were as they regarded me.

Mrs. Sugiyama saw us to the door and then walked us down to the gate which a serving girl was opening. "I'll see what I can turn up about your husband," the colonel said in a confident voice as we were getting into the staff car. "Don't get your hopes up, but we *might* even find a way to bring him back here."

"Oh, how kind you are!" Mrs. Sugiyama called, coming toward the car. "How truly satisfying it is to be with Americans!"

The colonel knew how I felt and as we drove away he nudged me and said in his pleasant growl: "Relax. I'll find you a house. And it'll be a hell of a lot better than that one too."

And I must say for him that he did, and it was. As it turned out, my house was close to Mrs. Sugiyama's and often as I passed hers I found it pleasant to make mental comparisons.

I never saw her again, though, nor was her house ever taken over as a U.S. Occupation residence. And since the colonel finished his tour in Japan soon after our house-hunting experience together, I never learned if Mrs. Sugiyama's husband survived the Philippines and got home again. But if he did, he too must have found the Americans satisfying. For in those occupation days I seldom passed his home without seeing a U.S. Army vehicle parked out in front of that big black gate.

50.

Dependent Housing

Our family life in that expropriated house in Tokyo was ostensibly that of conquerors—the life of ease amid the ruins. Just as our Army had procured the house for us, painted and furnished it, sodded its ruined lawns, installed a pumphouse, reinstated the furnace, replaced the urinal in the "powder room" with a more acceptable piece of plumbing, and generally "Westernized" the place, they undertook its upkeep.

Almost daily, in those first months, workmen appeared, either to complete the magical transformation or to repair previous mistakes. The house itself was a continuing misadventure and we were constantly having to call Dependent Housing for help to make it work as we conceived a house should work.

At first the Japanese journeymen who swarmed up our driveway in response to our calls were supervised by a GI technician, generally some vague Midwestern farm boy, overfed and sodden with authority, whose hamlike hands were capable of ruining every fragile bit of Japanese workmanship they came in contact with. But after a little while the native workmen came unescorted, occasionally singly or in pairs, more often in large swarming teams. And their initial visit to a house, their first tap of the hammer, their first turn of the screw and their first cup of tea in the kitchen of that house was as magical and mysterious a beginning as birth itself, and from that moment went into an active, enduring cycle of life: visits and revisits, poundings and repoundings, tea and more tea.

Sometimes they passed each other in the driveway, one team having just finished its job and the other answering a new call. And sometimes they passed each other in the house itself, a crew of electricians climbing over a crew of boiler experts who themselves had just worked through a team of telephone repairmen. But wherever their work might take them in the big house, they would all finally gather in the kitchen where cook-san had tea and cigarettes waiting and where many of them opened their little frayed brown bags that had once carried gas masks and took from them rice balls rolled in seaweed for an in-between-job snack.

Cook-san, like the workmen, like the little rompered women who visited us periodically to comb our lawn and pick the leaves out of it, like the other servants of our household, came to us from the Japanese government via Dependent Housing. We did not understand them and they did not understand us and at first we made each other very nervous.

Shelley was working half-time, now that she had a baby to think about, and she and I constituted the American staff of the *Time* and *Life* bureau in Japan. But sometimes I had the feeling that even half-time was too much for her as I listened to her on the office telephone where presumably she was gathering information or making arrangements for some story: "Hiroko-san?" I would hear her ask guardedly. "How is baby? Baby-san O.K.? Everything all right? *Daijobu?*" She would get no answer and her voice would begin to rise until at last one of our soft-hearted bilingual office staff would offer to take the phone, would talk for a moment with the flustered Hiroko, and would assure us that Seth was fine.

But gradually we came to understand each other, to shake down from our original positions of frightened servitors and equally frightened masters to something resembling a large feudal family on the Japanese order. Most of our original government-supplied staff, with their government-supplied supervisor who came periodically to mediate between us, was replaced by a more congenial group, untrained but eager to learn. Hiroko-san stayed on. It was the telephone which frightened her, not her master's voice. And she became that indispensable in any large domestic staff: the butt of all mistakes and irritations, hard-working, always smiling, always to blame.

But the center of our household was, of course, Seth. He was the only American who was home all day. And anyway, the Japanese, perhaps more than any other people, are great lovers and followers of children. It soon became obvious, even to Shelley, that no possible harm could come to him, surrounded as he was by loving servants and—as he grew older and began to talk—by neighbors, the ever-present workmen, even chance college students who got wind of his existence and came calling to practice their English on him.

One of the most fortunate of all the pleasant things that happened to us in Japan was securing Aiko-san as nurse for Seth. We knew very little of her background. But she brought into our household such a pleasant flavor of Japanese culture and quaint baby lore that her own gentle and old-fashioned breeding was quite obvious.

To be male and first-born is a combination in Japan that is the ultimate answer to marriage and prayer. And although Shelley tried hard to counteract it, Japanese tradition in this respect proved much too strong for her. This was made quite plain to me one day when I found Aiko and Seth in the tearoom, a charming little Japanese retreat in our mostly Western house, with its straw tatami floor and its lovely rice-paper shoji windows. For I discovered when I entered that the shoji panels had a series of finger holes pushed through the delicate paper.

"Aiko-san," I cried. "Who did that?" It was a needless question, for there stood Seth, two years old, wetting his finger in his mouth and readying himself for still another plunge.

248

Aiko was silent and I intercepted Seth as he went for the last shoji screen.

"Aiko-san," I persisted, "why did you let him do it?"

"In Japan," she answered reluctantly, "this is sometimes what babies do."

"But now," I said, "we must have all those shoji re-covered."

Again she was silent—and I had a sudden thought. "Aiko-san," I asked, "if Se-chan had been a girl baby would you have stopped him?"

Her face flushed and she nodded. "A girl baby, yes," she said. "But a boy baby—and a first-born, no."

We had a girl baby not long after that. It was in the spring of 1949. We named her Shelley, but Aiko called her Missy, a name that Seth's two-year-old tongue soon converted to Misty. Misty, though, received far more than the usual acclaim for a girl baby when she joined our household. By great good fortune her day of birth was also that of the Emperor of Japan.

51.

A Visit to the Admiral

It was considerable time after the end of the war before all the statistics of the Battle for Leyte Gulf had been gathered and added up. But by the time we sought out Admiral Kurita enough had been assembled to promote it from the category of "greatest naval battle of the Second World War" to "largest engagement ever fought on high seas." It was a tremendous encounter, ranging over an area of as much as five hundred miles, and was fought in four separate but related and sometimes simultaneous actions—all to repel one mighty Japanese operation.

The Imperial Navy code-named it *"Sho"* and mounted it against our penetration into the Philippines. It was their last chance to stop us and they knew it. They threw everything they had into it—and they very nearly succeeded. If they had, they might have pushed us right off the island of Leyte and set back our Pacific war effort half a year at least. The fact that they didn't was attributed by Admiral Sprague, who was in the thick of it, to the "definite partiality of Almighty God." From a distance of considerably more time and space—that is, Tokyo, some two years afterward—it seemed that at least some clue to their failure might lie closer at hand.

It was for this reason that I sent Shelley to interview Admiral Takao Kurita, who had commanded the Central Force, the spearhead, of the Japanese attack. *Life* was preparing a text piece on the Leyte Gulf battle, which was at that time the subject of some hot post-mortem discussions in the American press, and had cabled the query to me. As bureau chief I passed it on to Shelley, for she was not only my only American assistant but she already knew a fair amount about the battle.

She had been in Pearl Harbor as a correspondent attached to the Navy when the news came that Admiral Oldendorf had "crossed the T" of the Japanese Southern Force as it emerged from Surigao Strait south of Leyte—a cause for much back-slapping jubilation among the old-line Navy men, for they saw it as a sort of vindication of the "battleship mentality" then so deplored. And she had also had the opportunity to discuss the battle not long after its conclusion with Admiral Thomas Kinkaid, who commanded the defending force at Leyte, the American Seventh Fleet.

It was late summer of 1947, a lazy sunny afternoon, when Shelley and Kay Tateishi, our colleague and interpreter, set off by jeep to find the admiral. Chrysanthemums were beginning to bud and sprawling squash vines hung on the little unpainted thin-boarded houses on the outskirts of the city—houses all of the same vintage, a couple of years perhaps, built after the fire raids, and just beginning to weather a silver gray.

The admiral lived far on the edge of the city where fields

sometimes interrupted the ragged blocks of suburb. The roads were deeply rutted and dusty and Shelley told me afterward that they lost all sense of direction, of being in the city at all, even of time, as they drove and turned and backtracked, searching for the admiral's home.

They found it at last, a prewar semi-Western house typical of its prosperous residential neighborhood grown shabby in the years of war. It was set behind a rush fence with a torii-like gate and a single, twisted pine, and the sound of cicadas came from the garden behind. They asked at the front door for the admiral but were told that he no longer lived there, he had rented it, he lived with his family "out in back" and the servant pointed across a small strip of vegetable garden to a small shack.

They walked in the sunshine along a thin path through the vegetables that led to the admiral's cottage. Once the patch had been a Japanese garden, conventionally arranged of stunted trees and rocks and water, and by the door of the little house a red-leafed plum still stood, while on the other side a row of neat utilitarian pea vines climbed their bamboo sticks right up to the very edge.

The door itself was no more than a sliding glass window and as they stood hesitating in the narrow path they could look through it into a dark and cluttered entranceway where a woman sat working at a sewing machine. Kay raised his hand and then paused a moment before knocking, and Shelley too hung back. It was a pity to intrude. This was where the admiral had holed up, alone and in disgrace, after the battle and defeat.

For one smoke-filled and roaring hour in the southern seas this man had held the fate of tens of thousands in his hands. For that decisive hour, power and victory were his. Then he had let them go.

The hour had been midmorning, October 25, 1944. Five days earlier American forces had landed at Leyte. From all over the Philippines Japanese troops were rushing down to meet them. It was becoming obvious that the battle for the Philippines —perhaps even for Japan itself—would be settled right on Leyte. In Singapore the Japanese Imperial Navy clearly saw the threat.

They mustered every ship available from what was left of their original fleet—more than half the total force they had at their command when war began. And they devised a daring strike on Leyte: a decoy force of useless carriers denuded of their planes was sent far north along the eastern coast of Luzon to lure our fleet away. Then, to converge on our transports in Leyte Gulf, a two-pronged force of their largest ships, their heaviest fire-power, was sent to run the straits, one north, one south of Leyte, and to join in an irresistible pincer round our light forces there.

Their plan went very well. Admiral Halsey with his entire U.S. Third Fleet took after the decoy force and rushed to the north, out of the main area of battle, leaving our transports and landing protected only by a handful of baby-top carriers and a small screening force. The Japanese southern pincer managed to navigate the Straits of Surigao, but it was here that Admiral Oldendorf crossed the T and this force was destroyed.

Now it was up to Admiral Kurita with his Central Force. Under attack by our carrier planes and submarines when he began his run, he managed through great skill and unwavering determination to thread the reef-filled Straits of San Bernardino in the dark, to shake his enemy, and to emerge, the morning of the twenty-fifth, ready to attack. Battered, but still overwhelmingly superior to our remaining units guarding the gulf, he opened fire on Kinkaid's tin-plate force with the world's biggest naval guns, the heaviest-caliber fire that U.S. warships had ever been subjected to.

Desperately our flattops and their destroyer escorts dodged and fired and laid smoke screens, calling for help from our Third Fleet which was racing away to the north, delaying as they could their seemingly inevitable destruction and the destruction of our transports and our stocks of supplies on the beach.

Then, suddenly, the Japanese ceased fire. Calling his fleet about him, Admiral Kurita turned and retired, threading once more the treacherous Straits of San Bernardino, leaving the Gulf of Leyte stunned and quiet. Why?

Kay knocked. The woman rose and came to slide the door

open. Behind her in the dark, cluttered hall a little girl sat with some sewing in her lap. Obviously they were the admiral's wife and daughter and like so many upper-class Japanese women of that time were taking in sewing. The woman listened patiently while Kay told her what they wanted and then she bowed and shook her head as if in deep regret. The admiral was not well. He had been making trips into the country to sell the family possessions and buy food and he had aggravated a cold and now had an earache. However—she looked at Shelley; an American woman was still something of an oddity—she would ask.

She disappeared up the high step at the back of the plank-floored hallway, slipping off her shoes as she entered the tatami room behind. When she returned she repeated that her husband was ill, he could not hear well, but as they were Americans he would of course see them.

In spite of the warnings, Shelley was faintly surprised to find the admiral stretched out on the tatami floor in his summer kimono, a wet towel round his cropped gray head and a gray stubble running down his cheeks. He rose on one elbow to greet them while he held a large compress to his ear, and then lay back again, resting his head on a hard pillow. He was very thin of face, his body noticeably lean, but his eyes were clear and hazel, squinted at the corners and ready, it seemed, to laugh.

Shelley and Kay sat near him on cushions on the floor. They spoke politely of the weather, of his illness, of the admiral's life, now, in these postwar years.

The admiral laughed. "How do I live now? Ha, you can see; I am doing nothing. I suppose we shall do as they did in the olden days—live on from day to day on what we have, and when there is nothing left, pass on."

Then, with some diffidence, they began to talk about the battle for Leyte Gulf, how it had been with the American side and with his. The admiral lay back. He had increasing difficulty in hearing the questions so that Kay had to crawl forward and stay beside him on his hands and knees, hollering down into the admiral's ear. And for a while his answers were all prefaced with the caution, "My memory is not sure."

253

But soon, as Shelley talked and he came to realize that they were interested in the battle as an abstract thing—a sort of point in history turned at the battlements—something in which no particular good or evil was involved, his interest picked up and he seemed to hear better too. This was especially so when Shelley told him of the controversy in America over "Bull Halsey's dash north" and he understood that he was not to be made the butt of the interview.

"I did not know," he said. "I did not know that Admiral Halsey had taken his task force north. I knew nothing of the American side whatever."

Shelley leaned forward and began to draw on the tatami with her finger. "Here," she said. "Here we are at Leyte." And she drew a circle with her finger: "Leyte, and beside it Leyte Gulf, and above, Samar. Here is your fleet." She drew a wiggly line above Samar. "Here's Halsey . . . ."

Now the admiral, too, leaned forward, rising higher on his elbow, and began to draw rapidly on the tatami, invisible maps and maneuvers, until he came at last through the treacherous straits and rounded south along Samar toward Leyte Gulf. And with his finger on the tatami and his other hand supporting his head with the compress, he told of sighting the American ships, of opening fire, and of giving chase.

Now was the moment that Shelley knew she must ask the question she had come to ask: "Admiral Kurita," she said, "at that point, why did you turn back?"

The admiral looked puzzled and didn't answer directly, going back over the night's sail through the straits, the losses he had taken from air attack, the fact that he had been delayed.

Once more Shelley described for him the plight of Admiral Kinkaid in the gulf, his frantic maneuverings, his calls for help, the utter hopelessness of the American situation had Kurita pressed through with his attack.

The admiral watched her intently. For the first time the other side of the battle—the enemy's predicament—seemed to strike him. A look almost of shock went over his face and he repeated, half to himself, "I did not know. . . ." For a moment he was withdrawn, as though reviewing this new version of the battle.

Then he said slowly, "I did not realize I was so close to victory as you say. I had no intelligence, no air reconnaissance, practically no communications—only the knowledge I was able to acquire with my own eyes. . . ."

After a pause Shelley asked reluctantly, "Didn't you intercept a message from Admiral Kinkaid calling for help? Didn't you think it was unusual that he should send it in the clear? Didn't you realize he was desperate?"

"I heard the message," Admiral Kurita nodded, "and I did think it was unusual, very unusual, that he should send it in the clear. But I interpreted it to mean that help was coming to him very soon." He broke off and thought for a minute. "My force was scattered and I did not know what enemy ships were ahead of me or what was coming down upon me from the north. I only knew—it seemed impossible to complete my mission. The southern force was gone. So after a time, after a little while, I thought it best to reassemble and withdraw—before I should be caught between the two American forces."

He was silent, perhaps trying once again to place all those swiftly maneuvering ships in all that smoke. Then he said quite simply, "Now I can see that my decision was unfortunate, most unfortunate. But at the time, I can only say that at the time, my feeling was simply that we should pull back. . . .

"It is regrettable," he said. "Very regrettable . . . and I regret it very much. . . ."

There was nothing she could say to this and Shelley realized it was time to go. The admiral's face, which had become so animated as they talked, had changed; there was a cast of shadow over it once more. He lay back as they were leaving, hardly looking at them. He really was quite ill. Perhaps the excitement of reliving the battle had sustained him. And now that had passed.

52.

The White Mayor

Although our base was in Tokyo, much of my work took me on trips throughout Japan and on one of these I spent the night in Fukuoka in the officers' club of the local U.S. Military Government outfit. It was a Saturday and, as they did every weekend, Americans stationed out in the countryside came in to have a drink and enjoy the comradeship of fellow Americans. Such reunions were always good places for me to hear what was happening at the grass roots, though as an evening progressed and the bar boys kept the glasses filled, the stories sometimes grew so fanciful that they were not worth much as news leads in the bright light of the next day. But none could be safely ignored. And this was true of the one I heard that night about the White Mayor of Dazaifu.

A young artillery captain, somewhat drunk but still very articulate, told the story. He and his survey team had been out checking on the rice-rationing situation in his area; it never had been working too well and now he had reports of a complete breakdown. As they drove through villages, spot-checking as they went, the replies to their questions were all the same: nobody was getting enough government rice; the black market had it cornered.

Then at one village, a little place called Dazaifu, when they asked the question the answer was: "Everything's fine. No trouble at all since the White Mayor came to live with us."

Of course they asked what was meant by that but the Japanese just put their hands over their mouths as though they had already said too much. And when the survey team began to look around the town they found nobody at home of any consequence.

"By then we knew we'd find an American around there," the captain said. "The provost marshal put a watch on the town and at last they got him. He was a young kid out of Nevada, AWOL for more than a year. He wouldn't talk much, and the Japanese around Dazaifu wouldn't talk at all. But from all we could gather that kid was a hero down there—and he had more power in the whole area than General MacArthur and all the rest of us put together."

"What happened to him?" I asked. "Where is he now?"

The captain laughed. "That's what GHQ is asking us," he said. "He's gone. They had him in the Futsukaichi Stockade, getting ready to take him to Tokyo. And then the other night he disappeared—and so did the MPs' best jeep and about two hundred thousand yen out of the provost marshal's safe."

It was many months before I heard of him again. By then he had been retaken by the Army, given a general court martial and sentenced to twenty years. He was in the Eighth Army Stockade in Tokyo awaiting a review of his sentence when I first met him. The Army allowed me to see him if I promised not to write anything about him while his sentence was being re-examined. And he agreed to see me because he said the publicity might do some good. I wasn't sure what he meant by that when he said it. But as he told me his story it became clear that he meant good for the Japanese—or maybe it was for mankind.

His name was Danny Coalbrook. He was slim and tall. His eyes were startlingly blue and must have seemed unusual to the Japanese. His hair was light brown and thin and he kept it combed back tight, running a comb through it frequently as he talked and judging it by touch. His features were fine and his hands delicate. And once when he was talking about Japanese drama he mimicked several movements with the skill and feeling of a trained dancer. He spoke Japanese quite fluently, and all in all fell into that second—and by far less popular—of the two extreme groups of Americans stationed in the occupation: those who thought that nothing the Japanese did or had was any good; and the others who thought everything about them was perfect.

He was twenty-four years old when I saw him. He had been in Japan two and a half years: one of them on post, one at large, and the first half of the third—and the beginning of twenty—in prison.

The war had missed Coalbrook—that is, the part of it where you soldier. But it had provided the atmosphere of revolt and the opportunities to carry it out. Somehow as a boy he had always felt deeply for the underdog and this had often brought him into conflict with his father who owned a heavy-equipment business and believed in rugged individualism. When he finished high school the draft board classified him 4–F because of poor eyesight and the war gave him an endless choice of jobs with high wages. But he saw them as examples of exploitation rather than opportunities. He tried college, but after a couple of years a final family quarrel sent him packing.

"I'm going out where I can do some good in this world," he told his father the day he left. "I don't need you; I can make my own living."

He signed a contract with Pacific Naval Air Bases and was shipped to Barbers Point near Honolulu. He liked the people of the Pacific. "Something about them did things inside me the first time I saw them," he told me. He began an affair with a Hawaiian girl of Japanese origin. He quit Pacific Naval Air Bases and took a job as flight steward with Pan American, flying between Honolulu and Brisbane. Now he was earning $650 a month and living with his Hawaiian girl. She taught him Japanese.

The year the war ended he went home for a quick visit and was suddenly reclassified 1–A and taken into the Army. In November, 1945, PFC Danny Coalbrook, twenty-one years old, with seven thousand dollars of his own earnings in the bank, a fair knowledge of Japanese, and an urge to "do some good in the world," landed in Japan. His point of entry was Nagasaki. He was aghast at the devastation he saw there and emotionally disturbed by the poverty and pitiable conditions in which he found the Japanese living. "I don't know why it is," he said, "but I associate myself with these people, and when I saw the suffering there I resented it."

In 1946 he was working with an engineering aviation battalion, building a base near Zashonukuma. By the end of that year rotation had so depleted his company that he was taken off construction and moved into the mess as headquarters cook. He didn't like it. But in a week's time he was made acting master sergeant of the mess with one day on and three off.

As mess sergeant he had a weapons carrier at his disposal and he began to get out into the countryside and his growing knowledge of the Japanese language made his trips more and more absorbing. The Japanese liked him as easily as he liked them. They gave him melons and corn and cooked little cakes for him over smoky fires. He told them about America and about the vast farming and engineering projects he had seen and they told him about rice and rations and the trials of life. When he climbed back into his weapons carrier to return to camp there was always someone to tuck a bit of lacquerware under his arm or a melon under some rice straw on the seat beside him—"*presentos*."

Presentos in Japan are age-old and of unbreakable tradition: gifts which in due course must be replaced by gifts. As mess sergeant Danny Coalbrook had access to hoards, just the things for return *presentos*: sugar for sugar-starved children, cigarettes for a people rationed to ten a month, food in quantities for those who had never eaten its like before. Into the plentiful army larder Coalbrook reached deeper and deeper as his trips into the country created more and more friends. It was easy. He was drawing rations for between nine hundred and a thousand men and heavy rotation made departures and replacements so erratic that there was little accounting and no check.

In time Coalbrook, whose interest became increasingly rooted in the life of the nearby villages, went beyond the point of returning *presentos*. It was simply, as he put it to me, a case of the army having so much and these people so little. As his gifts grew larger, so did his stature with the Japanese. The little ones took him to see the bigger ones. He got to know the mayors and the prefectural bosses. The biggest black-market operators in the region came to meet him. They took him to parties and he spent more and more time off limits. But he turned aside all suggestions that he take part in their black-market activities. He was an idealist.

One night a small incident at the post changed this easy pattern. It was Thanksgiving eve and he was working late at night in the mess roasting forty turkeys. The battalion commander came in at that unusual hour with his Japanese secretary, Hanako-san. She was strikingly pretty. Coalbrook's senior officer asked him to broil two steaks. Coalbrook protested that it would mean taking turkeys out of the oven. They had words.

It was not really the cooking of the steaks that he resented, Coalbrook admitted, but rather his commander's attention to a Japanese girl. "Like everything else around here," he told me, "he thought that because he was an American and she was Japanese, what she had was his." In the days that followed the clash between them grew. In the end Coalbrook took Hanako-san away from his battalion commander and the battalion commander, Coalbrook says, began looking for something he could get on his mess sergeant. He would not have had to look far.

That Christmas Eve Coalbrook planned what he called "a real party" for his friends of the local village, and he invited twenty of his pals from his company to come along. "What we're going to do," he told the boys, "is share some Christmas spirit with these people." They drove out there in two weapons carriers loaded with forty cases of beer and Christmas rations for a hundred and fifty men. "They were full rations," he said, his face brightening as he recalled the night. "Everything from turkeys and cranberry sauce to the last of the fixings issued by the United States Army for a Christmas dinner."

Hanako-san had already reserved a hot-springs hotel a few miles out and a great assemblage from the village, together with the bosses of Yamaguchi prefecture, were waiting for them. "It was the best party those people ever had," Coalbrook said. "We showed them another side of the Americans."

A month later he was placed under arrest and confined to the battalion area with orders to be available for questioning on suspicion of black-marketing. His world began to tumble. "I was frightened," he said. "Two boys I knew earlier in the 32nd Division had been tried on charges like that and got ten years." That night he went AWOL.

Hanako-san took him to her home. "She comforted me. But I was in trouble and I knew it. I sent her off to get friends. She brought back a mayor and two city councilors. Americans underestimate the Japanese. They are quick to understand and fast to act, and their loyalty is beyond anything I have ever known. I didn't have to tell them much. They just knew. They brought a car and provisions. And before daylight, they had us in a mountain hideout."

Coalbrook and Hanako-san were married in a Japanese ceremony and began their new life in their isolated retreat. But ominous as was the outlook, Coalbrook would not yet fully accept his fate as irrevocable. He blindly hoped for a way out. It grew into an obsession, and one night he returned to his battalion and slipped into his old barracks after dark. They were all asleep in there but he woke two of his friends. What they whispered to him convinced him that there was no going back. He was wanted, they said, on suspicion of having taken fifty thousand dollars' worth of U.S. Army rations. The search for him was country-wide.

Coalbrook returned to his hideout and soon used up all his money. "You're a fall guy when you've broken the law," he told me there in the Eighth Army Stockade. "Once you're in trouble there seems nowhere to go but in deeper. I was broke. I borrowed money and was broke again. I had to do something, and I decided not to play around the fringes."

A couple of days later, dressed in full uniform, he went down to Sasebo, a major port on Kyushu. He talked with several of his old black-market friends and they agreed on a plan. Sasebo was the government's most important rice-collecting point for Yamaguchi prefecture. A good part of this rice, which was gathered from the farmers at government prices, simply fell into the hands of several large Japanese black-market combines. Their problem was to truck it back into the country and sell it illegally at enormous profits; without government permits their trucks could not get past the Japanese police check points. Coalbrook agreed to run a convoy through these controls. His take was 30 per cent. "It was easy," he said. "I sat in the first vehicle and simply waved the convoy of eight trucks past the Japanese guards. We were stopped only once, and when the Japanese saw my uniform they saluted and gave the signal to come on through. American military police never stop Japanese vehicles. In half a day we moved sweet potatoes from Kumamoto to Sasebo, reloaded with rice and ran it to Fukuoka. That night I went home with a million and a half yen in my pockets." A million and a half yen in those days was worth a hundred thousand dollars.

After that they decided to move. Hanako-san was sent off to choose the area. She picked the village of Dazaifu. Here they bought a house on a hill overlooking the village and Coalbrook redesigned it and carpenters were hired to rebuild it. The villagers came by twos and threes and the Coalbrooks shared their wealth and their kindness with them, and when their secret spread they knew it would be kept.

Once more during his free year Coalbrook went back to Kumamoto and moved another rice convoy to Fukuoka. Again his pay-off was more than a million yen. He had enough to live on for a long long time and now he settled down to be a big man in the village. His first community project was to pick out the two most run-down buildings on the main street of Dazaifu and persuade the owners that for civic reasons they ought to be rebuilt. He provided a plan for architectural changes and he loaned the money for the reconstruction. The village turned out and watched. And when the work was finished everybody was delighted and the town threw a party for him. The speechmakers praised his contribution to Dazaifu, but they also lamented that now they had two new shops but no merchandise to sell in them. The next day Coalbrook sent a delegation to Tokyo, well heeled with cash, to buy dry goods, kitchenware and other staples to supply both stores. These became the showplaces of the village and Coalbrook more and more the man of benevolence and judgment and action.

People came to see him—sometimes in delegations, sometimes as individuals—and sitting cross-legged on the floor and smoking his cigarettes and drinking his tea and whisky, sought his advice. The creek at the low end of town overflowed on the road each spring; Coalbrook directed a drainage project. In June every year cholera spread to Dazaifu; Coalbrook brought in DDT and gave a public lecture on wells and seepage and sickness. He showed how to cover food with screening and told the story of the fly and its dangers. He inspected latrines. And whatever he did, he did for others. He took nothing for himself. He became a living legend. Everybody talked about him. Parents and go-betweens consulted him on marriages. He was often the honor guest at birth celebrations. Family quarrels were settled in his home. Once a mother complained to him that her daughter was spending too much time with an American soldier in a neighboring village. Coalbrook went down there and had a furtive look at him and sent the girl away to her relatives.

But of all Coalbrook's accomplishments, his most noteworthy concerned the most important and most frequently discussed problem in the lives of the Japanese: the allocation of rice. "I saw the people of Dazaifu standing in line half the day in front of the rice shops and often going home empty-handed or without enough rice in their baskets to feed their families," he said. "I studied the system. And I began to see that all those SCAP announcements and all those press stories in the Japanese and American newspapers about how well the rice was being distributed were written by people who didn't know what was happening out there in the country.

"All the farmers are supposed to sell their rice to the government for rationing so that everybody can buy enough at the fixed price. But what I found was that the district bosses were getting to them first, and they paid about eighty times the government price to get it for the black market so of course the farmers went along with them. That meant everybody had to pay the markup price and even then they didn't get enough a lot of the time.

"I decided to change this in Dazaifu. First I went out into the countryside and bought ten thousand pounds of rice from the farmers so that the people could eat until I set up a new system. Then I called in the big bosses from Fukuoka and told them that they were not to buy any more rice from our area—and if they did they would never again get any help from me. They knew what that meant.

"At Dazaifu I began to explain the most important thing I had learned about a black market: a merchant who has to pay black-market prices for his food and supplies must charge black-market prices for his product. And so does the farmer. You can only break the cycle if you work out a system where everybody is sure they can buy and sell at the same fixed prices. A black market can only operate if everybody supports it; nobody really likes it except a few top bosses. So at Dazaifu I formed a committee of the best men I could find and sent them out into the country to carry the word. 'Tell the farmers,' I said, 'that the big bosses are not coming to see them any more, and now if they bring their vegetables and rice into Dazaifu instead of carting it to the big cities for a black-market deal we'll pay them fair prices and in return guarantee to supply them with anything they need at fair prices.' It took only about a week for it to begin to work. Word of it spread fast in the Dazaifu area and no one there ever had any trouble getting rice—or anything else —at a fair price."

He stopped his story here, that last day I saw him in the Tokyo stockade. "And that's it," he said, his voice suddenly becoming soft. But it wasn't that he was in any way kneeling to quarter, for after a moment's thought he added, "But whatever I did in that village, that was the best thing I ever did in my life."

They moved him to another prison soon after that, and I learned later that his sentence was cut to ten years. He must be out by now, his past forgotten in his own country, the few pages delineating his crimes buried in the enormous records of our years as occupiers of Japan. And it is unlikely that historians skipping through the tons of trivia written down as the official chronicle of those days will pause long over the exploits of a private first class who went absent without leave, played the black market and cleaned out the safe of the provost marshal who arrested him.

264

But these are not the things that are on his record in Dazaifu. There, his record is not written down on paper but rather in the hearts of the villagers who now remember the American enemy as good, only because such a bad one came to live among them.

53.

The Catfish

One night soon after I had first returned to Japan and was still living at the Tokyo Correspondents' Club, I was roused from sleep by a strange and gentle motion like that of a hammock swaying in the breeze. I had just become sufficiently awake to realize that it was perhaps an earthquake when a Japanese room boy opened my door and putting his head in called out: "*Namazu*-san." He laughed and went away.

Since you cannot always tell in Japan whether laughter comes from something funny or something tragic, I jumped out of bed and ran after him. But he disappeared. So I looked up "*namazu*" in my dictionary. "*Namazu*," it said: "catfish." The "san" made it "honorable."

Surely I had heard him wrong. He had not come to my room and opened the door in the middle of the night to shout, "Honorable catfish!"

But the next morning when I asked the headwaiter at the billet if he had felt anything unusual in the night he replied eagerly: "Earthquake!" Then he added, "But not big one. Catfish playing easily last night."

"Catfish?" I repeated. "What have catfish got to do with it?"

"In Japan," he said, pointing at his feet, "very big catfish underneath. When play—" he wiggled his hand like a swimming fish—"we have earthquake." He laughed too.

I learned later that both laughs were of the tragic kind. Everything about earthquakes in Japan from its earliest history has been tragic. And like so many other things on earth that are frightening and cannot—or at least could not—be explained, superstition has grown up around them. Some say that the islands of Japan rest upon a giant catfish, and when it moves the earth trembles and men die. In 1923, in a single quake, one hundred thousand died.

Long ago, pictures of the fish were hung in villages and posted on the walls of houses as talismen. And in out-of-the-way places, I am told, they still are. I have never seen them. But I did experience the play of the catfish, once, on a very large scale indeed, for this time—in Fukui in 1948—it brought on the most disastrous quake in Japan's last quarter-century. And I was sitting, literally, on its epicenter.

My presence there, as is so often the case when a correspondent is credited with occult powers which direct him to some great news event, was pure chance. I was planning one of my periodic journalistic jaunts out of Tokyo and Shelley suggested that I have a look at Fukui. The U.S. Military Government unit there, she said, was supposed to be one of the most successful in Japan and the city and prefecture had made noteworthy progress in recovery since the war. I marked it on my itinerary.

I had never been to Fukui before nor even heard very much about it. The city lies on the far western coast of Honshu, across from Tokyo, and it was not very often that Americans found reason to go there. So when Kay Tateishi and I wound up our jeep ride over the terrible rutted roads of the area and came into the sprawling city, we were astonished to find it so extensively rebuilt and to note the permanence of the construction which was in such contrast to the postwar shanties so common elsewhere. And even as we looked we could hear the din of building. It was this sound that rose into a resonance over the city and later so abruptly ended—to be followed by one of the strangest silences I have ever known—that is one of my sharpest memories of that day.

We arrived at noon. It was June 28, and I learned only after we got there that it was already a historic date in Fukui. For it was in that week, three years before, that the Americans fire-raided the city leaving it 97 per cent destroyed and in its ruins sixteen thousand dead. It was from these ashes that the new city had risen.

We had been billeted with the small military government unit stationed there. And having spent the afternoon seeing the phoenix-like city with its military governor, Colonel James Highland, we returned to the billet for dinner. It was a modest ferroconcrete building in the heart of the business section. We had joined a dozen or so American officers and civilian government specialists in their ground-floor mess.

All of us had finished and were sitting over our coffee. It was 5:14. Outside it was slightly overcast. Nothing else about the day or the weather was noteworthy enough to be remembered. There was no unusual wind or sound, no little warning tremors, no vague feeling of pressure which is sometimes reported by survivors of great natural disasters. The concrete floor just exploded with a brute thrust. Tables and dishes and cutlery flew into our faces and we were all hurled into a mad dance, bouncing and rebounding about like popping corn. Noises of crunching concrete and breaking timbers filled my ears. Among us all, only one found his voice, and that was for only one word. "Earthquake!" he cried, and his voice was pitched so high it was frightening.

Thick dust poured into the scene of dancing men and masonry and tables and pillars and walls. Everybody was trying to go somewhere. But it was like trying to run on a savagely flapping conveyor belt which was furiously changing directions. A few made for the low, open windows. But the sills were in such turbulent spasms that no one, I think, got out. The rest of us directed ourselves toward the one open doorway, falling over each other, leaping up and down, heading one way and being thrown another. When at last I got near the doorway and there was an opening in the struggling mass of men around me, I hurled myself at it. But the floor shifted, and instead of going out I smashed into the crumbling wall a yard farther along. Finally I made it, running madly from the building as pieces of it crashed to the ground near me.

I reached the open lawn. It was split into great fissures, opening and closing as the ground heaved. Scores of others, Japanese and Americans, were gathering there, all trying to stand or sit against the paroxysms of the earth. I tried to fling myself upon the ground as one does in combat, but it rose and threw me off. Then, abruptly, the frenzied eruptions stopped, and for a moment the earth just trembled gently and we all stood still. A great silence fell over the city. Perhaps it was for seconds. I remember it was unnaturally prolonged, an eerie quiet—the strained, unearthly kind that makes you feel something on the back of your neck. At last voices began to rise, the immediate little exclamations near us, and then the build-up of cries of grief and pain and prayer and fright. All over the city they rose until they reverberated like the continuing din that rings in your ears after the nearby blast of a high-explosive shell.

Where was Kay Tateishi? I saw him coming. He was one of the last to leave the building. This was because he had been trained never to leave a building during an earthquake but to get under a table or next to a support. He was panting when he reached me. "The tables wouldn't stay down and the pillars threw me off, so I made a run for it," he said, a little smile of disbelief mingled with the surprise and terror in his face.

More and more Japanese were coming into the American encampment. Many of them were injured, some making their own way and others being carried. The violence had begun again and those trying to reach the lawn area struggled unsteadily against the turbulence. A U.S. Army aid station was beginning to operate.

I went back into the building after my cameras. It began to rock and thump violently. Voices called warnings at me. I stood there feeling indecisive and alone. The convulsions lessened. I went on again. I was walking ankle-deep in white foam. The fire extinguishers had been thrown about and had released themselves. The stairs were askew. I ran up them. They too were covered with foam. I located the room where I had put my gear. At first I couldn't find my equipment. The bed, which had been near the door, was now across the room. It had collapsed. And the bookcases had been thrown about wildly and had spilled their books over the floor. Under a heap of them I found my cameras.

I raced down the hallway and gingerly climbed out the front window onto the porch roof to make an over-all picture of the city. When I got there I was astonished to see the great seven-story concrete Daiwa department store across the street collapsing slowly. Jets of dust were bursting from it. And elsewhere, as far as I could see, the town was knocked down and a brown dust rising.

Something froze my attention. Here and there, each way I turned, I saw thin gray wisps of smoke trailing up and bending into the dusty sky. I knew at once what they were. I was looking at the beginnings of the second stage of a Japanese earthquake. At the bottom of each thin gray column was a *hichirin*, a Japanese clay charcoal cooker. The quake had struck at dinnertime and all of them would be filled with burning charcoal. The houses had fallen upon them. All over the city fires were starting.

I ran back to the stairs and out. Kay was there, anxious and waiting. He too had seen the smoke tails and pointed at them. "Let's work while we can," he said. And we started at a run, I shouting film numbers and he scribbling notes against each as I shot.

Outside the compound people were running down the street in both directions, all of them, it seemed, looking over their shoulders at the horror behind them, not realizing that it also lay ahead. The roads were split into gaping fissures, some large enough to swallow a man, and every house was down. Now the red and yellow clusters of flames were beginning to sprout, but no one was fighting the flames. There was no water, and it was all so hopeless. Some sat in the ruins hardly moving and without looking; some crawled timidly into their collapsed homes to save things, often trivial things. One family doggedly carried watermelons from their broken house and laid them carefully in a row on the street. Others worked bravely and frantically to save someone trapped in the ruins. And all the while new paroxysms shook the ruins, frightening the rescuers and sometimes trapping them too.

It was the trapped who knew the full horror of that quake, and it was they whom I cannot forget. More than three thousand people died that day and most of them were burned to death, pinned in their homes by fallen roofs and timbers while rescuers worked frantically with bare hands to free them and their friends and families ran screaming, begging for a saw, an ax—just anything to cut them free—until the fires grew and spread and finally caught them.

Only once that day did we see an adequate rescue tool. We were photographing a flaming house when suddenly a man brushed by us carrying a saw. He disappeared into the smoke. Others followed him and we ran in too, and found a young man in there, lying on his back. He was pinned by one arm under the whole weight of the tumbled building. There was no choice, no hesitation, and no talk. The rescuers without a word sawed off the arm. Then, lifting him between them, they carried him out. And as they did he exclaimed to them repeatedly: "*Arigato. Arigato.* Thank you." I photographed him as they passed, and unaccountably he smiled and thanked me too.

By dusk a scorching wind was sweeping the fires toward us in a great semicircle and everyone was running for the old castle. Only within its moat, people called out, would there be safety. And there, amid the ruins of sixteenth-century Japan, we all crowded together, Americans and Japanese, looking out from the ancient battlements at the burning town. Some of the huge granite blocks of the old moat wall had tumbled down, and this disturbed many of the Japanese. "It is a bad omen," one of them said. "This city has burned down many times and we have had many earthquakes here. But never before have these big stones fallen into the moat."

"Perhaps it is because the town was rebuilt too fast," another added. "There is an old legend, you know, that a town built too fast will also be destroyed fast."

Almost all the fires had burned themselves out when daylight came. Already survivors were beginning to stream out over the hot roads toward the gray patches where their homes had stood. We were taking pictures of the injured being brought to a collecting point when we saw the young man who had lost his arm.

I was surprised at how comfortable he appeared and in what good spirits. And it seemed incredible that after such a brief and tragic meeting the day before he would recognize us. But he did. And when we knelt beside him I saw that he was pointing with his one hand at the ground.

"Last night," he said to Kay, "the catfish was certainly playing." He was laughing when he said it. But by then, of course, I knew what kind of laugh it was.

54.

Colonel Ishiyama's Family

One day near the end of 1948, Seth, now a household sentinel and a carrier of news from staff to family—and no doubt from family to staff—came to me with an observation which at his age was intensely absorbing. "Aiko-san," he said, his voice and manner underscoring the astonishing development, "is crying."

He found her for me, sliding open the panel door of the tearoom and pointing and exclaiming, "There!" Aiko rose from the tatami where she had been sitting, surprised and embarrassed.

"What is it, Aiko-san?" I asked. She shook her head, weeping anew, and we all sat cross-legged on the floor, Seth and I waiting a long time before she answered. But at last she told us with one word. "Papa," she said tearfully.

Shelley and I had by then learned a good deal about Aiko's family, and through the particulars of their history we gained a more intimate understanding of the tragic anxiety which was then a factor in the Japanese mood those years immediately following the surrender, where scarcely a family survived that did not daily search and hope and wait for husband, son or brother swallowed without trace by the war, or reported vaguely in some faraway prison.

In Aiko's immediate family there were two who did not come home: her father, a regimental infantry colonel, and her brother Kazuo, the family first-born, an army lieutenant.

Aiko's father, Torao Ishiyama, was a professional soldier, a graduate of Japan's military academy, who took his family with him from garrison town to garrison town, sometimes in Japan, more often in Korea and Manchuria. During this itinerant army life his family grew, two more daughters following Aiko and then a second son.

Her father, Aiko remembers, was not always honored by his command because he was proud and defiant toward those above him and unusually considerate to the ranks. He was, as a consequence, the slowest of his academy class to be advanced and earned the affectionate nickname among the men of "*kokuto hin*," the antique officer.

When the war in the Pacific started Colonel Ishiyama was moved from Korea to Manchuria and his family joined him there, being quartered in the great garrison town of Kiamusze. But after our landings on Luzon the colonel's regiment was hastily shipped to the Philippines to augment the crumbling Japanese defenses and there was no word from him after that.

Surrender came, and during those days of terror Mrs. Ishiyama fled south with her children to Korea, blackening her daughters' teeth and dressing the girls as unattractively as possible when the Russians swirled around them. They were stopped at Pyongyang, and there they stayed for ten months waiting for permission to return to Japan. They waited also, day after day, for news of father or brother. But there were only reports that the battle for the Philippines had been a bloody one and that there were very few survivors.

In June, 1946, they at last had orders from the Russians to move south. There was no transportation so Mrs. Ishiyama took her family on foot. They walked for three days and two nights until they reached the Thirty-eighth Parallel and crossed over. There the Americans gave them transportation to Inchon and put them aboard a ship to Japan.

In Japan they called upon their next of kin to help them; Mrs. Ishiyama's youngest brother, himself hard-hit by war, built them a tiny house near his own in a Tokyo suburb and there the three youngest went back to school while Mrs. Ishiyama worked at odd jobs to support them—sewing, mending, selling thread—and Aiko came to us as nursemaid.

It was still another year before they had any news of Colonel Ishiyama. And when it finally came it was nearly as ominous as the long silence. His regiment, which had not gotten beyond Formosa, had surrendered to the Chinese and now, somewhere in a China prison, Colonel Ishiyama was awaiting trial as a war criminal.

In time, Aiko's mother had a message from him. He was being held in Nanking, charged with the burning of a Chinese village. But the entire accusation was an error. Neither the colonel nor his regiment had ever been in that part of China. He wrote to his wife to do her utmost to find official documents that would prove it; they would be in the Ministry of War in Tokyo. On her success his life depended.

But the Japanese War Ministry was by then defunct. And the few dispirited guardians who were left in charge of what remained of the files could not cope with the task of locating records and witnesses. Mrs. Ishiyama worked desperately but unavailingly against this inertia. In those years of anguish, who cared for the anguish of one woman? A second letter came from her husband. He had received no papers, he wrote, and that week his trial was scheduled to begin. Without the papers he would be condemned.

That was the day that Seth found Aiko crying. We waited, sitting in the tearoom, until she could begin to talk. And at last, trembling with reluctance, she told me for the first time the full story of her father.

We drove at once to Aiko's home and got her mother and took her to the War Ministry building for a last desperate try. And by that night, goaded by urgency and the importance of an American uniform, whose correspondent's patch was not in-

telligible to the Japanese, the guardians found the needed papers.
I sent them at once to China by the first courier I could find.
Next day the courier put them into the hands of Frederick
Gruin, *Time*'s correspondent in Nanking. And Gruin that very
day delivered them himself to Colonel Ishiyama in prison.

In a week's time I had a message that Colonel Torao Ishiyama
had been tried and found innocent of all charges.

After that I often asked Aiko when her father was coming
home and she would always laugh and say "soon." But as
months went on the laughter died. For China was at war again
and the Communists were pushing steadily down from the north.
One day a major Chinese Communist victory above Nanking
was announced and the press was already speculating upon the
fall of the great city itself. I asked Aiko for news of her father.
"Papa," she said anxiously, "has been moved to a prison somewhere in Shanghai. But even though he has been tried and
cleared, he can't get transportation home. And if the Communists take China he may never get out."

At that moment a series of odd coincidences began: Nora
Waln, Quaker, writer, and good friend of ours, happened to
stop by. And when she heard our problem she suggested that
the Friends Society in Shanghai might help us. She wrote a
letter to a Japanese Quaker there named Saburo Yamanouchi.
At once I drove down to my office to find a courier, and there
a cable from New York awaited me: "In view of the situation
in China," it read, "think you ought to go there and reinforce
our coverage." I left next day.

When I got to Shanghai I went straight to the Friends' Center
and there the first person that I spoke to was Mr. Yamanouchi,
standing in the hallway almost as though he might have been
waiting for me. I gave him Nora's letter. "Ah," he said, "I do
not know Colonel Ishiyama. But if he is in Shanghai he will be
in the Second Prison Camp in Kiangwan. It just happens that
I am going there today."

As a Quaker he was permitted to enter the prison. He would
be glad to take me along, but I would need a pass. I could get
this at the Chinese Ministry of Information and at noontime he
would come and fetch me there.

At noon I waited, pass in hand, when suddenly Mr. Yamanouchi came toward me almost at a run. Behind him came a Japanese officer in a faded army uniform and on his face a look of some bewilderment.

"Here!" cried Mr. Yamanouchi, laughing. "We need not make the trip. Here is Colonel Ishiyama."

"How could it be?" I asked him, puzzled. "Where did you find him?"

Mr. Yamanouchi was delighted with my surprise. "It was so very easy," he explained. "I had to go to the old Japanese Association building for a moment on business, and there I saw this man. So I said to him: 'Are you Colonel Torao Ishiyama?' and he said, 'It is so. I am Colonel Torao Ishiyama.' And I said, 'But I thought you were in the Kiangwan Prison.' And he said, 'I am in the Kiangwan Prison, but today I have been sent to Shanghai on a pass to buy things needed for some prisoners who are to be sent to Japan this week.'"

I turned to Colonel Ishiyama. He seemed to me to be a man of dignity and humor but he was faded now, like his uniform, the sharp structure of his brows and slanted cheekbones somehow softened by years of imprisonment. "And are you to be sent back?" I asked him. "Is his repatriation really going through?" I repeated to Mr. Yamanouchi.

The colonel shrugged in reply, and though I could not understand all of his soft answer, I read its meaning easily: "Who knows? Perhaps, perhaps not." And Mr. Yamanouchi translated: "It is just a rumor."

I took from my pocket a picture of Aiko-san and gave it to the colonel. He held it for a moment, and then he sat down on a bench and stared at it and then at me in a way I shall not forget. He arose, and for a while Yamanouchi translated and I answered a stream of questions. About his son, had there been news of him? I shook my head and he nodded his understanding; about his family; about his home. Then his face became severe. "Aiko's manners," he asked, "are they proper? Does she do all that is asked of her in your family?" I reassured him: Aiko was a daughter he could be proud of. With that deep look he bowed to me, and then we parted.

Late that day, after Colonel Ishiyama had faithfully taken himself back to prison, the Chinese Ministry of Information found out for me the facts about the repatriation. There were a few Japanese prisoners of war who were scheduled to sail for home on a Chinese repatriation ship, the *Hai Liao*, but there were only twenty-six of them and Colonel Ishiyama's name was not among them.

"Maybe, though," said the Ministry of Information with fine Chinese logic, "there could be twenty-seven instead of twenty-six and your Colonel Ishiyama might be the twenty-seventh. The *Hai Liao* sails at nine o'clock tomorrow. You come there and perhaps you will see Colonel Ishiyama."

I was scheduled to leave for Tsingtao the next day and made a late and hasty visit to the port area—in time to see the stained and aging *Hai Liao* pulling away from the dock. She had brought reparations war matériel from Japan to China and now, rather than return empty, was repatriating twenty-six or twenty-seven Japanese POWs. I hoped it was twenty-seven. And it was. For standing in the rusty waist-deck of the ship was a gathering of Japanese prisoners, and one of them was waving at me. It was Aiko's father.

One last fateful experience awaited him on his journey home, I was to learn later. When he arrived at Maizuru, that port of entry through which repatriated Japanese stepped first upon their homeland, Colonel Ishiyama saw his eldest son rushing toward him through the crowds on the dock. "How good of you to come all this way to meet me," he cried as they threw themselves at each other. "How did you know I was arriving?"

"But I didn't know you were arriving," cried Kazuo. "I thought you had come down to meet *me*. I have been a prisoner in the northern Urals for almost three years. Only now, at this moment, have I arrived in Japan."

It has been years since we've seen Aiko. She is married now and has a family of her own with a son and a daughter spaced two years apart, like ours she used to care for. And Torao Ishiyama has at last come to rest in a small village near Tachikawa where he is again the center of his family and runs a little rice-wine and soy-sauce shop which is now a crossroads and often a guest house for a stream of men who once served under their beloved "*kokuto-hin*."

PART VII

55.

The Chinese Choice

When I returned to China that winter of 1948, the Communist forces had already encircled Peking and were ranging well south of the ancient capital. On the Shantung Peninsula they had formed a great arc around the old treaty port of Tsingtao and were closing in to take it with its formidable naval base so strategically placed midway between Shanghai and Mukden. Here, since 1945, when the Japanese surrendered its modern docks and installations, the United States had maintained its Western Pacific fleet. But now, unless we too were to become involved in the war in China, the time had come for us also to give up the facilities. The order to withdraw came Thanksgiving week.

I was staying at a little Dutch-owned hotel which stood just above the harbor. Its proprietors had already gone and most of the Chinese staff had disappeared after them. The dining room was closed and the stoves in the rooms were no longer fired and we all gathered in the dark lobby to eat and to share the only source of heat in the hotel, an old Dutch stove which we stoked with coal ourselves.

Very few guests remained, and the half-dozen or so I joined round the stove in the lobby that morning might have been the last of them. They were all missionaries and they had lived and worked in China most of their adult lives. In the past few days they had come by ricksha and on foot from the interior, and now they were on their way out.

We were waiting for breakfast and we all sat idle and silent gazing out the windows at the frost-covered roofs below us that slanted down the hill to the harbor. At the end of the slope were the waiting ships that would take us away, and beyond just a few miles off, was a fringe of islands. These—although it seemed incredible—were already in the hands of the Communists.

Behind me someone spoke and I turned back into the dark room. An old man in a long Chinese gown sat swaying slowly in an old rocking chair. "Well, it's all over," he said. He brightened a little when he saw he had my attention. "Not much more we can do," he added. Then he leaned forward as though to confide in me. "You know," he said, "two weeks ago a Chinese soldier came into the mission compound and lived with us for a few days. He was the son of our wash amah. We've known him since he was a boy. A Christian. The last year or two he's been a radio technician with the Chiang Kai-shek forces. One day he said to us, 'What am I? I am like all the other Nationalist soldiers. I have three choices. I can desert and try to flee south with my family. I can remain here and wait for the Communists to come and shoot me. I can travel north now and join them; and when they come in my family will be protected and cared for.' The day we all left for Tsingtao he brought us food for our journey—and then he went north to join the Communists." He sat nodding at me for emphasis, and then he added: "It wasn't much of a choice—under the circumstances."

General Robert Soule, whom I had known as a colonel when he led the attack which liberated the Los Banos prison camp in the Philippines, was now the military attaché with our embassy in Nanking. He had on his wall a great map of northern China marked with the fighting fronts and the units engaged, and that day when I visited him I began to copy onto my own map such information from his as might serve me when I went forward.

The general stopped me. "If you're going up there," he said, "don't count too much on what you see here." He waved vaguely at his map. "We keep marking it up but almost all our reports are from Chinese sources and very few of them are dependable now. These positions," he said, running his finger along a crayon line, "are shown here as unbroken defenses. But they're not that at all. There is no line. Just units, mostly independent of each other, and we're never sure they're where they say they are—or even whose side they're going to be on next."

I had never before known a military campaign like the one I found in the vast wheatlands of Anhwei which stretched out from Pengpu. General Soule had prepared me to expect no line, but my earlier experiences in military engagements had fixed my thinking and I had, in fact, continued vaguely to visualize one— though broken. Instead I found the defending troops rolled into small, independent forces, dug in here or coming to rest there, or moving on again, out of communication with their command, bumping into friendly units or the enemy and bouncing off again as aimlessly as amoebas in a puddle.

Somewhere on those great prairies the evacuated Süchow garrison, clumped with forces representing three separate army groups, was encircled and reportedly fighting its way south toward still another army group, the Twelfth, which had come out of Hankow in support of the besieged garrison and was itself encircled. Small remnants of these groups, together with various other units in the area, confused and increasingly dispirited by rumors of defeat, were the amoebas.

Into these we drove, my young interpreter, Li, and I, twenty miles north of Pengpu. We had been carried to the end of the line at Chao Pai Chia in an armored train, our party increased by one, an English-speaking major who had been sent by headquarters to help us with our mission and who was eager to accommodate us when we told him that our goal was an area of combat. He persuaded the railroad command to provide us with a truck and driver and we headed out through the wheat stumps, across the roadless flatlands.

A smoke-smudged horizon bent round us and out there somewhere heavy guns thudded and soon we began to pass villages where there had been action. The villages were all small ones, rising like tiny atolls in an ocean of stubble, most of them completely destroyed by flame and shell, their bleak adobe-mud huts tumbled and scattered about.

Those villages which were not destroyed were full of troops and around each was a circle of spider holes, dug deep in the Japanese fashion. As we approached, a soldier standing up to his chest in a hole would challenge us, and then we would be passed into the hamlet. Late in the day we entered a large one. It was crowded with soldiers, some of them busily extending a network of trenches which wound through the thin alleys and under the houses. Every hut was packed with troops, and against the adobe walls rough lean-tos made of kaoliang reeds sheltered more men huddled in the cold.

Only a few villagers remained, running at the call of each imperative military voice, their houses commandeered, their heaps of straw being chewed away by the artillery horses, and their rice and vegetables and whatever livestock they had left disappearing into the cooking pots which boiled and simmered wherever rifles were stacked and men squatted in the heat of the smoky fires.

The village had changed hands a couple of times in the course of that strange warfare, and the experience had left its mark on the few survivors we found there. "Who is better?" Li asked one of them, "the Nationalists or the Communists?"

"Both are good," the farmer answered quickly. "Only the people are bad."

When we were introduced to the commanding general and had photographed him, I asked if we could remain for a few days and cover his troops in whatever action might develop. He was an expansive man and he threw out his arm in a great arc as he invited us to share his hospitality. And I began at once to document the scene of the encampment in pictures as a prelude to what might later follow.

After a while, though, the major, coming out of the headquarters hut, motioned me to join him and we walked over to Li.

"Now we must go," he said when we were all together.

"Go where?" I asked quickly.

"Go back to the railroad," he answered. "The truck is waiting for us."

"But we're not going back now," I said in some astonishment. "The whole point of our coming here was to see some action. The general has invited us to stay as long as we want."

Li stood silent and the major shook his head. "The general misunderstood you and now we must go," he said. "This is a poor village. There is no place for you to sleep and the food is very bad. It is better for you to go back to Pengpu."

"But we're here to cover a war," I protested. "I don't care about the facilities! Let's talk to the general again."

"If we don't go now," he replied earnestly, "we'll miss the train, and no one knows when the next one will run."

"But I don't want to go!" I exclaimed. I was annoyed.

"Please," he pleaded. "We must go. We cannot stay."

I persisted. "But why?"

"Because," he answered slowly, and now plainly in anguish, "this general . . . these troops. Today they are Nationalist. But what they will be tonight or tomorrow . . . I cannot promise."

I made a show after that of taking a few more pictures. But sometime before dusk we were back in the truck, rolling toward the railhead.

56.

The Ferry to Hong Kong

As China continued to shrink before the Communist forces, the government withdrew from Nanking and moved south. And the foreign embassies and consulates followed them, carting their desks and papers and their emblems of state eight hundred miles to Canton. It was as far as they could go and maintain their vital communications and supplies from the West, but it was an ironic choice for them. For Canton was the first Chinese port ever opened to foreigners, and here, in the end, they all gathered again to watch the death of that fabulous foreign China they had helped create.

Nearby was Hong Kong, tiny jeweled island off the China Coast, symbol of British glory and the strength of the West. For years its expansive trade and the awe which its military power inspired were reflected on the great city of Canton. Now the tide was turning and the roles reversing. I felt it at once when, after following the government to Canton, I sailed down the Pearl River to Hong Kong.

It was Saturday night and the visitors to the mainland of China had finished with their parties at the Peninsula Hotel, their family reunions in the New Territories, their movies in the neon-lighted theaters of the glistening and modern China coastal port, and were returning to their homes across the bay on the hills of Hong Kong. The ferry crowd was large and predominantly Chinese. Some were coolies, clerks and shopkeepers, but most, on this weekend night, were China Coast upper class, lavishly clothed in Western evening dresses and dinner jackets or tweedy in Chinese-tailored British cuts, bilingual in Chinese and British-English. Sprinkled in smaller number were the British: men and women who could be distinguished from the well-dressed Chinese only by their more constrained manner and their Western faces. Such was the effect of a century of British Crown Colony rule.

There was pressure at the cashier's window as the last-minute rush to catch the ferry sent people fumbling their coins onto the payment counter and forced them to wiggle jerkily through the highly polished brass turnstiles. In his cage the unblinking cashier made change like a machine and kept his foot poised on the brake that could freeze the turnstile against anyone guilty of short payment.

The barefoot newsboys were hawking the latest edition in an

English screech: "Red Chinese Forces Mass Near New Territories Frontier!" A sturdy Chinese, a young man with a brown
face and a well-cut caramel-colored Harris tweed jacket, stopped
impatiently to buy and glance at the headlines. Then he dashed
into line, slipped a coin along the cashier's counter and pushed
against the turnstile. He was stopped abruptly as the cashier's
foot touched the brake. The brass bar smacked into his stomach
and he grunted and his face grew red.

The cashier, a Eurasian wearing the uniform of the British
ferry company, waited impassively for the additional coin. Still
red with anger and hurt pride the little man threw down another
ten-cent piece, bouncing it on the counter, and again thrust himself at the turnstile. The face of the cashier did not change but
his foot was slow to release the brake. The Chinese turned and
yelled at him: "You've got your money," he shouted. "What are
you sitting there for?" Holding the bar in his hands he rattled
it hard. "Dirty British bastard!"

The line of hurrying passengers backed up behind him and
the curious who had already been admitted gathered at the other
side of the brass rail. Aware of what he had said, the dapper
little Chinese said it again. "Dirty British bastard! Let me
through."

A ruddy, heavily built Englishman, wearing the ferry company
uniform with the gold-embroidered crown of British authority
on his cap, pushed through the crowd. He reached over resolutely and grasped the Chinese by the arm, turning him half
around.

"Come along. Get along out of here," he commanded. "We
can't have that kind of language on this ferry."

The Chinese swung about and seized the wrists of the Englishman who was holding him. "Put me off, then," he challenged in a
high voice, his face a foot below the Englishman's. "Put me off."

For another moment they stood holding each other and then
the official released his grip on the Chinese. But the Chinese
still held on. Nearby was a British major and gathered in the
crowd were also several soldiers and sailors in British uniforms.
The ferry official, his face beet-red, looked about. No one said
anything. There were no gestures of help. Then he lowered his

voice a notch: "I shall let you through this time. But mind you don't use such language here again."

The Chinese held fast to the official's wrists. "I'll mind nothing," he shrilled. "Put me off."

"Come, come," urged the Englishman. "We can't have a scene here."

"Put me off," the Chinese challenged again, his jaw out and his lips quivering. It was a threat directed at the Englishman but it was made for the benefit of the crowd.

The official signaled the cashier to release the turnstile and the Chinese, dropping the official's wrists, walked through. The official followed him. So did the crowd. The midnight ferry was still waiting—waiting for the official's signal to depart. The Englishman walked with the Chinese. "I shan't hold you this time," he said in an official voice, "but let this be a warning. No more such talk on ferry property."

Still keeping his face ugly the Chinese pulled from his tweed coat pocket the newspaper he had just bought and flipped it open in front of the official. He flashed the headlines under the golden crown and, turning it so that all could see, he shouted, "Your warnings are nothing but a death rattle." Then he walked toward the ferry followed by the crowd.

He was watching from the ferry railing, newspaper under his arm and an unpleasant smile on his face, when the ferry official signaled the craft to cast off.

57.

The Net

"At night," it was a French saying, "Indo-China belongs to the Viet Minh."

The French political adviser who shared my flight between
Hanoi and Saigon, that day I entered what was then Indo-China,
said that to me with a frown. And I accepted it as one of those
piquant exaggerations made to newcomers. It was the spring of
1950. Red armies had swept China to her final borders and
Communist strength was growing in all Asia. But it seemed incredible that the French could not keep control within the European settlements of their own colony.

That, however, I was to learn at once, was the case. For when
we came into the Saigon airport a few miles from the French
capital—and military headquarters—French officials rushed us
from the plane directly into waiting cars. "There is no time for
customs," they explained. "It is late and you must join the military convoy into the city. After dark the Viet Minh will take
over all the roads."

On the Saigon River in the heart of the colonial city, a few
blocks from my luxurious French hotel, lay two American destroyers, the *Stickell* and the *Anderson*. They had been sent to
Saigon as a display of our solidarity with the French and to
show their flags for the thirty miles of winding waterway that
led up from the sea and then to lie among the French warships
moored in impressive strength upon the coffee-colored river. To
celebrate this show of our allegiance, Admiral Russell Berkey,
senior American naval officer in the Far East, had flown from
Tokyo and there were fifteen-gun salutes and military parades,
colorful garden parties and formal dinners.

But late that night heavy mortar shells began to fall among
the ships. In the darkness I ran down to the Bund and found
the river front, where the polished review had been held a few
hours earlier, a scene of war with soldiers and sailors taking
cover near the docks and the gun crews on the ships alerted to
return the fire. But they never did. "How *can* we fire?" exclaimed
the French port commander who had rushed over to apologize
to the American destroyer commanders. "Here, at night, we are
just sitting ducks. We cannot shoot back. If we do we would just
kill the innocent; the Viet Minh are already gone."

Next morning at the hotel I shared a breakfast table with a
French businessman. I asked him how it could be that the Viet

Minh could move through the city—even lug and fire eighty-one-millimeter mortars—without detection. "Surely, somebody must see them!" I said.

A waiter was at that moment at our table and my companion kept silent until he had gone. Then he said in a low tone, "What can we do? That boy who has been serving us might very well have been shooting those guns last night. Maybe he wanted to and maybe he was ordered to. In either case it would mean death for anyone to tell us about it."

Wilson Fielder, a *Time* correspondent, had come to Saigon at the same time as I and we worked together. He had been born in China and he loved the country and its people. And it was he, using influence and charm, who managed permission, in strict military secrecy, for our story on the Plaine-des-Joncs. This was a vast region of marshes extending westward from Saigon almost to the Cambodian border. Its malarial swampland, cut and recut by rivers and streams and impassable to wheeled and land-tracked equipment, sheltered the most powerful Viet Minh force in the south. Attacks against them had been made in the past but they had accomplished very little. Now the French command was determined to clean them out, once and for all.

The operation was to be a co-ordinated infantry, naval and air sweep around the entire infested region. "A great roundup," the briefing officer told Wilson and me, sweeping a circle with his arm, "and the pulling of the drawstring when we have them in the net."

We flew from a base in the Saigon River in a small pontoon plane which the French called a sea otter. As we rose above it the Plaine-des-Joncs looked more like an ocean with patches of grass and jungle floating upon it than land with lakes and rivers. But the illusion vanished as we flew westward, for now a great grassland spread below us. And around it in a giant circle curved a broad band of blue smoke. The operation had begun; the troops, and craft upon the rivers, were sweeping the area with fire.

"The net," our pilot yelled at us above the roar of the engine. "It is being laid."

288

Seventy miles from takeoff he put us down on one of the principal waterways of the marsh, a sluggish winding river called the Cai Rung. A fleet of French vessels waited there, filling the river from bank to bank and disappearing with it as it curved into the jungle. They were mostly of American origin: LSTs, LCIs and nests of smaller landing craft. Both sides of the river were thick with bivouacs of Legionnaires and African Goumiers, who lived largely off the land and looked it.

At the end of the day, as I wandered among them taking pictures, the scene struck me as something remembered from a painting, or perhaps a poem, of ancient times, with campfires glowing and men sharpening their weapons by the light of them while others, the Moslems, turned toward Mecca in prayer, the night before the battle.

In dawn darkness we began to move, some of the troops fanning out across the marshlands and the rest of us loading into the vessels. When the light came we were all under way. From time to time some of the craft turned into smaller streams and the jungle growth thickened and the chatter of birds and monkeys grew very loud. Now and again we heard a single rifle shot. "Viet Minh," the commander of our LCI muttered, raising his eyebrows. "Signals that we are coming," he said in disappointment.

Twenty miles up the river Wilson and I went ashore with a unit of the Goumiers led by a French captain. For hours we walked with them through the marshes and along the dikes, keeping our voices low while the pointmen out in front advanced with caution. "Soon, very soon," the captain told us, "the Viet Minh will be squeezed and we will have a fight."

The houses we passed were of reeds and leaves, built high upon skinny poles. They were empty of people, but chickens and pigs scratched and rooted under them and in some the cooking fires still smoldered. The Goumiers gave them all a cursory search, and when they decided that they had harbored Viet Minh they put the torch to them. Behind us our march was marked with trails of smoke.

At midafternoon a pointman came running back to the captain. The head of the column had exchanged signals with the

Legionnaires. We quickened our pace to make the contact for this meant the closing of the net. Overhead, French fighters crisscrossed the air, providing reconnaissance and communications for our converging forces. We could hear shooting in the distance.

When we sighted the advance men of the Legionnaires they called out to us: "The Viet Minh! Have you seen them?" And our men called back: "The Viet Minh! Where are they?" And the men shrugged back and forth and grumbled to each other.

We joined forces and went on together, side by side, tightening our circle as we pushed in toward the center of the ring. Late in the day we passed a headquarters unit of the Legionnaires at rest by the trail, some beginning to set up a bivouac for the night. Our captain stopped and talked with their officers. Then he waved to us and started off again, leading his little column into an overgrown rubber plantation. When we caught up with him he gave us a peculiarly French look of gloom.

"The mission is accomplished," he said. "The drawstring has been pulled. *Alors!*" And he waved his hand, pointing through the rubber trees.

We looked. Standing in a circle of misery and fright was a little group of Vietnamese: six women and a dozen children.

As we walked up to them the captain pointed again at the cowering group. "*Victoire magnifique!*" he cried with bitterness.

"But these . . . !" Wilson exclaimed.

"These," the captain mocked. "The splendid victory. As always, the army of the Viet Minh caught in our net!"

58.

The Caldron

Once, in Korea, during a roundup of political suspects, I saw a woman in a circle of others waiting her turn to be questioned by the police. She knelt on carefully placed sharp-edged rocks and her hands were folded over her head. Her child crawled beside her, crying and begging and trying again and again to reach her breast, but she dared not lower her arms to help him. And when at last I could no longer restrain myself and lifted the little boy to nurse she could not bring herself to look at me, or at him. For what kind of evil trick was this in this compassionless world?

It is in scenes like this that I remember Korea.

History calls the Koreans a gentle people and their domain "the land of the morning calm." But by the time I got there, soon after the end of the Japanese war, both had changed, perhaps for the same reason: the brutalities of invading armies had over the ages left their mark upon the soul of the country.

In my first hour there, as I drove from the Seoul airfield to the city, I passed a crowd shouting and jeering in front of a police way station. I went in to learn the cause and there on the floor, back-lighted from a barred window, was a ribbon of glistening black moving snakelike toward the threshold where I stopped. Then, at its source, I saw the bodies of three men just shot. "Bad men. Very bad men," I heard a voice explain.

And in my last hour there, as I waited for the jeep which was to take me to a plane to carry me away, I saw a Korean army trailer with bodies of civilians heaped in it, the Western-shod foot of one of them jutting over the edge. A group of Korean soldiers lounged beside it. One of them was talking and, having mechanically tapped a cigarette and put it between his lips, he reached out with equal preoccupation and scratched a match on the sole of the projecting foot—without interrupting his story or distracting his companions.

Two years after my first visit to Korea and almost two years before the Korean War broke out, I went there from Tokyo to photograph an insurrection in the south. It was October, 1948. Our army of occupation was gradually being reduced and sent home, our bases closed or turned over to the Korean government, and an American military advisory group was in the early stages of organizing a South Korean Army as a counterforce to the one in the north that had been trained and equipped by the Russians.

The revolt began when a small Communist cell in a Korean Army regiment stationed at the southern tip of the peninsula killed their officers in the night and roused the local citizens to riot against the politicians and police who had oppressed them for so long. It was a purely local movement, brutal and bloody while it lasted, but soon put down.

Four days later when I entered the town with three other correspondents we found the entire population gathered on the playing fields behind the school. Here the loyalist army who had suppressed the insurrection were retaliating for the cruelties of the rebels with the same brutality and disregard for justice. In little groups scattered over the grounds, soldiers and police with rifle butts and clubs were extracting confessions from kneeling men.

One of the survivors from the police force, rifle slung from his shoulder and wearing a Japanese helmet, performed a fantastic jig around his victim, alternately smashing the man's face with his rifle stock and butting it, animal fashion, with his helmeted head until the man fell prostrate and was revived and at last "confessed." Then he, like all the others who succumbed, was led off to a ditch beyond the field and there destroyed by rifle fire—without a record of his name, his crime, or who had questioned or dispatched him.

Meanwhile, the women and children watched. And of it all, for me the most terrible part of the ordeal was the silence of those watchers and the restraint shown by the men themselves who knelt before their captors—and their utter silence as they were led off to be shot. Never a word of protest, never a scream for pity, never a murmur for God's help. Again, the centuries were upon them; what good would it do?

These uprisings in Yosu and Sunchon made it clear that the country was divided by more than an arbitrary parallel. There was a hatred in the land, of Korean for his brother, that lay beneath the surface, seething, and erupting now and again in bouts of slaughter like the ones we had witnessed. In the months that followed the boiling tempo quickened and there were many violent clashes, especially along the line of separation. And in the north the Communists kept watching, like a sorceress stirring up the pot.

It was in June of 1950 that the caldron overflowed and waves of hate came splashing down across the parallel.

59.

The Yellow Road

I was in New York when the war started in Korea and I was returned there so quickly that one day I saw the faces and heard the voices and felt the varying degrees of surprise and concern of Americans at home as they reacted eight thousand miles away from the event, and in the next it seems—with the help of that incisive editor, time, which reaches unerringly into the memory and extracts those images which are to be lost—I was walking down the center of a yellow road, its surface dashed with the season's first rains and trod into a sticky paste. One side of it was clumped with Korean troops, their helmets hung with sweet potato vines, their faces dull and silent and their steps urgently hurrying them southward. On the other trailed a thin line of young American soldiers heading north, bent under weapons, walking as if their feet hurt and looking as though they had groped their way through a dark passage and had just emerged, peering about and wondering where they were.

It was the fifth of July, 1950, and though the war was already ten days old, it began that day for me—on this road. It began there also for the other Americans who plodded along it. For that was the day that the first U.S. troops were committed to battle in Korea. These were the troops. And this was the road that led them to it.

The road, for all its yellow mud and the squalid villages it served, was marked on our military maps as "principal and all-weather." It was an ancient highway from the southern port of Pusan to the Yalu River. For the past five years, though, it had been sheered off by the Thirty-eighth Parallel just north of Kaesong. And now the North Korean invaders were coming along it, cutting it shorter piece by piece. So far there had only been South Koreans to deter them. Now we were moving in.

In a farmyard by the side of the road near the village of Pyongtaek we spotted a command post. In a war, a command post is anywhere a commander stops to read or send a message, look at a map, or brew coffee. They were brewing coffee when we joined them, and keeping an eye on the sergeant who was working the radio in the communications jeep. "Negative," he called out to a question as we arrived. "I receive nothing north of us." There were five of us correspondents and he greeted us with a grin as we passed him.

A lieutenant colonel welcomed us. He was Harold Ayers,

battle-seasoned officer with North Africa, Sicily and France behind him. But his command now, the 1st Battalion of the 34th
Infantry Regiment of the 24th Division, was just twenty-four
hours old.

We asked Colonel Ayers what was ahead of us, up the road,
and he told us Colonel Smith's battalion was out front. He
opened up his map for us. "Up here," he said, "just south of
Osan. Dug in on either side of the railroad. We had a message
from him this morning that he'd sighted tanks.

"When those North Koreans come along they're going to
run right into him," he said. "It'll be the first time they've hit
Americans—and I think they're going to get a surprise." He
smiled a little and so did we. We were eager to witness the first
engagement.

We headed for Smith's battalion along the empty highway.
We had not gone far before we met a South Korean cavalry
unit coming toward us at a gallop. As they passed some of the
riders shouted at us in English, "Tanks! Tanks!" their horses
skittering off the road as a jeep came from behind us, speeding
north. In it we had a glimpse of an American bazooka team
and we followed. The first of the monsoon rains had come and
the drizzle changed to a downpour. All around us clouds closed
in, black and foreboding.

We caught up with the bazooka team on a rise when their
jeep stopped and spun around and the men spilled out and ran
crouching into a bean field. Again we followed, as more jeeps
came piling up behind us and more men came running into the
fields and crawling through the green vines in the drenching
rain.

One bazooka team sprawled for action on a small knoll.
Off to their right were the straw-thatched huts of a little village
and above them, looking oddly out of character, the Western
spire of a church. Then, suddenly, straight ahead, black as the
storm and apparently sitting there all the while, we saw a
tank astride the railroad track, its cannon slowly sweeping us
in a semicircle, cold and implacable, like some monster in its
squat deliberation.

We flattened into the mud, although I was so startled I

295

thought for an instant that image must have been conjured from the storm. The bazooka men, though, were better trained and more sensible. They took the tank under fire.

The charge was laid exactly on the target, spilling off the turret with a blood-red splash. Seemingly it accomplished nothing. "Get in closer," voices urged, and the men crawled forward and fired again, their aim equally true and the effect equally futile.

Now a second tank came crawling up the tracks. The bazooka team took them both under fire and both the tanks returned the fire, one of them shooting its cannon and the other its fifty-caliber. After a while I saw some of the bazooka men running, bent almost double, carrying a body. "They got Shadrick," one of the men said in terrible surprise as they reached us. "He's dead!"

The rest of the bazooka men were now retreating from the field toward the road.

"Where are you going?" we asked, astonished at the withdrawal.

"We're out of ammunition," one of them answered. "The charge we've got don't do a thing to those tanks anyway."

And so, incredibly enough, we all withdrew, bowling down the road in that black rain, surprised and with a new humility, peering around us with that unpleasant feeling that comes when you don't know where the enemy is and expect him at the next turning.

By the time we found the CP the blackness of night had taken over from the storm without making much impression that the day had gone. Men were digging in around the building and some artillery pieces were being placed below it. Despite the heavy rain, the windows had been removed to prevent injury from flying glass and inside the room was soggy, hung with wet clothing and shoes, and stacked with weapons.

Colonel Ayers sat by a table where a spot of light fell from the cupped bulb hanging overhead. Several officers were grouped around him reading a map, and nearby Sergeant Loflen, who had been on the radio that morning, crouched by a field phone, cranking and calling into it. His face was strained and he looked

296

quite different from the easy smiling soldier we had seen earlier in the day.

It was just 10:30 when three soaked and shivering soldiers came into the room. They were from Smith's battalion. Haltingly they told their story: they had been overrun that morning. Tanks had come upon them followed by infantry. They had fought until they were out of ammunition. Then it was each man for himself. It had taken these three all day to get through the enemy. They knew no more than this.

Sometime in the night I must have dozed, for someone was shaking me. "Better wake up," he said. "We may have to move fast."

The room was astir as men who had been sleeping woke and began gathering up their equipment and checking their weapons. The word had not been used but everyone knew it. We were being enveloped. Now and again the building shook violently as the artillery emplaced nearby increased its fire. And the report of small arms came closer and closer as we abandoned the CP, and in the rain and darkness joined with the withdrawal along the road which we had traveled so confidently that morning.

And so ended that first day of our war, our heads turned southward again along that yellow highway, on a journey that was to continue week after week, sometimes with abrupt and costly pauses in fields and hills, in towns that few Americans had ever heard of: Chonan, Chonui, Chochiwon; Taejon, Yongdong, and Taegu. Now, again, they mean nothing except to those who fought there and survived. And even for them the perspective is narrowly subjective—limited and distorted by a wary eye to a bend in the road, the next thatched hut by the wayside, the lip of an embankment from which rise silent puffs of dust.

60.

Where the Road
Turned

Wilson Fielder came up from Hong Kong to cover the Korean
War. He loved Asia and he could not stay away from the vortex
of her suffering. He arrived as I was leaving to take my film of
those first days of battle out to Tokyo to be sent to *Life,* and he
asked me where along the fighting front I thought he should
go. I said, "Taejon." That was where General Walker had told
me we were going to stop and fight. "We've got reinforcements
coming," the general had said. "Until then what we need is
time. We're going to buy that time at Taejon."

"When you get there," I said to Wilson, "look for Colonel
Ayers and the 1st Battalion of the 24th."

He nodded and we parted then, Wilson and I, with a promise
to meet again in battle. But we never did. I was delayed a day in
Tokyo—the day that it took Wilson to reach Taejon. And when
at last I got a place on a plane bound for Korea I met another
correspondent coming out. "It's a slaughter over there," he said.
"I think your new man Fielder got it yesterday. I heard reports
that he'd been killed.

"I'm not sure," he added as I stared at him. "Look for a soldier named Tex Kimball. I've been told he said he was with
Fielder when he was hit."

I landed at Taegu that afternoon and set out for Taejon and
the front. Tex Kimball was my goal—or Wilson, if the reports
had lied.

Along the way I met a British correspondent, Mike Gigantes,

and I asked him, as I asked everyone, for Kimball or for Fielder. "I know where Kimball is," he said. "I just did a story on him. He's a headquarters driver for the 24th Division but he likes tanks and he's gone AWOL and attached himself to the 1st Cavalry. They're up near Yongdong. I'll take you up to him."

We tried the roads, but things were going bad for us at Taejon. And as in every military reverse, the roads behind were clogged and traffic at cross purposes. We found a train. All day we traveled, stopped and backed, and traveled again.

Sometime in the middle of the night we jolted to a stop and I awoke. I heard a babble of low voices and looked out. There was no station. It was dark except for glimpses of a few covered lights on the ground. I left the train and there was a feeling of many men around me, an undertone of murmur. Here and there the undertone was pierced by cries for water and of anguish and pain.

The scene took substance. A few men walked about. But there were many on the ground, sitting, lying, some asleep, some talking in low voices, some just gazing into the star-filled heavens.

"What outfit's this?" I asked a soldier who was pacing back and forth along the tracks. He stopped and peered at me as though to make out my features. "Outfit?" he repeated. He seemed not to understand. He walked away.

I asked another, "What outfit is this?"

"We're nothing any more," he answered quietly. "We're all mixed up. Whoever's made it and whatever's left, I guess. Anything that got out of Taejon."

"Any from the 1st Battalion of the 24th—Colonel Ayers' outfit?"

"Not many, I guess." He paused. "Not many."

"Colonel Ayers?"

He shook his head.

"Did you see a correspondent named Wilson Fielder?"

He shook his head.

And so I started through the crowd, calling here and there, stepping over bodies, turning whenever I heard a voice, asking for Wilson Fielder, for Colonel Ayers.

299

Abruptly someone grabbed me, almost smothering me. I could feel him shivering and sobbing and I got him down on the ground. He clung to me and through his sobs he cried, "I made it, Carl. I made it."

I got my flashlight free and turned it on his face. It was a wasted face, spent, with eyes so red they seemed to be bleeding. I didn't recognize him. Then I realized—it was Lester Loflen, Colonel Ayers' sergeant.

"Where are they all?" I asked him.

"They're gone," he rasped. "They're all gone. Dead."

"Colonel Ayers?"

"We got separated. I don't know."

"Wilson Fielder. The *Time* correspondent? Did you see him?"

But he shook his head. He didn't know. Nor did anyone else that I could find. The train began to move. I got on board.

We left the train at dawn and found the road again and got a lift to Yongdong. Mike said the tank outfit where Tex Kimball had attached himself was just up there.

Yongdong was under artillery attack. Shells were falling in the streets and we could see where ours were landing in the green hills just beyond. "Just up here," Mike said. "The outfit's dug in at the north end of town." And so we ran.

But we were running into fire. We could see buildings ahead of us exploding. When we reached a cavalry command post sign I yelled to Mike to stop. "Let's find out what we're running into," I protested. But he was impatient to get on. "It's just up here a little more," he urged. "Let's make a run for it."

And so we stood a minute, each of us turned slightly from the other, tense and ready, like runners on the mark. And in that way we parted.

When I entered, the cavalry command post was in crisis, ready to pull out. The enemy was south of us, almost encircling the town, and their tanks were coming down the highway from the north. And while I stood there panting in the door I heard the order given to withdraw. By noon we had abandoned Yongdong, lucky to get out. And by that hour Mike Gigantes had been wounded and was already a prisoner.

I never did find Kimball, for he too was captured at Yong-dong.

I never did find Wilson, either, although I went on searching for him and for Colonel Ayers. In the end I did find Ayers and learned from him a little of what happened. Wilson had joined him at the beginning of the battle for Taejon, and had stuck with him through the fighting, through the encirclement and retreat until they reached a point of safety in the hills.

Then Colonel Ayers, looking down into the city, saw some Americans still trapped there. He took a small group back in to try to lead them out—and Wilson went in with them.

There, where the road turned, in some nameless village short of the town, the North Koreans came upon them. Their group was split and Ayers never saw Wilson after that. He himself made it—after many days—back through the enemy to safety. But Wilson never did show up.

"Perhaps he'll make it too," Ayers told me hopefully, when we still had hope.

He didn't, though. Long afterward, along that yellow road, we found his body.

61.

The Gook

I first saw them in a medic's tent near Waegwan, the old man kneeling by the boy and the captain yelling at the old man. It was later, after the old man and the boy were gone and the captain himself was lying on the cot, that he told me this story:

Days before, his outfit had been fighting thirty miles north, near Kumchon. And one night their position was overwhelmed and the captain was separated from the rest. He remembered every detail. But what he remembered most clearly was a certain view, a cluster of ripening rice stalks bent heavily with swelling grain framing it like a pastoral scene through an arch. There was the immediate dark green of the stalk just above the water and, as the eye rolled upwards toward the leaves, a growing stain of yellow. At the top the fruit hung dark against a brilliant, cloudless sky, one edge of which was daubed with just a touch of hazy mountaintop.

It was an unusual view, for it was from the water level of a paddy field. And the reason the captain remembered it in such detail was that he had seen nothing else since the first faint light of morning. By late afternoon the strain and pain of forcing his back into an inverted bend to keep his mouth and nose above the water had created steady muscular spasms. These threw out little circular ripples which floated off through the rice stalks. Sometimes the captain would follow these with absorption. Sometimes he would watch the grain above, and the sky with its fringe of mountains. But always he was obsessed by one great fear: sleep. He was exhausted. The great pain of hunger had subsided into a gnawing ache. He had satisfied his thirst with revolting drinks from the evil-smelling paddy water. And now, despite every determination, moments of sleep would sneak upon him and his body would slowly soften, his quivering muscles relax, and his head sink into the black water. Each time he would waken, thrashing and choking. And then he would lie rigidly still, listening.

Sometimes he heard voices and footsteps along the paddy pathways. And once he heard shouts and splashings in a neighboring paddy field, and a scream and a sharp volley from a burp gun. Then he would sink his elbows deeper into the soft mud and lower his head until the water made a cool line just below his nose.

Time and again he tried to escape in fancy. He played tricks with his mind, painstakingly sorting from his memory moments of his life which he struggled to live again. But it was always the same. No matter where he started or how he concentrated, the scene would slip away. Then, in spite of himself, he would relive yesterday. He always started with the scene near Kumchon when he passed the word to his tired, sweat-stained men: "The enemy has infiltrated in strength behind us. Many are dressed as civilians. We're going to shoot our way out."

He remembered how well the men took the news. And when the Koreans hit and overran them, he watched again in agony as his own men went down. Each moment of the battle and his escape was relived: the close-in fighting and killing, the hide-out on the outskirts of the town, the thirst, the wandering, the dodging through the night.

And now as darkness came again the captain struggled out of the paddy field and in an aching crouch moved along toward the fringe of mountains. The pain of hunger was back and he ate some of the bitter grains from the unripe rice. All night he walked, cursing the moon as it rose in the sky. By dawn he was into the hills and stunted trees and could go no farther. He sat, intending to rest for but a moment. Almost immediately he was asleep.

He was awakened by someone rolling his shoulder. He grabbed for the forty-five under his arm. A hand held his wrist. "Easy, Captain," said a voice. And the captain looked into the drawn, unshaven face of an American soldier. Behind it were two others. "We're moving up higher," said the soldier. "We'll help you along." That was the only greeting. The captain nodded and was helped to his feet, stiff and stumping like a man on stilts. The climb grew steeper and the trees thicker as they labored up the eroded foot of the mountain. But after a mile or so the captain quit. He just sat down slowly, his head rolling, his eyes coated, and an arm reaching below him for support like a blind man feeling for a chair. When the men knelt near him he was already asleep.

They made no further effort. They sat where they were, each suffering in his own painful way the cumulative effect of exhaustion, hunger, thirst and the debilitation of dysentery. Each knew that someone must stay awake. But there was no longer the strength nor the will to discuss it. They all slept. One was a corporal. The other two had not yet earned a stripe. They were young men, but the strain and stain of battle made them look

303

older. Their unshaven faces were drawn and yellowed, their lips cracked and encrusted.

It was the corporal who woke first when the old Korean with the black horsehair hat and long bamboo-stemmed brass pipe approached along the forest path. "Gook!" he shouted, and was on the Korean, menacing him with the butt end of his rifle, when the others awoke. The Korean raised his hands, dropping his pipe in fright. He was unarmed and the corporal thought the better of what he was doing and lowered his rifle. "God-damn gook," he muttered, ashamed of his threat against the old man.

The others were on their feet now and gathered around the Korean making signs of eating to him. He pointed up the mountain and they followed, moving slowly along the rugged path. Abruptly they came upon a shack hidden in the trees. It had weathered mud walls and a thatched roof. It was empty. The Korean brought them water and eggs while they watched him, watched his fine-boned yellow hands and the food in them. The Americans snatched at the eggs and broke them and drank from the shell, gulping. It was not enough to satisfy them but with the water the grip of hunger relaxed and in the cool shack they stretched out on the floor and slept.

It was early twilight when they awoke and the old Korean was gone. Rested and refreshed they became a fighting unit again, assuming rank and discipline. They cleaned their weapons, took stock of their ammunition, placed a guard. Below them at a distance they could hear the dull reports of artillery.

"As soon as it's dark," said the captain, "we'll move on higher." And then, as the men crouched by the door waiting for the word, they were hit.

"It's another ambush!" shouted the corporal.

"Run for it," commanded the captain.

As they broke for the trees across the little clearing the fire was concentrated on the open doorway. Through the hysterical noises of shouts and intense firing, the confusion and the purple flashes in the dusk, the captain ran zigzag, keeping low, sweating. He could see the corporal's heels before him but the other two had fanned out wider. He did not see them hit nor hear them go down, and when he reached the brush he simply grabbed the corporal and pushed on.

304

They stayed together, moving up the mountain, stumbling, supporting each other. The sound of the pursuing firing receded and sputtered out. It was strangely quiet. They were winded and sat silently on the ridge top, listening, seeing the long dark outline of the valley below them and, over the hills to the south, the intermittent bright flashes which marked the new outline of the war.

"It was the old man, the gook," said the corporal bitterly. The captain nodded and said nothing.

Now for uncounted days and nights the captain and the corporal walked and struggled, hid and slept. Always they were hungry, frequently tortured by thirst, constantly weakened by dysentery. One night they tumbled into an abandoned ruin of another mountain shack. When they awoke a Korean was sitting between them. The Americans reached for their weapons but these were little more than involuntary actions. They were both too weak for more.

The Korean, a young lad, sat there squatting on his heels, smiling, shaking his head, holding a hand out against the weapons. Then he rose and turned away and the corporal watched him narrowly.

The Korean came back with a gourd of water and some tinned rations. Patting them affectionately he smiled again. "Yongdong. American," he said. He opened them and they all ate in silence.

When he finished, he pointed to the earthen floor and made a sign for them to sleep. And in pantomime he showed them that in the morning he would take them southward over the mountains. Then he reached for the corporal's carbine, opened the bolt knowingly, checked the magazine and crawled over to a fire position.

Behind the Korean's back the corporal pointed slyly at the captain's forty-five. The intent was clear and the danger obvious, but it reached the captain through a vague dreamlike haze. He closed his eyes. When he looked again the corporal was asleep. Soon he slept also, while his mind still grappled with the problem of surprising the Korean.

They awoke late in the afternoon. The Korean was still sitting in the doorway, carbine across his lap. When he saw them move he grinned again and pointed at the food and water. Then he

turned back to his business of watching. Once more the corporal
signaled the captain, pointing at his weapon and then meaning-
fully toward the door. But the captain's mind was clearer now
and he shook his head.

"Where you from?" he asked the Korean.

The boy understood. "Chonan," he replied. He was good-
looking, with dark skin and white teeth and long black hair. He
wore the black, baggy pants of the Korean peasant and an
American Army shirt. Suddenly he smiled. "American," he said
pointing southward. Then: "We go."

From then on it was the Korean who was in command. He
chose the trails, picked the hideouts, foraged for food and sat
the longest with the carbine. But as the corporal's strength
grew, so did his distrust. "Jump him," he urged the captain.
"Or let me jump him."

"He's taking us south," the captain said.

"Yeah," whispered the corporal. "But he's a gook."

The captain did not answer, but his indecision was heavy
and it made him edgy.

The sound of fighting was close now and one night from a
mountaintop they looked down into the battle. Tracers marked
the positions of the lines and the tempo of fire indicated the
expansion of the war since the battle at Kumchon. All night
they moved cautiously down the mountain toward the American lines.

When it began to grow light they stopped in the trees near
the base of the mountain. The Korean made the sign. They
would wait there. And that night they would go through. "Maybe
fight," he grinned. The captain made his decision. He reached
out and shook the boy's hand. "You're a good boy, Joe. A
soldier," he said.

The corporal was sullen, but when the captain selected their
defensive positions for the day he took his, back to back with
the Korean, without speaking. All day they sat thus, warily,
listening for Korean patrols, thinking of the night's dash ahead
of them. At dusk they were moving again, leaving the steep
hill country and the shelter of trees, advancing cautiously across
level ground and slipping into a small deserted village. They

306

could tell by the feeling that it was between the lines—that it belonged to no one.

At the far side they peered out beyond the shelter of the broken walls, across the low furrows of a sweet potato field to the scrub-covered rising ground and the outline of the ridge toward which they were heading. Immediately they were spotted by a North Korean patrol and drew back, crouching as they heard the warning shouts and the firing. To stay there was to be trapped.

"We're going to have to run for it," the captain commanded hoarsely. "From the sound of the firing, we've got troops over that ridge. It's each man for himself."

Then, looking at the Korean, the captain asked carefully and slowly: "Do you understand? Americans there," he emphasized by pointing. "We all run. If anyone is shot," and he patted the ground to be sure he was understood, "the others go on. No chance for the wounded."

The Korean raised his head a little and looked about. The firing was closer now. He nodded. "O.K.," he said.

The captain looked at the corporal. "Let's go!" he shouted.

As they rose, thundering and slipping through the potato field, the crack of firing and the whine of bullets picked up for the kill. The Korean was in the lead, the corporal behind him, and the captain last. They ran crazily, looping, darting, twisting. Then the young Korean was hit. He went down in convulsions. Over him jumped the corporal and then the captain.

Hardly two paces beyond, the captain stopped, flung himself back on his hands and knees, rapidly felt over the boy's body. He looked up to see the corporal standing at a distance bolt upright in the field, his whole body silhouetted, doing a kind of crazy dance of indecision as he checked himself, turned, and swayed.

Then the corporal came. Running straight back for them at a crouch, he reached out and grabbed the Korean under the arm. The captain took the other arm and now, half-dragging the wounded boy, they stumbled on. Behind them the firing increased. Then suddenly ahead of them came a shout and a challenge in English. They drove madly, blindly toward it. A body loomed from the field, a big one with a rifle. It said:

"Keep acoming, boys. Come right on through us." The American patrol closed around them.

They lowered the young Korean. He was badly hurt. "Through the belly," said the captain to the aidman who was already reaching for the Korean. "Gook," said the aidman professionally as he began bandaging.

Back a little way a jeep came and picked them up. It was soon after they arrived that I found them in the medic's tent. The Korean was lying under a bottle of plasma and the captain sat on the cot beside him with a gauze sponge in his hand, gently wiping the bloody foam from the boy's lips. The corporal sat crouched on a box at the foot of the cot, his head in his hands, dozing.

At the farther end of the tent was an old Korean in GI clothes and white sneakers. "Is he the interpreter?" the captain asked me. "Let's get him up here." The old man came at the call and looked at the boy on the cot. Then he lowered himself on his knees beside him and held his hand. Sometimes he spoke in Korean but the boy never answered. Only his eyes moved, watching the old man's face.

"He's badly hurt," said the captain. "Talk to him. Get his family and where he lives."

The old man nodded in response to the captain's voice but he did not answer his question.

"He saved our lives," said the captain, his voice rising. "Took us all the way from Kumchon. But we never knew his name." Then more urgently: "Can't you find out who he is?"

The old man nodded again, but he just held the boy's hand.

When they moved the boy to the operating section the interpreter went as far as the tent flaps and then waited there silently. The captain took out a cigarette and sat on the cot watching him. "He's seen a lot of this," he muttered at last. "Hard. Like all Koreans."

When the word came from the operating room it was the old interpreter who brought it over to us, squatting again by the cot as though the patient were still lying there. The corporal awoke and suddenly began to cry. "He's dead, Captain. He's dead," he repeated.

The captain sat motionless for a moment and then lowered

his face to the old man. "He saved us, that boy," he said intensely. "He died for us." And he jabbed his finger at the corporal and himself. The old man just nodded.

"Look at me!" the captain roared into the old man's face. Rising from the cot and grabbing the Korean by the arms, he yelled: "Don't you understand? Don't you know what I'm saying? He's dead. And now his family will never know what happened to him—how he died."

Gently the old man moved his arms free. Then looking into the captain's face he said slowly: "I understand. I know who he is. I have known him for seventeen years. He was my son."

62.

Home

All these are now memories: the road from Pyongtaek to Taegu, and the longer one that stretches back through China and Japan and Europe and finally home.

That last day when I left Korea I traveled once more along the yellow highway, passing the towns and hamlets we had fought for and had lost and now were ours again. The seasons were coming into circle too, and I could see a few men and women bent to the tilling of the soil, and children were playing around broken farmhouses, their shouts of joy ringing strangely clear and new across the land.

And suddenly I felt a surge of gladness that I had been there, that I had seen it all and felt it all. And I was glad too, despite all I knew of men's inhumanity and brutality, to be a man, living among men. For I knew then, with that moment's insight, that this is my home, this world, this war-torn world. And this is my time and place in it.

Each of us has a role, a time, a place. Those who are most fortunate discover what it is.

I once visited an old American missionary woman who had elected to remain in China after the rest of her mission had been repatriated to the United States. She stayed because she had twelve Chinese orphans dependent upon her and she lived with them behind a gray stone wall, filthy with defecation, in the worst slums of Shanghai. By the time I met her she was reaching the end of her life and had lost all outward marks of her origin and nationality.

Standing in the passageway to her narrow compound as she unbarred the rotting wooden door for me, she looked like some ancient Chinese witch, her face yellowed and her teeth gone, her gown spotted with food and muddy about the hem. She kept her orphans alive on a tiny pension and by gathering broken bottles and selling the glass. And they returned her love and shielded her from the Japanese who occupied the city. She was ready to die, but she said that she would not, as long as these children needed her. And thus she lived, unaware of her own drama, while history moved outside the gray stone walls.

All of us live in history, whether we are aware of it or not, and die in drama. The sense of history and of drama comes to a man not because of who he is or what he does but flickeringly, as he is caught up in events, as his personality re-acts, as he sees for a moment his place in the great flowing river of time and humanity.

The sense of drama can be strong, as in the Chinese beggar woman who keeps alive by it. Awareness of history may come to a Turkish doctor when he sees a man dying in the Korean twilight, or it may come in the quiet of Midwestern farm-lands when one feels the earth turn round, or as it came to me when I heard those children shouting as they played by their broken homes.

I cannot tell you where our history is leading us, or through what suffering, or into what era of war or peace. But wherever it is, I know men of good heart will be passing there.